JOHN PAUL II

The Story of My Life

JOHN PAUL II
The Story of My Life
Collected Memories

Compiled by Saverio Gaeta

Foreword by Rocco Palmo

Introduction by Angelo Cardinal Comastri

Pauline
BOOKS & MEDIA
Boston

Library of Congress Cataloging-in-Publication Data

John Paul II, Pope, 1920-2005.

[Vi racconto la mia vita. English]

John Paul II : the story of my life : collected memories / John Paul II ; compiled by Saverio Gaeta ; notes to the English edition by Mary Lea Hill.

p. cm.

Includes bibliographical references (p. 265).

ISBN 0-8198-3992-2 (pbk.)

1. John Paul II, Pope, 1920-2005. 2. Popes--Biography. I. Gaeta, Saverio, 1958- II. Hill, Mary Lea. III. Title. IV. Title: Story of my life.

BX1378.5.J6275 2011

282.092--dc22

[B]

2010031931

Excerpts from *Crossing the Threshold of Hope* by His Holiness Pope John Paul II, translated by Vittorio Messori, translation copyright © 1994 by Alfred A. Knopf, a division of Random House, Inc. Used by permission of Alfred A. Knopf, a division of Random House, Inc.

Excerpts from *Gift and Mystery* by Pope John Paul II, copyright © 1996 by Libreria Editrice Vaticana. Used by permission of Doubleday, a division of Random House, Inc.

"Marble Floor," "Over This Your White Grave," "Song of the Inexhaustible Sun," from *The Place Within: The Poetry of Pope John Paul II* by Pope John Paul II, translated by Jerzy Peterkiewicz, copyright © 1979, 1982 by Libreria Editrice Vaticana, Vatican City. Translation and notes copyright © 1979, 1982 by Jerzy Peterkiewicz. Used by permission of Random House, Inc.

Cover design by Rosana Usselmann

Cover photo © Photographic service—L'Osservatore Romano

"P" and PAULINE are registered trademarks of the Daughters of St. Paul.

Originally published and copyrighted by Libreria Editrice Vaticana, Citta del Vaticano.

English edition published and copyrighted by Daughters of St. Paul, Boston, MA.

English edition © 2011, Daughters of St. Paul

Published by Pauline Books & Media, 50 Saint Pauls Avenue, Boston, MA 02130-3491

Printed in the U.S.A.

www.pauline.org

Pauline Books & Media is the publishing house of the Daughters of St. Paul, an international congregation of women religious serving the Church with the communications media.

1 2 3 4 5 6 7 8 9   15 14 13 12 11

"*I find myself before you without notes.*
I must find the notes within me,
because everything that I want and must tell you
is written in my heart."

—*John Paul II*

Contents

PART THREE

Twenty-Seven Years
in the Heart of History

Foreword

Joseph Stalin once famously asked, "How many divisions does the Pope have?" Had he lived to see Karol Wojtyła, he would have known the answer. Chances are he wouldn't have liked it.

You are about to "put out into the deep," into one of the great stories of our time as it has never before been told. It's the chronicle of a man who, born of humble roots, grew through adversity; a man who had an indelible impact on millions and changed the course of history. Yet five years after Pope John Paul II returned to the Father's house, what remains most remarkable about his life isn't its result, but the pilgrim age that formed, strengthened, and saw him called forth to be his era's leading witness to the world.

Beyond the autobiographical reflections contained in these pages, the testimonies of others reinforce that, in an age that craves authenticity and is perhaps not as hostile to religion itself as lacking evidence of genuine faith, the 264th Successor of Peter was the real deal. What he preached before crowds as large as 5 million, he practiced in the "bubble" of his Vatican apartment.

Many stories could illustrate this, but one serves well to sum it all up. In early October 1979, hours into his first visit to the United States, a threat was placed on the Holy Father's life. It would be two years before the wider world came to see that not even the Pope was immune to an assassin's bullet, but organizers of the trip scrambled to make emergency plans, which largely entailed confining John Paul in armored cars or behind rows of police, scuttling the open-air walkabouts that would be the only chance for most of the gathered throngs to see him up close.

As he emerged to celebrate a Mass in my hometown of Philadelphia, the Secret Service stood by a waiting car to drive the Holy Father a stone's throw to the temporary outdoor altar. At the time, it was the largest gathering in the city's history—over a million people filled the massive boulevard linking City Hall, our cathedral, and the art museum, site of the famous "Rocky steps." Prodded toward the limo—and well aware of the threat—John Paul looked instead toward the crowd and said, simply, "The Pope will walk."

And so he walked, causing further panic among the planners by darting from side to side of the asphalt aisle that, for a moment, became Peter's processional route. If Christ could walk to Calvary, fully knowing what awaited him there, who was his Vicar to do anything else?

Indeed, it was no accident that the homily at his funeral centered on the two simple words of the Lord's call, not just to the Roman pontiff but to every Christian of every age—"Follow me!"

While even his immediate predecessors were carried on a throne borne on the shoulders of attendants, "the Pope will walk" quickly became the *modus operandi* of John Paul's reign. Even though his travels were often mistaken as spectacles to be admired, their true purpose was never to entertain, but to encourage. He undertook 104 foreign trips—with enough mileage between them for three trips to the moon—to "walk" to the ends of the earth so that God's people might feel a bit more confidence and joy in their walk of daily life, the Christian's mission-field in a challenge-ridden world.

At every turn, the philosopher-pope, whose own experience bore witness to the truth of the Gospel, never failed to employ his sizable arsenal of charisma and conviction to call for humanity's most powerful tools of change, which tend to be the quietest ones and are available to everyone.

Without knowing his story or hearing the emphasis in his voice, one could simply write off John Paul's teaching as a political message or "tough talk" to the faithful. Over the years, many have aimed to do just that. But peace is no mere slogan when you've endured wars; the need to respect life and cherish human dignity hits home when you've had friends killed, tortured, and exploited under totalitarianism's heavy hand; hard labor for little reward gives new meaning to the need for justice, and, most of all, extolling the virtues of love, family, and commitment is never a rote act when your own were gone at an early age. As each of these threads ran through his life, so he passed their lessons forward, that the world he left behind might have life, and have it more abundantly.

Yet even this was just part of the puzzle. In his wake, the life and witness of this spectacular figure tends to be compartmentalized— John Paul the poet, the politician, the ecclesiastical governor, the "rock star." Still, however one tries to piece it together, every last facet of the man was drawn from the same place—John Paul the Christian, the witness, the priest and pastor of souls. Miss that, and you miss *everything*.

For all his many divisions, the pope is not unlike the rest of us—no occupant of the post will ever be perfect, nor be able to invest himself everywhere he would like. He, too, has to choose his priorities and emphases, knowing he isn't eternal and can't be omnipresent.

And for all that, John Paul chose us—the young people who became his own, the generation he inspired to carry his fearlessness and faith forward. Sure, he loved us. More importantly, he looked to us, called out for us—*he believed in us*—to walk where he couldn't and to continue the Lord's work of being salt and light in this world.

Though today we may take John Paul's inspiration for granted, we shouldn't. The notion of a pontiff directly reaching out to a group that wasn't ordained or professed—and, in many cases, was discouraged or wavering in its adherence to the faith—never won over the Vatican bureaucracy, with its score of departments with "better" ideas to take up the Pope's time and energy. But this special bond between John Paul II and the youth of the world reflected the Pope's understanding of something deeper: Christ's charge for Peter to "confirm [his] brothers." It sprang from the instinctive awareness of an eternal camp chaplain that the young are a "letter of Christ—his calling card." To invest in us was to sow the seeds of the Church's future.

As you'll soon read, the Holy Father once observed that while day's end means sleep for the old, "the young are always different . . . for them when the sun goes down, it means the songfest begins." Even as he is now looking down on us from the window of the Father's house, the story of John Paul II continues in the many songs he brought to life—every soul he touched; each vocation he inspired; every path to peace, hope, responsibility, and belief his witness played a part in building. As he taught us so well, none of these takes place in a vacuum, but in a family of faith—the Church—that can never be its best until we give it the best of ourselves.

He looked for us, and we came to him—and we're grateful and all the better for it. As we return to his life, here in his own words, may each of us come away renewed and reinspired—not only to continue the mission of Karol Wojtyła, but by the wholehearted, life-giving yes Christ asks of each of us: the very walk of fearless love our *Pope from Galilee* always and everywhere called us to follow, that never easy but always sweet journey that can transform this earth.

John Paul the Great, thank you, we love you—pray for us!

Rocco Palmo
November 1, 2009
63rd anniversary of Karol Wojtyła's
ordination to the priesthood

Introduction

JOHN PAUL II ACCORDING TO . . . himself.[i] With this charming remark we could summarize the sense of the following pages. This is a true and proper "autobiography" of Pope Wojtyła, one he actually wrote day after day. In his almost twenty-seven years of pontificate, there were in fact about 15,000 discourses and documents that he pronounced or wrote for the most varied circumstances. In this tome of texts, besides their completeness and depth of teaching, the fact stands out that the pontiff—whenever he had the opportunity—would deviate briefly from the principal theme to refer to episodes of his own life, or to recount his own intimate sentiments and thoughts.

It can well be said that in this book edited by Saverio Gaeta, Karol Wojtyła recounts for us his whole life—from his early years to his episcopacy, up to the beginning of his pontificate when he cried out: "Do not be afraid! Open the doors to Christ," and even until the last extraordinary moments of his agony. In the meantime, scrolling before us are the frames of this existence that singularly marked the history of the last century; be it his initiatives in Poland during the communist regime, or the entreaties he launched during the hundreds of pastoral visits to every part of the world, up until his last appeals for peace among peoples and the rights of every human being.

---

i Giovanni Paolo *secondo* . . . se stesso. This first sentence of Cardinal Comastri's introduction begins with a play on words, a pun in Italian that does not translate easily into English. *Secondo* can mean *the second* and also *according to*. We have included both meanings.

From where do these impassioned *confidences* spring forth? They come to us from the Holy Father himself who on November 3, 1981, turned to the doctors of the Gemelli Hospital who had assisted him after the attempt on his life and said: "I find myself before you without notes. I must find the notes within me, because everything that I want and must tell you is written in my heart." This affirmation was his way of being and of presenting himself that all of us have come to know and appreciate; of one whose days were sprinkled with prayer that beat with the same rhythm as his breath.

Pope Wojtyła thus reveals himself as a man and a priest who, having become a pontiff, did no more than incarnate his own human and priestly vocation within the same preceding horizon of faith and witness, in a total unity of life, action, and teaching. In these pages each one of these aspects stands out: the depth of his soul and the completeness of his thought, his multiple pastoral initiatives and the social work he promoted for the sake of the most acute needs of our time.

Reading this text, which in many places sounds like a real and proper novel, I returned in thought to the many personal episodes during my relationship with John Paul II. I recall in particular the incredible day in Loreto, September 5, 2004, the last trip that the Pope made outside of Rome. There were so very many people, and especially the young people of Catholic Action. They were there for the beatification ceremony of the Spanish priest Pere Tarrés i Claret and of the Italian laypeople Alberto Marvelli and Pina Suriano. We were somewhat apprehensive because the Holy Father's health was not the best. When Pope Wojtyła reached the altar I approached him, wanting to encourage him by saying: "Be strong, Holy Father." But when he saw how moved I was, it was he who caught me off guard by saying: "Courage, my son!"

His lucidity was intact until the end. A couple of days after I had been established definitively in the Vatican, on April 1, 2005, Bishop Stanisław called me and invited me to go to the Pope's apartment for our last greeting. At the Pope's bedside, his secretary touched the pontiff's arm saying: "Holy Father, Loreto is here." The Pope looked at me and corrected: "No, Saint Peter's." He thus recalled my change of seat, and then tried to bless me and encourage me in my new assignment.

Today, as Archpriest of the Basilica of Saint Peter, I feel a great responsibility for the pilgrims who come to render homage at his tomb in the Vatican Grottos, which has in fact become a small sanctuary. Each day about ten thousand to twelve thousand people come here and leave an enormous number of notes. Many are written in dialogue form, as coming from children who are speaking with their father: "Pope John Paul, you who so loved families, protect mine." "John Paul, I entrust to you my son who is far from the faith; bring him back to God." "I am expecting a child. Let everything go well. I entrust this child to you from this moment on." Among the many notes, I recall a touching letter from a little girl who had heard in the news about the war: "John Paul, you are in heaven and the bombs are thrown from heaven: stop them."

In these notes we can find the entire vocabulary of human sentiments that are perfectly correlated with the whole gamut of sentiments expressed by Pope Wojtyła throughout the arc of his life. And in these pages we find them again in an integral manner, in this journey that leads us by the hand to the great and profound heart of John Paul II.

Angelo Cardinal Comastri

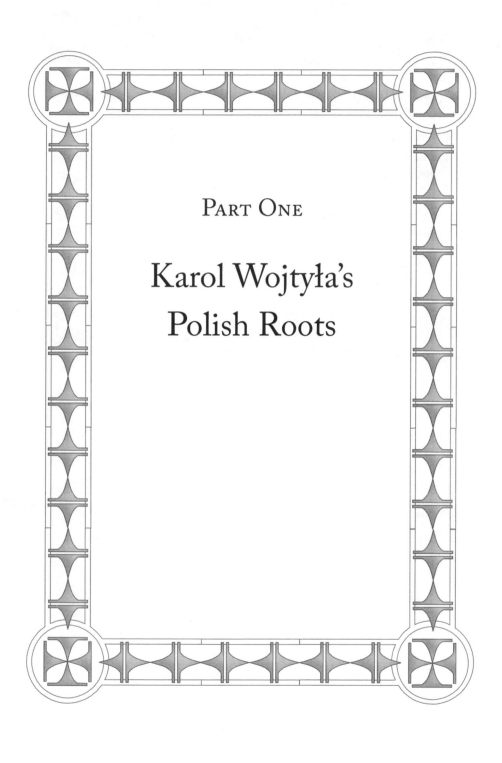

PART ONE

Karol Wojtyła's Polish Roots

Childhood at Wadowice

ACCORDING TO WHAT I WAS TOLD, my birth took place between five and six in the evening. Then, at almost exactly the same time, fifty-eight years later, I was elected Pope.[1]

I was born May 18, 1920. On a day that is so important for a person, I go back in memory to my parents, who have been dead for many years. I remember with gratitude my father and my mother, who gave me life. As I think of my parents, in a special way I want to give thanks to God, Lord and Font of life, for this first and fundamental gift.[2]

> It was during these months that Poland received back its independence, with the treaties of Versailles (1919) and Riga (1921), which freed them from the dominion, respectively, of Austria and Russia.

I was born in a time of war, but I knew nothing of it. Yet I have always had great admiration for those who won that war.[3]

> His father, also named Karol, was born in 1879 and was forty years old when his son was born. In 1904 he was an administrative official at the army barracks in Wadowice, a city of fifteen thousand.

My father was admirable and almost all the memories of my childhood and adolescence are connected with him.[4]

People often sing to the pope: "Long life! Long life! May you live a hundred years!" It is difficult at those moments not to think of my mother, the woman who gave me birth. If I am alive, it is because she gave me life. Naturally, my father also, but the labor of transmitting life is borne by the mother above all.[5]

> His mother, Emilia Kaczorowska, born in 1884, was thirty-six years old when he was born. At the moment of his birth she asked the midwife

7

"to open the window so that the first sounds that would be heard by her newborn would be songs in honor of Mary, the Mother of God. And so the midwife went from the bed to the window and opened the shutters. At once the little room was flooded with light and the songs of the vespers of the month of May, provided by the church of Our Lady in front of his birth house."[6] *Only a month after his birth on June 20, he was baptized by the military chaplain Father Franciszek Zak and received the names Karol (Charles) and Jozef (Joseph).*

We know how important the first years of life, of childhood, and of youth are for the development of human personality and character. These are the very years that bind me inseparably to Wadowice, to the town and the area around it. When in thought I look back over the long path of my life, I reflect on how the surroundings, the parish, and my family brought me to the baptismal font of the church of Wadowice, where I was given, on June 20, 1920, the grace to become a son of God, together with faith in my Redeemer.[7]

I express today my gratitude for the divine life I received at the baptismal font in the parish church at Wadowice. With the sacrament of rebirth in water and the Holy Spirit, a new life began for me: supernatural life, a gift from God, a gift that transcends the dimensions of natural existence.[8]

I give thanks to the Lord for the first anointing with the sacred chrism that I received in my hometown of Wadowice. It took place during my Baptism. Through sacramental washing we are justified and grafted into Christ. For the first time we also receive the gift of the Holy Spirit. This anointing with chrism is a sign of the outpouring of the Spirit, who gives new life in Christ and renders us capable of living in the righteousness of God.[9]

I am convinced that never at any period of my life was my faith a purely "sociological" phenomenon resulting from the habits or customs of my environment, in a word, from the fact that others around me "believed and acted like that." I have never regarded my faith as "traditional," although I have conceived a growing admiration for the tradition of the Church and that living share of it that has nourished the life, history, and culture of my country. Nevertheless, when I look objectively at my own faith I have always observed that it has had nothing to do with any kind of conformism, that it was born in the depths of my own "self," and that it was also the fruit of my intellectual search for an answer to the mysteries of man and of the world. I have seen more and more clearly that faith is a gift.[10]

Name days always draw the attention and the benevolence of those closest to us—members of the family—upon the person who bears a given name. This name reminds us of the love of our parents, who, on giving it, wished to determine somehow the place of their child in that community of love which the family is. They were the first to address him with this name, and together with them, his brothers and sisters, relatives, friends, and companions. And so the name marked out the man's path among men; among the men closest to him and fondest of him. My beloved parents gave me the name Karol (Charles), which was also my father's name. Certainly, they could never have foreseen (they both died young) that this name would open up for their child a way through the great events of the Church of today.[11]

Today I want to venerate Saint Charles Borromeo, whose name I received at my Baptism. I have made pilgrimage to his tomb in Milan a few times, as well as to places connected with his life, like Arona. His heart rests here in Rome in the church dedicated to him, Saint Charles (San Carlo al Corso). This detail is very eloquent; it testifies that this cardinal and pastor of the Ambrosian [ii] Church of Milan was at the same time a servant of the universal Church.[12]

> *At home there were also the first child, Edmund, born in 1906, and another baby named Olga, who died, most probably only a few days after birth, in 1914. Due to this last pregnancy, which ended so dramatically, much damage was done to the heart and the kidneys of Mamma Emilia, which led to her death on April 13, 1929.*

I was not yet the age for my first Communion when I lost my mother, who did not have the joy of seeing that day she so anticipated:

[ii] The Ambrosian rite is one of the ancient liturgical traditions within Roman Catholicism. It is proper to the Archdiocese of Milan and originates with (or pre-dates) Saint Ambrose (339–397). The rite is similar to the Roman rite, but has distinctions of rubrics, calendar, breviary, and chant.

she wanted two sons, one a doctor, the other a priest. My brother was a doctor and, in spite of everything, I have become a priest.[13]

> Over this your white grave
> the flowers of life in white—
> so many years without you—
> how many have passed out of sight?
> Over this your white grave
> covered for years, there is a stir
> in the air, something uplifting
> and, like death, beyond comprehension.
> Over this your white grave
> oh, mother, can such loving cease?
> for all his filial adoration
> a prayer:
> Give her eternal peace—
>
> — "Over This, Your White Grave" (Kraków, 1939)[14]

When he wrote the verses of this poem dedicated to his mother, Karol was nineteen years old and had also lost his adored brother, Edmund, who died in Kraków on December 5, 1932.

My brother Edmund died from scarlet fever in a virulent epidemic at the hospital where he was starting as a doctor. Today antibiotics would have saved him. I was twelve. My mother's death made a deep impression on my memory, and my brother's perhaps a still deeper one, because of the dramatic circumstances in which it occurred and because I was more mature. Thus quite soon I became a motherless, only child.[15]

Now Karol had only his father, who left the army in 1927 with a modest pension.

For me, it was my father who in a special way made me aware of the activity of the Holy Spirit, precisely when I was your age. If I found myself in some difficulty, he would suggest that I pray to the Holy Spirit; and this teaching of his has shown me the path which I have followed to this day.[16]

One day my father gave me a prayer book which contained the *Prayer to the Holy Spirit*. He told me to recite it daily. So, from that day on, I have tried to.[17]

The small town of Wadowice always represented for Karol the place of memories and his first affections.

I want to thank Wadowice for those schools from which I received much light—the elementary school and then the magnificent Wadowice High School dedicated to Marcin Wadowita.[iii] [18]

I remember, above all, the Wadowice elementary school, where at least a fourth of the pupils in my class were Jewish. I should mention my friendship at school with one of them, Jerzy Kluger—a friendship that has lasted from my school days to the present. I can vividly remember the Jews who gathered every Saturday at the synagogue behind our school.[19]

And the parish of Our Lady of Wadowice would remain for him the cradle of his faith.

Here, in this city, in this ancient parish church, I heard Peter's confession[iv] (of faith) for the first time. It came from the baptistery, the altar, the pulpit, and the school. It was all wrapped up in the life of this Christian community. This confession formed its life, as it forms the Christian life of the entire world. This confession came to me as a gift of the faith of the Church. It gave my life a direction that began in the Father, and in the Son, opened itself to the Holy Spirit, to the inscrutable mystery of God. My mother's hands taught me this mystery, as she joined my baby hands in prayer, showing me how to make the sign of the cross, the sign of Christ, who is the Son of the Living God.[20]

As children we all waited for Saint Nicholas on account of the gifts that he brought to us. . . . I remember that as a child I had a personal

---

iii Marcin Wadowita, also known as Wadovius or Campius (1567–1641), born in Wadowice, was a priest and theologian and, successively, student, professor, chancellor, and benefactor of the Jagiellonian University.

iv This reference is to Peter's response when Jesus asked what people thought about his identity: "You are the Messiah, the Son of the living God" (Mt 16:16, NRSV).

connection with him. Naturally, like every other child, I waited for the gifts that he would bring to me on December 6, but this expectation had a religious dimension, too. Like all the children of my age, I nourished a veneration for this saint who unselfishly bestowed gifts to the people, and so manifested his loving concern.[21]

It has always been clear to me that the Church is the place where the sacraments are dispensed and received. From my first years at primary school, preparation for first Confession and first Communion taught me that a sacrament "is a visible sign of invisible grace, instituted by Jesus Christ for our salvation." That is how the catechism put it.[22]

The years of my childhood and adolescence passed in an atmosphere of faith, of faith handed down and freely continued. I was very conscious, sometimes agonizingly so, of the "last days" especially of the "judgment of God." In the catechism in use at my primary school, the "last days" figured in the chapter on Christian hope, which discussed successively death, judgment—personal and final—heaven, hell, and purgatory. At the center of this catechetical eschatology lay—or at any rate that was my impression—the judgment of God.[23]

The liturgy is also a kind of *mystery* play, acted out on stage. I remember the deep emotion I felt when, as a fifteen-year-old boy, I was invited by Father [Kazimierz] Figlewicz to the Sacred Triduum at Wawel Cathedral, and I was present for the Tenebrae[v] services, anticipated that Wednesday afternoon of Holy Week. It was a profound spiritual experience for me, and to this day I find the Triduum very moving.[24]

Here in Italy there has been much development of the oratories since the time of Saint Philip Neri. In Poland there were other organizations, and I went often to them. From my childhood I was a good altar boy.[25]

In the parish in Wadowice where I was born, our very zealous pastor would often read passages to us from the encyclicals of Pope

---

v Prior to the liturgical reform of Vatican II, Tenebrae (Latin for darkness) was the celebration of Matins and Lauds (late evening or early morning) of Thursday, Friday, and Saturday of Holy Week. The series of psalms and readings were accompanied by the gradual extinguishing of a number of candles representing the loss of Christ to death. One candle remained, or was restored, as witness to the resurrection.

Pius XI. However, what interested me more than his encyclicals was the fact that he was a mountain climbing pope *(Papa alpinista)*. [...] I wanted to own up to this in order to mention the tie between a great Italian pope who called himself a Polish bishop[vi] and this Polish bishop who is to be called an Italian pope.[26]

The Saint Vincent de Paul Society Councils have spread beyond France to all the countries of Europe and to the world. Before the Second World War, while a student, I myself was part of one of them.[27]

The pride of his Polish origins was not only a purely nostalgic sentiment, but it also represented the awareness of belonging to a fearless people.

I am the son of a nation which has lived great experiences of history, which has been condemned to death several times by its neighbors, but which has survived and remained itself. It has kept its identity, and it has kept, in spite of partitions and foreign occupations, its national sovereignty, not by relying on the resources of physical power, but solely by relying on its culture. This culture revealed itself in the circumstances to be a power greater than all other forces.[28]

The painful experience of the history of my own country, Poland, has shown me how important national sovereignty is when it is served by a state worthy of the name and free in its decisions; how important it is for the protection not only of a people's legitimate material interests, but also of its culture and its soul.[29]

The faith traditions of his homeland also accompanied him throughout his life.

Many years ago I was a child like you. I, too, used to experience the peaceful feelings of Christmas, and when the star of Bethlehem shone, I would hurry to the crib together with the other boys and girls to relive what happened two thousand years ago in Palestine. We children expressed our joy mostly in song.[30]

---

vi Pope Pius XI (1857–1939) was born Ambrogio Damiano Achille Ratti. He was appointed apostolic visitor and then nuncio to Poland, Lithuania, and Silesia. He was consecrated bishop of Lepanto in the Warsaw Cathedral in 1919, but transferred to Adana, Italy, in 1921. Though a studious man, he was an ardent mountain climber as well, ascending the Matterhorn and Mont Blanc, among others.

I remember a song I used to sing in Poland as a young man, a song which I still sing as Pope, which tells about the birth of the Savior. On Christmas night, in every church and chapel, this song would ring out, repeating in a musical way the story told in the Gospel. It says: "In the silence of the night, a voice is heard: 'Get up, shepherds, God is born for you! Hurry to Bethlehem to meet the Lord.'" The same story is told in the beautiful hymn "Silent Night," which everyone knows. That is a hymn which moves us deeply by reminding us that Jesus, the Son of God, was born of Mary, born to make us holy and to make us adopted sons and daughters of God. It is a hymn to the creative power of the Holy Spirit. It is a song to help us not to be afraid.[31]

Jesus' words in today's Gospel bring me back to my youth and remind me of a song we used to sing in my home parish at Wadowice. The words of that song are very simple, but at the same time very profound: "Come, Holy Spirit, we stand in need of your grace. Make us grow in the heavenly knowledge you have revealed. Make it easy for us to understand it, and by our perseverance may it remain in us. Enlightened by that truth, we shall be confirmed in goodness."[32]

A traditional Polish Lenten practice comes to my mind that has been carried out with particular devotion since the seventeenth century. It is called the *Amaro pentimento*, which means "bitter regret." Allow me to repeat the words that I have heard and sung since I was a child; they remain deeply impressed in my memory:

> "Come, bitter regret, pierce our hearts.
> Let go, my eyes! Well up, springs of sad tears!
> The sun and stars recede, shrouding themselves in mourning.
> The angels cry sadly. Who can describe their grief?
> The cliffs harden; the dead arise from the earth.
> I ask what is it, what has happened? All creation is stunned!
> In the presence of the passion of Christ,
> We are filled with inexpressible regret!
> Jesus, shatter without delay the hardness of our hearts!
> Quench the ardor of my passions as I enter the depths of
>   your passion."[33]

I remember taking part in many processions of this type when I was a child. I led them as a priest and bishop. The Corpus Christi procession was a great yearly event for the people who participated.[34]

He prepared himself to receive his first Communion and, in 1946, he expressed his feelings regarding that day in a sweet, poetic synthesis.

I remember as though it was yesterday—together with the other boys and girls of my own age, I received the Eucharist for the first time in the parish church of my town. This event is usually commemorated in a family photo, so that it will not be forgotten. Photos like these generally remain with a person all through his or her life. As time goes by, people take out these pictures and experience once more the emotions of those moments; they return to the purity and joy experienced in that meeting with Jesus, the one who out of love became the Redeemer of man.[35]

In a child's single look
fixed on the gentle Host
I met the heavenly Father
looking at me with love.
My eyes
like some discovered flower
trembled before this gaze
in which the world was seen,
His glory beyond power.[36]

Dating back to those days, to those long walks with the priest and then with friends, his characteristic sportsman's nature began.

When I was a child, I used to skate; as a young man, a priest, and a pope, I still ski. [. . .] And I tell you that the period of childhood that you are living was for me a time of the most beautiful memories. These memories of the time of childhood are very important for us.[37]

I see that you are intelligent people and, as they say, rather curious. You have some curiosity, I think justifiable curiosity. You want to know, as children, what the Pope did when he was a boy. Now, I think that being boys it is better not to think of the possibility of becoming pope. It will frighten you.[38]

Your visit makes me feel young again among the young; because it awakens in me dear memories of a long time ago when I too was able to play games of soccer as many young people do.[39]

I have always given (and continue to give) great importance to the ancient principle: "a sound mind in a sound body." Physical effort, particularly in sports, will achieve this. Another motive for me, so important with regard to these various sports, was always the love of nature: the lakes, the woods, the mountains, whether in summer or in the other seasons, but particularly in the winter when we made trips using our skis.[40]

When I see Scout troops, I think immediately of tents; their lives as Scouts spent under the tents. I know a bit about life in a tent because I spent many a vacation living in a tent.[41]

Hikers: you all know well what that means. I know, too, through my own personal experience. [. . .] Mountaineering is not just a healthy bodily discipline, vigorous and demanding, which prepares and disposes us to overcome physical weaknesses but, undertaken in the most complete way as you do, it is a school of life where you learn to practice generosity, solidarity, and camaraderie, self control, a sense of initiative and of risk. It is even more: seeing it as you do from the viewpoint of faith, it becomes a privileged way of discovering God in the marvels of his creation and awakening the desire to meet God on the mountain heights that reach to the edge of heaven.[42]

On May 6, 1938, in Wadowice, the archbishop of Kraków, Adam Stefan Sapieha, arrived to confirm the students who had just passed their exams for high school.

The inheritance of my Baptism was then strengthened and solidified in the sacrament of Confirmation. From here sprang up also the gift of my vocation—Christian, priestly, and episcopal.[43]

My religion teacher, Father Edward Zacher, chose me to give the address of welcome [to Archbishop Sapieha]. It was the first time I had the opportunity of being in the presence of that man who was so highly regarded by everyone. I know that after my speech the archbishop asked the religion teacher what university course I would be taking upon completion of secondary school. Father Zacher replied: "He will study Polish language and letters." The archbishop apparently replied: "A pity it is not theology."[44]

University Student and Worker

I entered for the first time the halls of the university as a ten-year-old elementary school student to attend my older brother's graduation; he received a doctorate in medicine from the Jagiellonian University. I can still see that ceremony as if I were attending it today.[45]

On June 22, 1938, he became a student at the same university.

Because of this, my father and I moved from Wadowice to Kraków and set up house at 10 Tyniecka Street, in the Dębniki district. The house belonged to relatives of my mother. I began my studies in the faculty of philosophy at the Jagiellonian University, taking courses in Polish language and letters, but I was able to complete only the first year, since the Second World War broke out on September 1, 1939.[46]

Ever since I was a child I have had a very special bond with Wawel Cathedral. I don't remember when I went there for the first time, but since that day I have felt particularly drawn to and personally attached to it. In some way, Wawel encompasses the entire history of Poland. I lived through the tragic period when the Nazi governor Hans Frank established himself in Wawel Castle and the flag with a swastika flew over it. For me that was a particularly painful experience. But in the end, the day came when the flag with the swastika disappeared, and the Polish flag returned.[47]

I will never forget the day of September 1, 1939. It was the First Friday of the month. I had gone to Wawel for confession; the cathedral was completely empty. That was perhaps the last time that I was able to enter the church freely.[48]

The bombardments began then. I would serve the Mass during the bombardments, between the bursts of antiaircraft artillery.[49]

The time of violence began; a terrible time, above all for my country. I cannot forget the Holocaust of the Jewish people. I testify that Divine Providence led me by the hand during the war. And it was then that I discovered my priestly vocation. Right in the midst of that tragic experience of the war, I found the way for my own life. At the same time, I shared the sufferings of so many people in my country and all over Europe.[50]

A year later the university was closed by the occupying power, and its teachers, many of them elderly and eminent, were deported to the concentration camp at Sachsenhausen.[51]

If I think back on my life, I can say that the war is certainly an unforgettable experience of danger and fear. I had not yet turned twenty when, in Europe and the world, the tempest of the Second World War was unleashed. It was a time of constant fear for the bombardments, deportations, and reprisals. So, I know only too well what it means to experience terror.[52]

I too was twenty, like you. I enjoyed sports, skiing, and acting. I studied and I worked. I had desires and worries. In those years, now so long ago, when my native land was wounded by war and then by the totalitarian regime, I sought the meaning for my life. I found it in following the Lord Jesus.[53]

My youth, in its most decisive moments, was fraught with difficulties. It was a time of war, and ours was an occupied country. This was a great trial for the entire nation, and especially for its youth. At the same time, however, it was a time of affirmation of the highest values, lived many times to the point of heroism, many times at the cost of one's own life![54]

I think of the Warsaw uprising in 1944—the desperate revolt of my contemporaries, who sacrificed everything. They laid down their young lives on the burning pyre. They wanted to demonstrate that they could live up to their great and demanding heritage. I was a part of that generation, and I must say that the heroism of my contemporaries helped me to define my personal vocation.[55]

I carry the most profound impression in my memory of that unique year of study before the war: the atmosphere of the university, the names of the famous professors that I had the honor to study under, and the faces of my friends, most of whom I have been separated from by the events of the succeeding years.[56]

The Second World War is a historic event, and some of us, myself included, have experienced firsthand the occupation and oppression of our country. It was not easy to work day after day in difficult circumstances. It was not easy to study at the university. It was not easy to see suffering and injustice on such a worldwide scale, and at the same time to continue to live the virtue of hope, trusting God and trusting other people. It was not easy to make room for the voice of the Lord calling me to a total self-giving in the priesthood and to study in secret under all kinds of limitations in preparation for that consecration. But no true vocation is easy! What I learned in those and other hard moments was to judge all things in the light of Christ: the way, the truth and the life of every individual and of all peoples.[57]

> *To avoid deportation to forced labor camps in Germany it was necessary to have the identification card from the German authorities, a release as a "socially useful" worker.*

I began in the autumn of 1940 to work as a laborer in a stone quarry attached to the Solvay chemical plant. This was at Zakrzówek, about half an hour from my home in Dębniki, and every day I would walk there. [...] The managers of the quarry, who were Poles, tried to spare us students from the heaviest work. In my case, they made me the assistant to the rock-blaster: his name was Franciszekłabuś.[58]

During the summer of 1941 I was transferred to work in the boiler system of a so-called water purifying plant.[59]

Providence willed that, for a certain period of my life, even I would experience hard labor in a quarry. I therefore can testify from my own experience about the difficulties this work entails. Physical strength is not enough; a person also needs dexterity, control over one's nerves, quick reflexes, and courage. It isn't enough to know how to maneuver the machinery; one needs to have familiarity with the mountain itself, to come to know its secrets and also its hidden dangers. Above all, one needs solid moral gifts to hold up under the strain of a day passed with the jackhammers, chisels, and mallets. There are, then, the sudden accidents that in a few seconds can transform the workplace atmosphere into a scene of tragedy. I experienced even this, and they were moments that will remain stamped on my soul for the rest of my life.[60]

Among the most beautiful experiences of my life will always be those moments of solidarity and friendship I was able to enjoy with my coworkers when I was a laborer. It was an experience profoundly human and deeply comforting. We never lacked work, nor the sad and difficult moments that accompanied it. In these moments the friendship and solidarity we lived helped and comforted us. And these friendships, these signs of solidarity, that I witnessed firsthand as a laborer, remain in my soul even now as most precious.[61]

The Pope has no fear of men of work. They have always been particularly close to him. He has come from their midst. He has come from the quarries of Zakrzówek, from the Solvay furnaces in Borek Fałęcki, and then from Nowa Huta.[vii] Through all these surroundings, through his own experience of work, I make bold to say that the Pope learned the Gospel anew. He noticed and became convinced that the problems being raised today about human labor are deeply engraved in the Gospel, that they cannot be fully solved without the Gospel.[62]

I, too, have been a worker: for a short period of my life, during the last world conflict I, too, had direct experience of factory work. I know, therefore, what the commitment of daily toil in employment by others means. I know how heavy and monotonous it is; I know the needs of the workers and their just demands and legitimate aspirations. And I know how necessary it is that work should never be alienating and frustrating, but should always correspond to man's superior spiritual dignity.[63]

---

vii The Nowa Huta district of Kraków was constructed as a secularized city of workers; however, Bishop (later Cardinal) Wojtyła set about to harass the authorities until he was able to establish the great Marian "Ark Church," consecrated May 15, 1977. Other churches followed.

Forty years have passed, but I recall those years as if they happened yesterday. This experience of life as a laborer, with its positive aspects and also its miseries, while at another level, the deportations of my fellow Polish citizens to extermination camps, has profoundly marked my existence. From that time, the mystery of human existence has occupied the first place in my reflections, and I feel irresistibly moved to speak in defense of human dignity, sustained by the mysterious action of Christ, who is our God, but who became our brother to save us.[64]

Someone has asked me if I ever had the desire to become a trade union representative. I must say that I felt the vocation to the priesthood, and followed it. But the conditions then were very particular. There was the war, and the occupation. So, I think that it is a beautiful vocation to help one's brothers and colleagues; it is a Christian vocation that I myself did not feel called to. Others have felt it. For example, at this time much is said about the strikes in Poland, and I refer to the example of this vocation as lived by my fellow countryman, Lech Wałęsa. This is how Providence distributes the calls; he gives to each one a vocation.[65]

On February 18, 1941, young Karol's father also died, leaving him alone.

The violence of the blows that had struck [my father] had opened up immense spiritual depths in him; his grief found its outlet in prayer. The mere fact of seeing him on his knees had a decisive influence on my early years. He was so hard on himself he had no need to be hard on his son; his example alone was sufficient to inculcate discipline and a sense of duty.[66]

I remember that day so very clearly: I returned home from work and found my father dead. My friendship with the Kydryńskis was a great comfort for me at the time. Our friendship then grew to include other families, especially the Szkocki family.[67]

The time arrived in which a change of direction was outlined for Karol to give way to his vocation. The idea of becoming an actor, which at times had piqued his interest, had little by little been gratified. His last appearance on the theatrical scene was in March 1943, in the leading role of Samuel Zborowski *by Juliusz Słowacki.*[viii]

After my father's death, I gradually became aware of my true path. I was working at the factory and devoting myself, as far as the terrors of the occupation allowed, to my passion for literature and drama. My priestly vocation took shape in the midst of all that, like an inner fact of unquestionable and absolute clarity.[68]

During that time I stayed in contact with the *theater of the living word* which Mieczysław Kotlarczyk had founded and continued to direct in the underground. . . . It was all quite simple. The scenery and decoration were kept to a minimum; our efforts were concentrated essentially on the delivery of the poetic text. The recitations took place before a small group of people whom we knew and before guests who, because they had a particular interest in literature, belonged in a sense to the "initiated." It was essential to keep these theatrical get-togethers secret; otherwise we risked serious punishment from the occupying forces, even deportation to the concentration camps. I must admit that that whole experience of the theater left a deep impression on me, even though at a certain point I came to realize that *this was not my real vocation.*[69]

When I was a university student I read various authors. At first I turned to literature, especially plays. I read Shakespeare, Moliére, the Polish poets Norwid, Wyspiański, and obviously, Aleksander Fredro. My passion, however, was to become an actor, to step out onto the stage. Often I considered the roles I would have liked to play. Kotlarczyk and I would amuse ourselves by assigning possible parts to each other and wondering who could best play particular characters. These are things of the past. Later someone said to me, "You have talent . . . you would have been a great actor if you had only stayed in the theater."[70]

From my earliest childhood I have loved books. It was my father who introduced me to reading. He would sit beside me and read to me,

---

viii Juliusz Słowacki was a Polish playwright who attempted to preserve and promote Polish history and culture through the power of the word. His five-part dramatic poem *Samuel Zborowski* (1844) extolled the efforts of a sixteenth-century nobleman to advance the Poland of his day.

for example, Sienkiewicz and other Polish writers. After my mother died, the two of us remained alone. He continued to encourage me to explore good literature, and he never stood in the way of my interest in the theater. If not for the outbreak of war and the radical change that it brought, perhaps the prospects opening up for me through academic study would have absorbed me completely. When I told Mieczysław Kotlarczyk of my decision to become a priest, he said, "What are you doing? Do you want to waste your talent?"[71]

My acquaintance with Kotlarczyk began in the years between the end of the '20s and the beginning of the '30s in our common city of birth, Wadowice. I knew him as a pioneer of an original type of theater, understood in the noblest sense of this word. He expressed the heart of Polish and Christian traditions, traditions that had been passed down to us through all our literature, above all the great romantic and neo-romantic works. [. . .] [Our relationship] began in unusual circumstances, and in an unusual work of his theater in Kraków that brought to light the "Rhapsodic Theater." It was during the time of the German occupation. [. . .] During that period the concept of the *theater of the living word* arose. This theater created by him worked in Kraków under clandestine conditions until the end of the occupation.[72]

It is during the years of one's youth that each person's personality becomes clearly defined. The future is in a sense already made present, and the years to come are viewed as being well within one's reach. These years represent the most favorable time for an especially clear discovery of the person and of his characteristics and the abilities hidden within. It is during this period that life is seen as a promising plan and each person has the role of the leading character in it.[73]

Before entering the seminary, I met a layman named Jan Tyranowski, who was a true mystic. This man, whom I consider a saint, introduced me to the great Spanish mystics and in particular to Saint John of the Cross. Even before entering the underground seminary, I read the works of that mystic, especially his poetry. In order to read it in the original, I studied Spanish. That was a very important stage in my life.[74]

Tyranowski created a group called the "living rosary" that was made up of fifteen youths. To each one was entrusted the daily recitation of a

mystery of the rosary. Even Karol was part of this group. Also at the
school of spirituality of Tyranowski, Karol read the Treatise on True
Devotion to Mary *in French by Saint Louis Marie Grignion de*
Montfort.

The reading of this book was a decisive turning point in my life. I
say "turning point," but in fact it was a long inner journey that coincided with my clandestine preparation for the priesthood. It was at
that time that this curious treatise came into my hands. The *Traité*
[*Treatise on True Devotion to Mary*] is one of those books that it is not
enough to "have read." I remember carrying it with me for a long time,
even at the sodium factory, with the result that its handsome binding
became spotted with lime. I continually went back to certain passages. . . . As a result, my devotion to the Mother of Christ in my childhood and adolescence yielded to a new attitude springing from the
depths of my faith, as though from the very heart of the Trinity and
Jesus Christ.[75]

Who were my models? They were many. I owe much to Saint
Francis of Assisi, who did not think himself worthy of ordination and
so remained a deacon, and to his [Franciscan] brother Albert
Chmielowski, his most faithful disciple in my country. Brother Albert
was one of those responsible for the spiritual renascence of Poland
toward the end of the last century.[76]

At a certain point in life, it is necessary to make a radical choice.
Without denying anything that is an expression of God's beauty or
of the talents received from him, we must be able to side with Christ
to witness before all to God's love. In this regard, I like to remember
the great spiritual fascination that the Holy Friar Albert exercised in
the story of my vocation! Adam Chmielowski was his name, and he
was not a priest. Friar Albert was a very talented and cultured painter.
Well, at a certain point in his life he broke with art, because he understood that God was calling him to far more important tasks. He came
to Kraków to make himself poor among the poor and devoted himself to serving the outcasts. In him I found special spiritual support
and an example as I was distancing myself from literature and the
theater because of my radical choice of the vocation to the priest-

hood. Later, one of my greatest joys was to raise him to the honors of the altar, and even before that, to dedicate a play to him, entitled: *Brother of Our God.*[77]

You cannot imagine with what great affection and admiration I drew near to the human, linguistic, cultural, and religious context of the life and works of Saint Teresa of Jesus. She, together with Saint John of the Cross, was for me a teacher, inspirer, and guide in the ways of the spirit. I was always motivated by her to nourish and maintain my interior liberty for God and for the cause of human dignity.[78]

If I look back at my youth, at those years lived during the occupation, terrible years—a real nightmare—I see that the source of my "foundational strength" was the Eucharist. It was thus not only for me, but for many others, above all for those whose lives were uprooted by the most unsupportable conditions.[79]

To live the Eucharist it is necessary, as well, to spend much time in adoration in front of the Blessed Sacrament, something which I myself experience every day, drawing from it strength, consolation, and assistance.[80]

I recall that when I was young like you are and I would read the Gospels, the strongest proof for the truthfulness of what I was reading for me was that in the Gospel there were no secret promises! Jesus presented his disciples with some very hard sayings: don't expect anything, no kingdom of this world, no seat at my right hand or my left in the ministries of this future messianic kingdom. The messianic King will go to the cross, and there he will be put to the test. Then the resurrection will give you strength; the power of the Holy Spirit will enable you to bear witness to the world about this Crucified One. But no secret promises! In the world you will be persecuted. This did a lot to convince me, because normally people seek to attract followers with promises—promises of a career, of monetary gain—this will come to you, you will get that, and that, and that. . . . [81]

A light was beginning to shine ever more brightly in the back of my mind: the Lord wants me to become a priest. One day I saw this with great clarity: it was like an interior illumination which brought with it the joy and certainty of a new vocation. And this awareness filled me with great inner peace.[82]

A day came when I knew for certain that my life would not be fulfilled in human love, the beauty of which I have always felt deeply.[83]

I owe a profound debt of gratitude to several priests, especially to one of them, now very old, who in my early youth brought me closer to Christ by his goodness and simplicity. He was my confessor, and it was he who knew at what precise moment it was right to say to me, "Christ is calling you to the priesthood."[84]

Clandestine Seminarian

In the autumn of 1942 I made my final decision to enter the Kraków seminary, which was operating clandestinely. I was accepted by the rector, Father Jan Piwowarczyk. The matter had to be kept strictly secret, even from those dear to me.[85]

Immediately I found myself up against an obstacle. My literary training, centered on the humanities, had not prepared me at all for the scholastic theses and formulas with which the manual was filled. I had to cut a path through a thick undergrowth of concepts, analyses, and axioms without even being able to identify the ground over which I was moving. After two months of hacking through this vegetation I came to a clearing, to the discovery of the deep reasons for what until then I had only lived and felt.[86]

I studied metaphysics on my own and tried to understand its "categories." And I did understand. Even without the help of my professors, I understood. As well as passing the exam, I was able to realize that metaphysics and Christian philosophy gave me a new vision of the world, a deeper perception of reality. Up to then, I had only done humanistic studies linked to literature and letters. Through metaphysics and philosophy, I found a key, the key to an understanding and perception of the world. A much deeper, I might even say, ultimate perception.[87]

The seminary of Kraków prepared me for the priesthood. It is a great thing to prepare someone for the priesthood. The period during which this took place was a special, exceptional one. I had quite a strange seminary education; when someone asked me if I had six years of seminary, I reflected: what years? At any rate, seminary means preparation for the priesthood, and the Kraków seminary did this for me, for which I am very grateful.[88]

I am often asked, especially by young people, why I became a priest. Maybe some of you would like to ask the same question. Let me try briefly to reply. I must begin by saying that it is impossible to explain entirely, for it remains a mystery, even to me. How does one explain the ways of God? Yet, I know that at a certain point in my life, I became convinced that Christ was saying to me what he had said to thousands before me: *"Come, follow me!"* There was a clear sense that what I heard in my heart was no human voice, nor was it just an idea of my own. Christ was calling me to serve him as a priest. And you can probably tell I am deeply grateful to God for my vocation to the priesthood. Nothing means more to me or gives me greater joy than to celebrate Mass each day and to serve God's people in the Church. That has been true ever since the day of my ordination as a priest. Nothing has ever changed it, not even becoming Pope.[89]

I give you my own witness: I was ordained a priest when I was twenty-six years old. Fifty-six years have passed since then. So how old is the Pope? Almost eighty-three! A young man of eighty-three! Looking back and remembering those years of my life, I can assure you that it is worthwhile dedicating oneself to the cause of Christ and, out of love for him, devoting oneself to serving humanity. It is worthwhile to give one's life for the Gospel and for one's brothers and sisters![90]

You have decided to build a just society, free and prosperous, in which each and every person can enjoy the fruits of progress. In my youth, I also lived with these same convictions. Young students, I have proclaimed this with the voice of literature and art. God wished this desire to be toughened in the fire of a war whose atrocities did not spare my family. I saw these convictions trampled on in many ways. I feared for them, seeing them exposed to the tempest. One day I decided to confront them with Jesus Christ. I understood that he was the only one to reveal to me their true content and value. I thought to defend them with him against I did not know what inevitable stresses. All of this tremendous, valid experience has taught me that social justice is real only if it is based on the rights of the individual.[91]

You asked me when I began to think about becoming a priest. This is a question about my vocation, certainly, but also about my conversion, because when one decides he wants to become a priest, a call from Jesus is necessary first. During his earthly life Jesus made these calls with his own words, words that could be heard with the sound of his voice. Now, instead, he calls with a voice heard interiorly, one heard in the heart and the conscience. To follow these words means to be converted, to begin to walk according to the words of Christ. This is essential for everyone who wants to become a priest, as it is for every Christian. Every Christian is such due to the grace of the sacrament of Baptism; at the same time, one continually "becomes" Christian by converting oneself and following the words of Christ, who calls some to the priesthood, some to the religious life, and all to be Christians, good Christians. I have received this call. I was not young like you; I was a university student during the difficult moments of war, a difficult time for my country.[92]

Secretly, during the occupation, I began . . . studies at the clandestine school of theology at the Jagiellonian University. Amid the terrible trials of war, I gradually discovered within myself the vocation to the priesthood, and I found myself on a new way. My studies at the school of theology in 1942 signified the beginning of this way. This way passed first through secrecy, and then, in January of 1945, in the regular studies at this school. This was the second chapter of my experience as a student, one very different from that done before the war, and in a certain manner it completed it.[93]

I used to take books with me to the factory during my eight-hour shift, during the day or at night. My workmates were rather surprised, but not scandalized. Indeed, they said, "We will help you, you can rest, and in your place we will keep an eye [on the boilers] instead of you." So I was also able to do the exams with my professors.[94]

When I left the factory to follow my priestly vocation, I brought with me an irreplaceable experience of that world and the profound importance of friendship and of vibrant solidarity with my working companions, something precious that I treasured in my spirit.[95]

I shall remember as long as I live the men with whom I was linked in the same work yard, whether in the stone quarries or in the factory.

I shall not forget the human kindness that my fellow workers showed toward me. I shall not forget the discussions we had, in free moments, on the fundamental problems of existence and of the life of workers. I know what value their home, the future of their children, the respect due to their wives, to their mothers, had for these men, who were at the same time fathers of families. From this experience of some years, I drew the conviction and the certainty that man expresses himself in work as a subject capable of loving, oriented toward fundamental human values, ready for solidarity with every man.[96]

I am grateful for having had that opportunity to reflect deeply on the meaning and dignity of human work in its relationship to the individual, the family, the nation, and the whole social order. Those years allowed one to share in a specific way in God's creative activity and to experience work in the light of the Cross and Resurrection of Christ.[97]

During the fifty-eight years I lived in Poland, I had little hospital experience: only as a boy, because my older brother was a doctor, and then due to an accident that happened to me toward the end of the war. And that was it.[98]

In fact, on February 29, 1944, an automobile hit him, leaving him unconscious on the side of the road.

I was walking toward the Solvay along Konopnicka Street. There were no sidewalks at that time. That was it. The next thing I knew I was in the hospital with my head bandaged.[99]

After the accident I worked in the bicarbonate plant. I left work at the beginning of August 1944 and resumed the third year of studies at the metropolitan seminary.[100]

Here I want to confide in you something very personal. I find myself in a parish dedicated to Our Lady of Mount Carmel. I want you to know that during my youth, when I was as you are, she helped me: I cannot say how much, but I would say in an immense way. She helped me to find the grace proper to my age, to my vocation. Since I am visiting a parish dedicated to her, the Virgin of Mount Carmel, I want to say this; I want to testify to this, so that this testimony will be profitable, useful for each of you young people. I speak of a very special aspect of the spiritual riches of the Virgin Mother of Christ, because her Carmelite mission, begun on Mount Carmel in the Holy Land, is tied to a piece of cloth. This cloth we call a holy scapular. I owe much from my youth to the benefits of this Carmelite scapular. That the Mother is always solicitous, preoccupied for the "clothes" of her children, that they are well dressed, is a beautiful thing.[101]

In Kraków, on Rakowicka Street, there was a monastery of Discalced Carmelite Fathers. I spent time with them and once made my retreat with them. . . . For a time I also considered entering the Carmel. My uncertainties were resolved by the archbishop, Cardinal Sapieha, who in his typical manner said tersely: "First you have to finish what you have begun." And that is what happened.[102]

The closeness of my bishop, especially during the years when I was living in his residence, had a great influence on my formation for the priesthood.[103]

I went through the seminary under Cardinal Sapieha. At first I was a cleric, and then I became a priest. I had great trust in him, and I can say that I loved him just as other priests loved him. It is often written in books that Sapieha was in some way preparing me—perhaps it is true. This too is a bishop's responsibility: to prepare those who can eventually succeed him.[104]

During the time of the occupation, the metropolitan archbishop set up the seminary, clandestinely, at his residence. . . . I took up my lodging in this unusual seminary, with the much-loved Prince Metropolitan,[ix] in September 1944 and was able to stay there with my fellow students until January 18, 1945, the day—or rather the night—of the liberation. It was in fact at night that the Red Army reached the outskirts of Kraków. The retreating Germans blew up Dębniki Bridge. I remember that terrible explosion: the blast broke all the windows of the archbishop's residence. At that moment we were in the chapel for a ceremony with the archbishop. The following day we worked quickly to repair the damage.[105]

---

ix Adam Stefan Cardinal Sapieha, Archbishop of Kraków (1867–1951), called Prince Metropolitan, actually was a prince by birth. He was also known as the Unbroken Prince because of his unflagging resistance to the German occupation.

When the war was over, I thought to myself: the Lord God allowed Nazism twelve years of existence, and after twelve years the system collapsed. Evidently this was the limit imposed by Divine Providence upon that sort of folly. . . . If communism had survived for longer and if it still had the prospect of further development to come, I thought to myself at the time, there had to be meaning in all this. . . . "The miracle on the Vistula," that is, the triumph of Piłsudski in the battle against the Red Army, muted those Soviet ambitions. After the victory over Nazism in 1945, though, the communists felt reinvigorated and they shamelessly set out to conquer the world, or at least Europe. . . . There was a sense that this evil was in some way necessary for the world and for mankind. It can happen, in fact, that in certain concrete situations, evil is revealed as somehow useful, inasmuch as it creates opportunities for good.[106]

As an ecclesiastical student in the major seminary of Kraków, during those first postwar years, I was able to share in the life of the academic society of the university. For a while I was even vice president of the "Brotherly Aid" group of the students at the Jagiellonian University. After I finished my studies and was doing research for a doctorate in theology, I continued to keep in contact with the athenaeum. In November 1953 I was given a certificate in the field of moral theology. This was the last certificate issued by the school of theology of the Jagiellonian University before the exclusion of that school—after almost six centuries—from the organization of the university, the oldest alma mater in Poland. My alma mater![107]

At the beginning of my fifth year, the archbishop decided that I should go to Rome to finish my studies. And so, a little earlier than my companions, I was ordained a priest on November 1, 1946. That year our group was of course not very large: we were seven in all.[108]

After the anticipation and the prayerful preparation during the month of October, I remember with emotion the rite of my ordination by the archbishop of Kraków, Adam Stefan Cardinal Sapieha, in his private chapel. From that moment on, I let myself be led by the Lord on the road he opened up to me day after day.[109]

Vividly before my mind's eye pass the images of that day long ago, when early in the morning I presented myself at the archbishop's residence in Kraków, on Franciszkańska Street, to receive priestly ordination. I was accompanied by a small group of family and friends. With emotion I see again the floor of the private chapel of the metropolitan archbishop; I hear the chanting of the *Veni Creator Spiritus* and the Litany of the Saints; I await the imposition of hands; I accept the invitation to proclaim the Good News, to guide the people of God, to celebrate the divine mysteries. They are indelible memories, that I relive this day with inexpressible gratitude toward the Lord.[110]

The chapel in the episcopal residence in Kraków has a very particular significance for me. In it I was ordained a priest by Cardinal Sapieha on November 1, 1946, even though ordinations usually took place in the cathedral. . . . I personally witnessed the habitual practice of the Prince Archbishop of Kraków, Adam Sapieha. . . . I tried to imitate his incomparable example. In the private chapel I not only prayed, but I also sat and wrote. There I wrote my books. That's where I wrote *The Acting Person*, among other titles. I am convinced that the chapel is a place of special inspiration. It is an enormous privilege to be able to live and work within the climate of this Presence—a Presence which draws us like a powerful magnet.[111]

This day is one fixed with an indelible seal in my memory. It was, in fact, on the feast of All Saints forty-four years ago that I received the gift of the priesthood of Christ and became the servant of the Eucharist. I recall with perennial devotion those who accompanied me toward this ministry. I am united to them in the mystery of the Communion of Saints.[112]

I have been pope for two years; I have been a bishop for over twenty years, and yet the most important thing for me still remains the fact that I am a priest; the fact of being able to celebrate the Eucharist every day. I am able to renew Christ's own sacrifice, by giving back, in him, all things to the Father: the world, humanity, and myself. The correct dimension of the Eucharist consists, in fact, in this. That is why I have always living in my memory this interior development as a result of which "I heard" Christ's call to the priesthood, this special "come and follow me." Confiding this to you, I invite you to listen carefully, each one of you, to these evangelical words. It is in this way that your humanity will be formed completely, and that the Christian vocation of each of you will be defined. And perhaps you will also hear, in your turn, the call to the priesthood or to religious life.[113]

The priest is a man of the Eucharist. In the span of almost fifty years of priestly life, the celebration of the Eucharist continues for me to be the most important and sacred of all moments. And what predominates for me is the knowledge that I celebrate at the altar *"in the person of Christ."* Never, in the course of these years, have I missed the celebration of the most holy sacrifice. If it did happen, it was only for reasons that were independent of my will.[114]

When I think of the Eucharist, and look at my life as a priest, as a bishop and as the Successor of Peter, I naturally recall the many times and places in which I was able to celebrate it. I remember the parish church of Niegowić, where I had my first pastoral assignment, the collegiate church of Saint Florian in Kraków, Wawel Cathedral, Saint Peter's Basilica, and so many basilicas and churches in Rome and throughout the world. I have been able to celebrate Holy Mass in chapels built along mountain paths, on lakeshores and seacoasts; I have celebrated it on altars built in stadiums and in city squares. This varied scenario of celebrations of the Eucharist has given me a powerful experience of its universal and, so to speak, cosmic character. Yes, cosmic! Because even when it is celebrated on the humble altar of a country church, the Eucharist is always in some way celebrated *on the altar of the world.*[115]

One of you asked me what the pope would be doing if he were not the pope. I don't know. Certainly, I would have become a priest, because this is the greatest reality of all: to be a priest "in the person of Christ," to offer his sacrifice, substituting myself for Christ the priest. Certainly, even if I were not the pope, my principal duty would be to preserve, protect, defend, increase, and deepen my aspiration toward the good, the true, and the beautiful.[116]

To respond to the boy who asked the second question, if being the pope is easy or difficult, I would say above all that for the pope, the most important thing is to be a priest. Every day I can celebrate the

most holy Eucharist, I can pronounce the words of Eucharistic consecration, and I can do this "in the person of Jesus." The other things
come after, like an additional vocation, as a bishop or as the bishop of
Rome, who is one of the bishops of the world, but a special bishop
because Peter's ministry is entrusted [to me] by Jesus. So, more than
speaking of a difficult or easy duty, I can say to you only that all things,
even those that are difficult, with the grace of the Holy Spirit, with the
grace of God, become possible—I don't say easy, but possible. Nothing
is impossible for God.[117]

Having been ordained a priest on the feast of All Saints, I celebrated
my first Mass on All Souls Day, November 2, 1946. On that day every
priest may celebrate three Masses for the benefit of the faithful. So in
a sense I celebrated three "first" Masses. It was a deeply moving experience. I celebrated the three Masses in the crypt of Saint Leonard,
which in Wawel Cathedral at Kraków is the front part of the so-called
episcopal cathedral of Herman. . . . Other "first Masses" followed: in
the parish church of Saint Stanisłaus Kostka at Dębniki and the following Sunday in Wadowice, at the Church of the Presentation of the
Mother of God. I also celebrated a Mass at the Confession of Saint
Stanisłaus in Wawel Cathedral for my friends in the Rhapsodic Theater
and for the clandestine group UNIA[x] to which I was linked during the
occupation.[118]

To Rome to Become a Teacher

*The date set for Father Karol's departure for Rome was November 15,
1946. There he remained for nearly two years, deepening his theological
studies.*

When the set day arrived, I boarded the train with great excitement.
With me was Stanisław Starowieyski, a younger colleague who had
been sent to take his whole course of theological studies in Rome. For

---

x UNIA, a clandestine organization composed primarily of young intellectuals, was an
attempt to form leaders and society in general for a new independent Poland.

the first time I was leaving the borders of my homeland. From the window of the moving train I looked at cities known previously only from my geography books. For the first time I saw Prague, Nuremberg, Strasbourg, and Paris, where we stopped as guests of the Polish Seminary on the Rue des Irlandais. We stayed there only briefly, since time was pressing, and reached Rome in the last days of November. Here we first enjoyed the hospitality of the Pallottine Fathers.[119]

I have come to visit this place and this community of Saint Vincent Pallotti because my personal story is marked by many important encounters with the spiritual sons of Saint Vincent Pallotti. Wadowice, my birthplace, is the center for the Polish Pallottines. I frequently came in contact with them, during my youth and also in my ministry as a priest and later a bishop. But there is a special reason that I feel bound to this place and this community. Even today I recall, not without emotion and gratitude, that day in far-off 1946 when, as a young priest, I arrived in Rome to complete my studies at the Pontifical Athenaeum[xi] and was welcomed into your community. Even though my stay was not a long one, it was sufficient for me to remember the atmosphere of serene fraternity that was palpable here.[120]

After a month and a half at the convent of the Pallottines on Pettinari Street, he transferred at the end of December to the Belgian College on Quirinale Street.

The Belgian College of Rome welcomed me forty years ago. I hold a memory that moves me with gratitude—the hospitality from which I benefited during my two years of theological study in Rome right after my ordination to the priesthood. Their house was at 26 Via del Quirinale. Cardinal Maximilian de Fürstenberg was the rector at that time. . . . Until today the Lord has guided me along pathways that I would never have been able to foresee, and has had grace ready for me continually, even the grace to be able to accept greater responsibility in the Church. But the period I spent as a young priest and student in the

---

[xi] The proper name for this Roman university is the Pontifical Athenaeum of Saint Thomas Aquinas. It is commonly known as the Angelicum in reference to Saint Thomas' epithet, Angelic Doctor.

Belgian College in Rome remains in my mind as a happy and fruitful time. It was almost like an Advent, a period of maturation, of preparation for service in the church, and a period of discoveries and exchanges that in turn enriched me. Yes, I owe a lot to this college for the scientific formation it promoted in me, along with the theological teachings received at the Angelicum, and for the education that has directed me toward an openness to the pastoral reality.[121]

During the audience granted to young priests and seminarians of the Belgian College, when Pope Pius XII, approaching each one present, came to me, the rector of the College said that I came from Poland. The Pope stopped for a moment, obviously moved, and repeated, "From Poland," and in Polish he said, "Praised be Jesus Christ." This happened in the first months of 1947.[122]

Many years ago, I myself was a "foreign student" here in Rome, which makes it easy for me to feel particularly near to you and to know well your situation, and not just by hearsay. I, too, experienced the difficulties of learning a foreign language, the unknowns of getting used to a new place, the distance from my loving family, from my friends, and from my homeland, which I had left behind. In a situation like this, moral effort is imperative in order to complete the studies you have chosen to make, and to arrive at authentic human and spiritual growth.[123]

Here I should like to refer to a conversation I had during my studies in Rome with one of my college companions, a young Flemish priest. He was associated with the work of Father Jozef Cardijn, the future cardinal, namely the so-called JOC (YCW), or Jeunesse Ouvrière Chrétienne (Young Christian Workers). The topic of our conversation was the situation in Europe after the Second World War. My colleague expressed himself more or less as follows: "The Lord allowed the experience of such an evil as communism to affect you . . . And why did he allow it?" His answer to this question I find significant: "We were spared this in the West, because perhaps we could not have withstood so great a trial. You, on the other hand, can take it." This remark by the young Fleming remained fixed in my memory. To some degree it had a prophetic value.[124]

After the last war, when I was studying in Rome, I served as a pastor—here in Belgium during the vacation—to a community of Polish emigrants. I knew then your loyal faith and your fidelity to God and to the Christian traditions of the fathers. I noticed also the scrupulous dedication you gave to your work. I also had the opportunity to know a good many families during the month that I carried out my pastoral work in this environment.[125]

In fact, during the summer he traveled to several European countries, as can be seen from this postcard to his friend Mieczysław Maliński:

I write to you from Paris, where I have now arrived after passing first to Marseilles and Lourdes. By order of the Prince [Archbishop Sapieha], I must dedicate this vacation to visiting France, Belgium, and possibly Holland, and to study of the various pastoral methods. This is a chance of a lifetime. What I get out of it will depend on the grace of God and upon my own powers of observation. Besides, I'm drawn not only to studying the pastoral methods, but also by the monuments that I can visit here.[126]

I came to Rome as a young priest to finish my studies. I had been ordained only a few weeks. I began right away to seek for what I had carried in my heart for a long time, because this unknown Rome I had carried deep in my soul as a dream, as an ideal. The long years of my studies and the strong Catholic tradition of my country had prepared me for this encounter with Rome. Above all, I had prepared myself by reading a book, written by a Polish author,[xii] concerning the first Christians of Rome: *Quo Vadis*. . . . I had carried within my heart for many years an image of the Rome of the early Christians, of the catacombs, and so, in November 1946 I roamed through the streets, in the churches, still unable to find that image which had been etched on my heart. Finally I reached the catacombs and I visited the first Christian basilicas, where finally I perceived the presence of the first generation

---

xii *Quo Vadis: A Narrative of the Time of Nero*, by Henryk Sienkiewicz, published in 1895, won the Nobel Prize for Literature in 1905 and is available in more than fifty languages; it was made into two major motion pictures in English.

of Christians. It was then that I recognized the Rome that lived in my soul.[127]

I will never forget the years, the months, and the days of my first stay in Rome. A place that was one of my favorites, one to which I returned often, was the very ancient ruins of the Roman Forum, still conserved today. How eloquent it was for me that beside the forum was the Church of Saint Mary, built directly on top of an ancient roman edifice.[128]

I arrived in Rome the first time almost forty-three years ago as a young, newly ordained priest. I looked in Rome above all for what our parish priest had described to us. I searched for these remains, the traces of the saints and martyrs, of these followers of Christ who testified to their faith with blood, with martyrdom, giving their lives. I still did not feel myself to be in Rome when I walked through the streets and the squares, until the moment I entered the catacombs and the basilicas—as that visit a week ago to Santa Maria degli Angeli, the ancient baths of Diocletian, a place of martyrdom. Today we add San Saturnino. This all makes me recall my first experiences seeing Rome forty-three years ago. I would never have imagined I would return as bishop of this holy city. Because we are here in these circumstances, I confide this to you. We find ourselves in a parish dedicated to a holy martyr, whose life was so well described to you by the pastor. We find ourselves in the relics of the beginnings of that first generation of whom we are all heirs, not only you Romans, but all Christians of the world.[129]

> But even his time of studies in Rome came to an end. After having passed the theology exam on July 3, 1947, he went on to defend his doctoral thesis, "The Doctrine of the Faith According to Saint John of the Cross," on June 19, 1948.

And then I immediately left for Poland. . . . As I left, I took with me not only a much broader theological education but also a strengthened priesthood and a more profound vision of the Church. That period of intense study close to the tombs of the Apostles had given me much, from every point of view.[130]

As soon as I reached Kraków, I went to the Metropolitan Curia to receive my first "assignment," the so-called *aplikata*. The archbishop was then in Rome, but he had left written instructions. I accepted the appointment with joy. Immediately I inquired how to get to Niegowić and made plans to be there on the day appointed. . . . And so I began my pastoral work in my first parish. It lasted for a year and consisted of the usual tasks assigned to a curate and religion teacher. I was put in charge of five elementary schools in the villages belonging to the parish.[131]

When I was a young priest, I taught religion in the schools. And several times, even when the class was noisy, as soon as I began to speak of Jesus, especially when I told the story of the passion, they all became silent.[132]

A memory comes to mind of when I was a young priest at the beginning of my new life. I was associate pastor in a country parish, very spread out, with many villages. Often, among ourselves we would note that the best priests were those on the outer limits [of the diocese]. Perhaps this can be a consolation to you priests who work in the outer areas of Rome.[133]

After a year, I was transferred to the parish of Saint Florian in Kraków. The parish priest, Monsignor Tadeusz Kurowski, entrusted me with teaching catechism to the senior classes of the secondary school and providing pastoral care to the students at the university. . . . There I began to give talks to the young people at the university; every Thursday I would speak to them about fundamental problems concerning the existence of God and the spiritual nature of the human soul. These were extremely important issues, given the militant atheism being promoted by the communist regime.[134]

As a young priest I led a retreat at the Camaldolese Fathers at Bielany for university students from Saint Florian's parish. I recall that on one occasion I went down to the church at a late hour. To my great surprise, I found the students praying there. And I came to know that they intended to take turns praying in order to insure their uninterrupted presence for the entire night.[135]

I must confess to you, parish priests, that I have never been a parish priest. I have only been a parochial vicar! And then above all I was a professor in the seminary and university. My experience is wider than that of a university chair. But even without a direct, firsthand experience as parish priest, I have always been in touch with many parish priests, and I can say that they have given me the experience that they had.[136]

From my early days as a young priest, I have spent many hours talking with students on university campuses or while hiking along lakes or in the mountains and hills. I have spent many evenings singing with young men and women like you.[137]

I have always enjoyed singing. To be honest, I sang whenever the circumstances allowed, but I enjoyed singing with young people most of all. The texts were varied, according to the occasions: around the fire we sang folk songs and scout songs. For national feasts, the anniversaries of the outbreak of war, or the Warsaw Uprising, we would sing military and patriotic songs. My favorites were *Red Poppies on Monte Cassino*, *The First Brigade*, and in general the songs of the Polish insurrection and resistance.[138]

Especially in the past, it happened often that I was a witness not only of these important personal milestones, but there was something else: the young confided the secrets of their hearts, especially those who willingly shared with me about their vocation to the married life and their family lives. I learned then the great truths about love and responsibility, and later dedicated one of my books to that subject. This book was born from the many expectations that arise from love, and spoke of the many efforts of people to make that love mature and grow, in order to construct on this love their entire existence in the familial community.[139]

Sharing as priest, bishop, and cardinal the lives of countless young people at the university, in youth groups, during our mountain climbing expeditions, in circles of reflection and prayer, I noted that a young person can begin to grow up perilously. This happens when they are left to trick themselves with the easy and comfortable principle that "the end justifies the means," when they begin to believe that the only hope to better our society lies in promoting struggle and hatred among the various social classes, to have the utopia of one classless society, which only leads to the creation of more classes. I am convinced that only love can bring us together and solidify our unity in diversity.[140]

I want to confide to you, on this subject, that the reflection on man and, first then, a peculiar and direct interest in the concrete man—each individual man—as a creature with natural and supernatural dignity, thanks to the convergent and provident action of God the Creator and the Son of God, our Redeemer—is for me a mental habit that I have always had, but that has acquired a clarity after the experiences of my youth and the call to priesthood and pastoral life.[141]

The young priest's life soon took a new turn.

During the vacation of 1951, after two years of work in Saint Florian's parish, Archbishop Eugeniusz Baziak, who had succeeded Cardinal Sapieha as archbishop of Kraków, directed me toward scholarly work. I was to prepare for the diploma qualifying me to teach ethics and moral theology. This meant that I would have less time for the pastoral work so dear to me. This was a sacrifice, but from that time on I was always resolved that my dedication to the study of theology and philosophy would not lead me to "forget" that I was a priest; rather it would help me to become one ever more fully.[142]

Two years later, in 1953, he obtained certification and began to teach, first at Jagiellonian University and then at the seminary in Kraków and at the Catholic University in Lublin. On November 15, 1957, he obtained the title of a certified professor.

This certification was the last one obtained in the school of theology at the Jagiellonian University. A short time later, it was suppressed by the communist authorities. This act was aimed at dividing the institutions, but its intention was also to put reason and faith in opposition. I am not speaking here of that distinction which was born in the later Middle Ages based on the autonomy of the sciences, but of the imposed separation that did violence to the nation's spiritual patrimony. Nevertheless, I retained the conviction that those attempts would never definitively achieve their purpose. This conviction was strengthened in me, thanks to my personal encounters with men of science, professors of various disciplines who expressed the deep desire for dialogue and the common search for truth.[143]

Circumstances have never left me much time for study. By temperament I prefer thought to erudition. I came to realize this during my short career as a teacher at Kraków and Lublin. My conception of the person, unique in his identity, and of man as such, at the center of the universe, was born much more of experience and of sharing with others than of reading. Books, study, reflection, and discussion—which I do not avoid, as you know—help me to formulate what experience teaches me. In these two aspects of my life and activity, the pastoral vocation prevailed over that of teacher and scholar; it gradually turned out to be deeper and stronger; but if the two vocations are a long way from each other, there was never any rupture between them.[144]

Every meeting of this kind sparks memories of my own experience in academic teaching at Kraków and Lublin. They were years enriched by study, contacts, and research, fired by the desire to identify and explore new paths for an evangelization attentive to the challenges of the modern age. The knowledge I acquired at that time was useful to me in my pastoral ministry, first in Kraków and later as Successor of Peter, in the service I continue to carry out for the entire people of God. In every phase and stage of university life and pastoral ministry, one of the essential reference points for me was attention to the person, placed at the center of all philosophical or theological research.[145]

It is particularly gratifying to find myself among you, on the occasion of this third international congress of Catholic universities and schools of higher learning. If you will permit me a confidence, I will say that I feel right at home among you, since I spent a number of years on the faculty of a Catholic university.[146]

You will allow me, I am sure, a former university professor, who dedicated long and happy years to university teaching in his native land, to talk to you for a few moments of what I consider are the two essential aims of all complete and authentic university formation: knowledge and conscience, in other words, access to knowledge and the formation of conscience.[147]

As one who for long years has been a university professor, I will never tire of insisting on the eminent role of the university, which is to instruct but also to be a place of scientific research. In both these fields, its activity is closely related to the deepest and noblest aspiration of the human person: the desire to come to the knowledge of truth.[148]

My dear professors: the Pope, who was once also a man of studies at a university, understands well the difficulties of your work, the great weight you carry, the harshness with which your commitment and your ideal are opposed. Do not let yourselves become discouraged by the daily tensions. You know how to greet each day creatively, without being too satisfied with the accomplishments of the past. Have the courage to explore new pathways with prudence.[149]

Bishop of Kraków and Cardinal

On July 4, 1958, he received the news of his nomination as Auxiliary Bishop of Kraków while on one of the customary excursions with young people, by whom he came to be called, confidentially, "uncle" (wujek).

As I entered the office of the primate, Cardinal Stefan Wyszyński, I learned that the Holy Father had nominated me auxiliary bishop to the archbishop of Kraków. In February of that same year (1958) Bishop Stanisław Rospond had died. For many years he had been auxiliary bishop of Kraków under the Metropolitan Prince, Cardinal Adam Sapieha. Upon hearing the words of the primate informing me of the decision of the Holy See, I exclaimed, "Eminence, I am too young; I'm only thirty-eight." To which he replied, "It is a weakness from which you will soon free yourself. I beg you not to oppose the will of the Holy Father." So I said only one word, "I accept."[150]

The next day I went to see Archbishop Eugeniusz Baziak at 3 Franciszkańska Street and handed him a letter from the cardinal primate. I remember it as if it were today. The archbishop took me by the arm and led me into the waiting room where there were priests sitting and he said: *"Habemus papam"*—"We have a Pope." In the light of subsequent events, one might say that these words were prophetic. When I said to the archbishop that I would like to return to Masuria to join my friends who were canoeing on the Łyna River, he answered:

"I don't think that would be appropriate." Somewhat troubled by this reply, I went to the church of the Franciscans and prayed the Way of the Cross. I often went there for this purpose because the stations are original, modern, painted by Józef Mehoffer. Then I went back to Archbishop Baziak renewing my request. I said, "I appreciate your concern, Excellency, but I would still ask you to allow me to return to Masuria." This time he answered: "Yes, yes, by all means. But I ask you, please," he added with a smile, "come back in time for the consecration."[151]

September twenty-eighth came. It was the memorial of Saint Wenceslaus, the day designated for my episcopal ordination. I constantly think of that great ceremony (in those days the liturgy was even richer than it is today), and I remember every single person who took part. There was a custom of offering symbolic gifts to the ordaining bishop, including a small barrel of wine and a loaf of bread. These were carried by my friends: Zbigniew Siłkowski, a schoolmate from high school, and Jerzy Ciesielski, now Servant of God; next came Marian Wójtowicz and Zdzisław Heydel. Stanisław Rybicki was probably also there. The most active one was certainly Father Kazimierz Figlewicz. The day was cloudy but later the sun came out. As if by some good omen—a ray of sunshine fell on the poor new bishop. After the reading of the Gospel the choir sang: "*Veni Creator Spiritus, mentes tuorum visita: imple superna gratia, quae tu creasti pectora. . . .*"[xiii] I listened intently to the singing of this hymn and once again, as during my priestly ordination, and maybe with even greater clarity, I became conscious that it was the Holy Spirit who effected this consecration. This was a source of comfort and consolation in the face of all the human fears associated with this great new responsibility. The thought filled my soul with deep trust: the Holy Spirit will enlighten me, strengthen me, comfort me, and teach me. . . . Did not Jesus make this promise to his Apostles?[152]

After Mass I went directly from Wawel Cathedral to the seminary where the reception was held for invited guests, but that same evening I went to Częstochowa with a group of my closest friends.

---

xiii "Come, Holy Spirit, Creator, come, / From your bright heavenly throne; / Come, take possession of our souls, / And make them all your own."

There, on the following morning, I celebrated Mass in the chapel of the miraculous image of Our Lady. Częstochowa is a special place for Poles. In a sense it can be identified with Poland and its history, especially the history of the struggle for independence. Here stands the national shrine called Jasna Góra—the Bright Mountain. *Clarus Mons*: this name refers to the light that dispels darkness, and it took on a special meaning for Poles during the dark times of war, partition, and occupation.[153]

Upon my return to Kraków from my first pilgrimage to Częstochowa as a bishop, I began work in the archdiocesan curia, and was immediately named vicar general. I can honestly say that I soon made friends with all those working for the Kraków curia. I felt very much at ease in the curia, and I recall the years in Kraków with deep gratitude and joy. Priests began coming to me with a great variety of problems. I worked with real enthusiasm. The visitation of parishes began in the spring. Gradually I became accustomed to my new role in the Church. Episcopal ordination brought new responsibilities. They had been expressed in a brief, synthetic form during the liturgy of ordination.[154]

I particularly enjoyed pastoral visitations. I liked them very much because they put me in direct contact with people. I had a strong sense that I was "forming" them. Priests and laity, young people and old, and the healthy and sick, parents with their children and their problems— all came to me with whatever was on their mind. That was life. I remember my first pastoral visitation to Mucharz, south of Wadowice. The parish had an elderly pastor, an excellent priest, a monsignor. His name was Józef Motyka. He knew this was my first pastoral visitation and he was moved by this. He told me this could be his last. He felt he should be my guide. The visitation embraced the entire deanery and lasted the months of May and June. After the summer vacation, I visited my home deanery, Wadowice. Visitations took place in the spring and in the fall. I did not manage to visit all of the parishes (there were more than three hundred of them); in spite of the fact that I was bishop in Kraków for twenty years, I didn't get to them all.[155]

During a visitation I would also administer the sacraments: confirming young people and celebrating marriages. I would meet separately with different groups, such as teachers, parish workers, and young people. There was also a special gathering in church for all married couples. Mass would be celebrated, concluding with an individual blessing for each couple. The homily would naturally be dedicated to the subject of marriage. I always felt moved when I encountered large families and expectant mothers. I wanted to express my respect for motherhood and fatherhood. From the beginning of my priesthood, I have always had a special pastoral concern for married couples and families. As a chaplain to university students, I regularly organized marriage preparation courses, and later, as a bishop, I promoted the pastoral care of families. These experiences, these meetings with engaged couples, married couples, and families, gave birth to my poetic drama *The Jeweler's Shop*, my book *Love and Responsibility*, and, more recently, my *Letter to Families*. There were also separate meetings with the clergy. I wanted to give an opportunity to each of them to confide in me, to share the joys and concerns of their particular ministry. I greatly valued these meetings; they enabled me to learn from the treasury of wisdom accumulated over many years of apostolic labor.[156]

Kraków, and especially the Kazimierz neighborhood, retains many traces of Jewish culture and tradition. In Kazimierz, before the war, there were several dozen synagogues which were in some sense great cultural monuments as well. As archbishop of Kraków, I was in close contact with the city's Jewish community. I enjoyed very cordial relations with the head of that community, which continued even after I came to Rome.[157]

On October 11, 1962, Pope John XXIII officially opened the Second Vatican Council in Saint Peter's Basilica.

Providence disposed that, when the hour of the Council struck, I was a new bishop, having received episcopal ordination on September 28, 1958. I had the singular grace of participating in this great event and also giving my own contribution to its works. In this way, from the earliest steps, through each successive stage of its development, and then into the work of implementation, Vatican II became the background, the atmosphere, the central inspiration for my thoughts and activities as the pastor of a beloved local church, to which the Lord in his goodness called me.[158]

I had the particular fortune of being able to take part in the Council from the first day to the last. This was in no way to be taken for granted, since the communist authorities in my country considered the trip to Rome a privilege and entirely under their control. If, then, under such circumstances I was given the opportunity to participate in the Council from the beginning to the end, it can rightly be judged as a special gift from God.... At the beginning of my participation in the Council, I was a young bishop. I remember that at first my seat was right next to the entrance of Saint Peter's Basilica. From the third session on—after I was appointed archbishop of Kraków—I was moved closer to the altar.[159]

During the first session of the Council, when I was still auxiliary bishop of the archdiocese of Kraków, I had the occasion to thank Cardinal Giovanni Battista Montini[xiv] for the generous and precious gift that the archdiocese of Milan had given to the collegiate church of Saint Florian in Kraków: three new bells (a symbolic and very eloquent gift, not least because of the names given to the bells: Virgin Mary, Ambrose-Charles Borromeo, and Florian). These bells had been requested by Father Tadeusz Kurowski, provost of the collegiate church of Saint Florian. Archbishop Montini, who had always shown great benevolence toward the Polish people, revealed a great heart for this project too, and much understanding toward me who, at the time, was a very young bishop.[160]

I also established friendships with the Germans: Cardinal Alfred Bengsch, a year my junior; Joseph Höffner of Cologne; and Joseph Ratzinger, churchmen of exceptional theological competence.[161]

On January 13, 1964, he was named archbishop of Kraków—after hav-ing been vicar capitular[xv] of the diocese for a year and a half following

---

xiv Giovanni Battista Cardinal Montini (1897–1978) became Pope Paul VI in 1963.

xv A vicar capitular, as mandated in the 1913 *Code of Canon Law*, is the administrator of a diocese left vacant by the death of the bishop or archbishop. When a bishop dies, jurisdiction of the diocese passes to the canons of the cathedral chapter. They in turn elect the vicar capitular, who then assumes all authority until a new ordinary is appointed. The 1983 revised code of canon law provides for the appointment of an apostolic administrator.

the death of Archbishop Baziak—and on June 26, 1967, he was raised to be a cardinal by Paul VI.

Father Bohdan Niemczewski, as dean of the Chapter of Canons, was later to be a strong advocate of my appointment as archbishop, despite the strongly aristocratic tradition there—archbishops of Kraków were usually chosen from among the aristocracy. And so it was a great surprise when after such a long line I, from the "proletariat," was named archbishop of Kraków.[162]

On January 13, 1964, I was named metropolitan archbishop of Kraków. The nomination was published shortly thereafter, and on March 8, Laetare Sunday, I solemnly took possession of the see in Wawel Cathedral. On the threshold I was welcomed by Professor Franciszek Bielak and Monsignor Bohdan Niemczewski, the mitred provost[xvi] of the chapter. Then I entered the cathedral, where I was to occupy the episcopal throne left vacant after the deaths of Cardinal Sapieha and Archbishop Baziak. I do not remember the details of the address I delivered on that occasion, but I do remember that my thoughts were filled with the emotion I felt for Wawel Cathedral and its cultural heritage, to which I have forever felt bound, as I have stressed earlier.[163]

I was consecrated bishop in the Cathedral of Wawel, and in January 1964 I inherited the great patrimony of the Bishop of Kraków. . . . I remember the old Kraków of the university years of my youth—and the new Kraków which, with the construction of Nowa Huta, has almost tripled in size. This was the Kraków in whose problems I participated as pastor, as bishop, and as cardinal.[164]

A new tradition was created. Every New Year's at midnight I would celebrate Mass with the Franciscans in Kraków. Then in the morning I would go to stay with the Ursulines in Zakopane for some skiing (there was usually enough snow at that time). Often I stayed with them until January 6, when in the afternoon I would leave so as to be back at the cathedral in Kraków in time to celebrate the 6:00 P.M. Mass.

---

xvi The provost (prior) is the superior or head of the group of priests (canons) of a cathedral. In some cathedrals the provost is allowed to wear a mitre similar to that worn by a bishop, as a sign of authority. This was common practice in European cathedrals.

Afterward, there was a gathering in Wawel during which we sang Christmas carols. I remember that one time I went skiing, probably with Father Józef Rozwadowski (who later became bishop of Łód?), and we got lost somewhere around the Chocołowska valley. So we had to run like madmen, as the saying goes, in order to get back in time.[165]

The bishops of Kraków enjoy a special privilege, reserved, as far as I know, to just four dioceses in the world. They have the right to wear the so-called *rationale*.[xvii] Outwardly it resembles the pallium. In Kraków it is kept in the treasury of Wawel Cathedral—a gift from Queen Hedwig. In itself this sign means nothing. It acquires significance only when the archbishop wears it. It then symbolizes his authority and his service: because he has authority, he must serve. In a sense, it is a symbol of the Passion of Christ and of all the martyrs.[166]

Admonition is another responsibility that certainly forms part of a pastor's role. I think that in this regard I did too little. There is always a problem in achieving a balance between authority and service. Maybe I should have been more assertive. I think this is partly a matter of my temperament. Yet it could also be related to the will of Christ, who asked his Apostles not to dominate but to serve.... I do think, though, that despite my reluctance to rebuke others, I made all the necessary decisions. As the metropolitan of Kraków I tried very hard to make those decisions in a collegial spirit, that is to say I consulted my auxiliary bishops and other coworkers. Every week we met for curial sessions during which all matters were discussed in the light of the greater good of the archdiocese. I used to put two questions to my coworkers: "*Which truth of faith sheds light on this problem?*" And then: "*Whom should we approach for assistance?*" Finding a religious motivation for our action and the right person for a particular task was a good beginning, offering hope that our pastoral initiatives would bear fruit.[167]

Since I was bishop of Kraków I have always wanted to keep up a privileged dialogue with seminarians, and it is easy to understand why:

---

xvii The rationale is a liturgical vestment worn on the shoulders over the chasuble. Once more widely used, it is now the privilege only of the bishops of Eichstätt, Germany, and Toul, France, and the metropolitan archbishops of Paderborn, Germany, and Kraków.

they are, in a very special way, the future and hope of the Church; their presence in the seminary testifies to the magnetic attraction that Christ exercises on young peoples' hearts. This magnetism in no way diminishes freedom; indeed, it enables them to fulfill themselves completely by choosing the greatest good: God, to whose exclusive service we dedicate ourselves forever.[168]

I learned long ago, when I was in Kraków, to remain close to couples and families. I also followed closely the process that leads two people, a man and a woman, to create a family, and with marriage, to become spouses, parents, with all the consequences that we know.[169]

At the end of the second and third Council sessions, in December 1963 and November 1964, he carried out two intense pilgrimages to the Holy Land.

We felt that since we are working in the Council for the renewal of the Church, we ought to turn directly to the Lord himself, of whom the Church is his Mystical Body. From this came the desire to visit the places where he was born, where he spoke and labored, where he also suffered and died on the cross, and rose from the dead and ascended into heaven. I do not consider my participation in the pilgrimage as something personal or private, but as a grace from Providence granted to me for others.[170]

One would be mistaken who wanted to consider the accomplishment of Vatican II any way other than as a response of faith to the word of the Lord brought forth by this Council. Furthermore it would be undesirable if the idea of the accomplishment of Vatican II would be used as a basis for a movement of renewal understood in a way that differs from that authorized by the Church.[171]

From that experience also came an important book, in which Karol Wojtyła, as cardinal, reflected on the implementation of Vatican II.

The Council was a great event, and for me it was an unforgettable experience. I returned from it deeply enriched. When I got back to Poland, I wrote a book in which I presented the insights that had matured in the course of the Council sessions. In those pages I tried to gather, so to speak, the substance of the Council teachings. This volume, which I entitled *Sources of Renewal: The Implementation of Vatican II*, was published in Kraków in 1972 by the Polish Theological Association (PTT). The book was intended as a kind of votive offering of gratitude for what divine grace, through the Council assembly, had worked in me personally as bishop.[172]

> *Subsequent studies engaged the archbishop from a philosophical point of view; others were more catechetical.*

In those years, my greatest involvement was with young people who asked me questions, not so much about the existence of God, but rather about how to live, how to face and resolve problems of love and marriage, not to mention problems related to work.... From our meetings, from my sharing in the problems of their lives, a book was born, the contents of which is summarized in the title, *Love and Responsibility*. My book on the acting person came later, but it was also born of the same source.[173]

When I wrote the book *The Acting Person*, the first ones to take notice of it, obviously in order to attack it, were the Marxists. In fact, my book represented an unsettling element in their polemic against religion and the Church. But, having arrived at this point, I must say that my concern for "the acting person" did not arise from the disputes with Marxism or, at least, not as a direct response to those disputes. I had long been interested in *man as person*. Perhaps my interest was due to the fact that I had never had a particular predilection for the natural sciences. I was always more fascinated by man. While studying in the faculty of literature, man interested me inasmuch as he was a creator of language and a subject of literature; then, when I discovered my priestly vocation, man became the *central theme of my pastoral work*.[174]

As a bishop in Kraków, I felt obliged to defend the faculty of theology at the Jagiellonian University. I held it my duty. The communist authorities maintained that this faculty had been transferred to Warsaw. Their pretext for this was that in 1953 the Academy of Catholic Theology had been instituted in the capital, and placed under state administration. That battle was won thanks to the fact that an autonomous Pontifical Faculty of Theology at Kraków was later established, followed by the Pontifical Academy of Theology. Sustaining me throughout this struggle was the conviction that knowledge, in its many diverse manifestations, is an inestimable patrimony for a nation. Obviously, in speaking with the communist authorities, it was the study of theology that I was arguing for, since its survival was under threat. Yet I never forgot the other branches of knowledge, even those apparently far removed from theology.[175]

As the communists suppressed all Catholic youth associations, a way had to be found to remedy the situation. The Servant of God, Father Franciszek Blachnicki, came upon the scene and initiated the so-called Oasis Movement. I became closely involved with this movement and tried to support it in every way possible. I defended it before the communist authorities, I supported it financially, and, obviously, I took part in its activities. During the summer vacation I would often visit the so-called oases, which were camps organized for the young people belonging to the movement. I would preach to them, speak with them, climb mountains with them, and sing with them around the fire. I frequently celebrated Mass for them in the open air. This all added up to a really intensive pastoral program.[176]

> *At the same time, within Poland and outside of it, he emerged as a pastoral figure even more attentive to the present problems and capable not only of dialogue, but also of strongly sustaining his own ideas. It is calculated that he made about fifty trips outside of Poland between 1962 and 1978.*

During the twenty years of my membership and participation in the work of the Polish Bishops Conference, I have learned a great deal, both from the individual members of this episcopal community, beginning with the eminent primate of Poland, and also from the community as such. In fact, the quality that particularly characterizes the Polish Bishops Conference is that unity which is the source of spiritual strength. The Polish episcopate, precisely through this unity, in a special way serves the Church in Poland and also the universal Church.[177]

It is, in fact, characteristic of a bishop to be the great unifier of the faithful around Jesus Christ in order to invite them to continue moving in convergent ways. In Kraków and at Rome, I always saw my role as bishop in this light.[178]

In my life as a bishop, beginning in Kraków, I was able to build many churches without any construction projects, because I had the parishioners build them. It was always the work of the community. I admired them for this. But I was useful for them, and necessary, too. In these situations I remember well having to fight: the bishop had to struggle with the civil authorities who were against this, who did not want the churches [built].[179]

I lived near a very ancient Franciscan church, and from time to time I went there to pray, to make the *Via Crucis*, and to visit the chapel of Our Lady of Sorrows. Unforgettable moments for me! One cannot fail to mention that from here at this magnificent trunk of Franciscan spirituality there bloomed the blessed Maximilian Kolbe, a special patron in our difficult times. Neither can I pass over in silence the fact that right here, in Assisi, at this Basilica, in the year 1253, Pope Innocent IV proclaimed as saint the bishop of Kraków, the martyr Stanisłaus, now the patron saint of Poland, whose unworthy successor I was until a short time ago.[180]

As archbishop of Kraków, I often paused before the wall of death and would walk through the rubble of the ovens in the crematories of Birkenau. I would always ask myself: "How far can the boundaries of hatred, of annihilation of men by men, of cruelty stretch?"[181]

Marian devotion, which is one of the principal characteristics of the spirituality of John Paul II, has ancient roots.

I myself come from a land and a nation whose heart beats—as also the hearts of the neighboring peoples—in the great Marian sanctuaries, above all in the sanctuary of Jasna Góra.[182]

Every nation draws life from the works of its own culture. We Poles, for example, trace ours back to the song *Bogurodzica* (*Mother of God*), the earliest Polish poetry to be written down, and also to the centuries-old melody which accompanies it. . . . The song *Bogurodzica* comes specifically from the Gniezno tradition in Polish culture. This is the tradition of Adalbert, Poland's patron saint, to whom the song is actually attributed. It is a tradition stretching back through centuries.[183]

All Polish believers go on pilgrimage to Częstochowa. Ever since I was a child, I too, often went there. In 1936 there was a great pilgrimage of university students, concluding with a solemn vow before the icon. Since that time, the pilgrimage has been repeated every year. During the Nazi occupation I made the pilgrimage as a student of Polish humanities in the department of philosophy at the Jagiellonian University. I remember it particularly because, in order to preserve the tradition, we went to Częstochowa as delegates: Tadeusz Ulewicz, myself, and a third person. Jasna Góra was surrounded by Hitler's troops. The eremitical Pauline Fathers offered us hospitality. They knew we belonged to a delegation. This was obviously a matter of great secrecy. Thus we had the satisfaction of having succeeded, despite everything, in maintaining that tradition.[184]

There is a custom—a beautiful custom—for pilgrims whom you have welcomed at Jasna Góra to make a farewell visit to you before leaving here. I remember many of these farewell visits, these special audiences that you, Mother of Jasna Góra, have granted me. . . . Our Lady of the Bright Mountain, Mother of the Church! Once more I consecrate myself to you "in your maternal slavery of love": *Totus tuus!*—I am all yours! I consecrate to you the whole Church—everywhere and to the ends of the earth! I consecrate to you humanity; I consecrate to you all men and women, my brothers and sisters. All the peoples, and the nations. I consecrate to you Europe and all the continents. I consecrate to you Rome and Poland, united through your servant, by a fresh bond of love.[185]

Totus tuus. This phrase is not only an expression of piety, or simply an expression of devotion. It is more. During the Second World War, while I was employed as a factory worker, I came to be attracted to Marian devotion. At first, it had seemed to me that I should distance myself a bit from the Marian devotion of my childhood, in order to focus more on Christ. Thanks to Saint Louis de Montfort, I came to understand that true devotion to the Mother of God is actually Christocentric; indeed, it is very profoundly rooted in the mystery of the Blessed Trinity, and the mysteries of the Incarnation and Redemption.[186]

On my episcopal coat of arms, the Gospel text just cited (cf. Jn 19:25–27) appears in a symbolic form. The motto *Totus tuus* was inspired by the teachings of Saint Louis Marie Grignion de Montfort.

These two words express total belonging to Jesus through Mary: *Tuus totus ego sum, et omnia mea tua sunt*, written by Saint Louis Marie, which translates, "I am all yours, and all that I possess is yours, my loving Jesus, through Mary your most holy Mother." The teachings of this saint had a great influence on the Marian devotion of many of the faithful, and on my own life. We speak here of a lived teaching, one of noteworthy ascetical and mystical depth, and expressed in a living and fervent way, that often uses images and symbols.[187]

The message of Divine Mercy has always been near and dear to me. It is as if history had inscribed it in the tragic experience of the Second World War. In those difficult years it was a particular support and an inexhaustible source of hope, not only for the people of Kraków but for the entire nation. This was also my personal experience, which I took with me to the See of Peter and which in a sense forms the image of this pontificate.[188]

Many of my personal memories are tied to this place. During the Nazi occupation, when I was working in the Solvay factory near here, I used to come here. Even now I recall the street that goes from Borek Fałęcki to Dębniki, a street that I took every day going to work on the different turns with the wooden shoes on my feet. They're the shoes that we used to wear then. How was it possible to imagine that one day the man with the wooden shoes would consecrate the Basilica of the Divine Mercy at Łagiewniki of Kraków?[189]

Kalwaria Zebrzydowska, the shrine of the Mother of God, reproduces the holy places of Jerusalem connected with the life of Jesus and that of his Mother: the "little way," as they are called. . . . I often came here alone and, walking along the "little ways" of Jesus Christ and his Mother, I was able to meditate on their holy mysteries and recommend to Christ through Mary the particularly difficult problems and singular responsibilities in my complex ministry. I can say that almost none of these problems were worked out except here, through ardent prayer before the great mystery of faith that Kalwaria conceals within itself.[190]

There is a third reason for my pilgrimage which I wish to mention. It is the prayer of thanksgiving for the four hundred years of the shrine of Kalwaria Zebrzydowska, which I have been associated with from childhood. It was there, praying as I walked along its paths, that I sought inspiration for my service of the Church in Kraków and in Poland, there that I made various difficult pastoral decisions. It was precisely there, among the faithful people at prayer, that I came to know the faith that guides me also on the Chair of Peter.[191]

For me, even devotion to Saint Joseph is connected with my experiences in Kraków. The Bernardine Sisters on Poselska Street, near the episcopal palace, have a church dedicated to Saint Joseph, where they have perpetual adoration of the Blessed Sacrament. In my free moments, I would go there to pray, and often my gaze would be drawn toward a beautiful image of the foster father of Jesus, an image greatly venerated in that church, where I once conducted a retreat for lawyers. I have always liked to think of Saint Joseph in the context of the Holy Family: Jesus, Mary, and Joseph. I used to invoke the help of all thee of them together for various problems. I understand well the unity and love that characterized the Holy Family: three hearts, one love. In a particular way, I entrusted to Saint Joseph the pastoral ministry to familes.[192]

The esteem that Paul VI had for him was made public when he was called to preach the spiritual exercises for Lent in 1976 at the Vatican for the Pope and the Roman Curia.

At the beginning of February 1976 I was telephoned by Monsignor Władysław Rubin, who told me that the Pontiff would like me to preach his retreat in March. I had barely three weeks in which to prepare my texts and translate them. The title that I later gave to those meditations was: "Sign of Contradiction." This theme had not been proposed to me, but it emerged at the end as a kind of synthesis of what I had wanted to say. In reality, it was not a theme, but rather a kind of key concept that tied together everything I said in the various conferences. I remember the days dedicated to preparing the talks, twenty of them, which I had to choose and put together all by myself. In order to find the necessary peace and quiet, I went to stay with the Gray Ursulines at Jaszczurówka. Until noon I wrote the meditations, then in the afternoon I went skiing, and in the evening I continued writing. That meeting with Paul VI, in the context of the retreat, was particularly important for me, because it made me realize just how necessary it is for a bishop to be ready to speak of his faith, wherever the Lord asks this of him. Every bishop needs to be prepared for this, including the Successor of Peter himself, just as Paul VI needed me to be ready and willing for the task.[193]

After the death of Paul VI on August 6, 1978, the analysis that he outlined with some friends was almost prophetic.

It seems to me—and this is confirmed by the statements of many people—that the Church, as well as the world, needs a very spiritual pope. This must be his first and indispensable characteristic, so much so that he might be the father of a religious community.[194]

Asia, Africa, Indonesia, and Latin America struggled with new problematic situations and were searching for a successor to Paul VI who could help them and, even more, understand them in their difficulties.[195]

At the last Mass that he celebrated before entering the Conclave (which opened August 25, 1978), he inserted into the prayer a meaningful expression.

We pray to you, almighty Father, that a man will be elected pope who is conscious of his inability to bear the weight of the responsibility of being vicar of your Son. Infuse in him the courage to say with Saint Peter: "Stay far from me, O Lord, for I am not worthy." But if he assumes such a responsibility, give him much faith, hope, and love, so that he can carry the cross that you will impose.[196]

And when on August 26, 1978, John Paul I was elected, Cardinal Wojtyła revealed his thoughts frankly to his friends.

Thanks to his piety and humility, I think that he is the ideal man, who will be open to the action of the Holy Spirit. It is this Pope that the Church needs today.[197]

Scarcely a month later, during the night of September 28, John Paul I died, and Cardinal Wojtyła offered a Mass of Suffrage for him in Kraków.

I have him still before my eyes. I see him that day, August 26, around 6 P.M. when everything already indicated that the votes of the Conclave were concentrated on Cardinal Albino Luciani. I see his face when he rose, turning toward the Cardinal Camerlengo[xviii] as he approached him. To the question of the rite, "Do you accept?" he responded: "I accept." And then he immediately chose the name John Paul I. What great joy, first among the College of Cardinals . . . then of Rome. . . . The joy of John Paul himself. . . . How much we expected from him, how much we counted on him! It seemed he would respond to our expectations with all his personality, human, pastoral, episcopal, and papal. He had become so quickly who he must be, thanks to his vocation.[198]

I recall how deeply his words touched the hearts of all who filled Saint Peter's Square. From the moment of his first appearance in the central balcony of the Vatican Basilica, he established with those present a current of spontaneous sympathy; his smiling face, his trusting and open gaze conquered the hearts of Romans and faithful throughout the world. . . . His words and his person entered into the heart of all, and for this reason the news of his unexpected death, which occurred on the night of September 28, 1978, was particularly overwhelming. The smile of a pastor, close to the people, who knew how to dialogue with the culture and the world with serenity and balance, had vanished. The few talks and writings he has left us as Pope enrich the considerable collection of his texts which, twenty-five years after his death, retain surprising newness.[199]

The last parish I visited in the archdiocese of Kraków was Saint Joseph in Złote Łany, a new residential neighborhood of Bielsko-Biała. In this city, Father Józef Sanak was the pastor of Divine Providence parish where I stayed. On my return from the pastoral visit, I celebrated

---

xviii The Cardinal Camerlengo is the chamberlain who prepares for and directs the Conclave to elect the next pope.

the holy Mass for the deceased Pope John Paul I. Then I went to Warsaw to participate in the meetings of the Episcopal Conference. After this I set off for Rome . . . not knowing that I would have to remain there.[200]

> On October 3, 1978, he took a flight to return to Rome and, on October 14, he once again entered the Conclave.

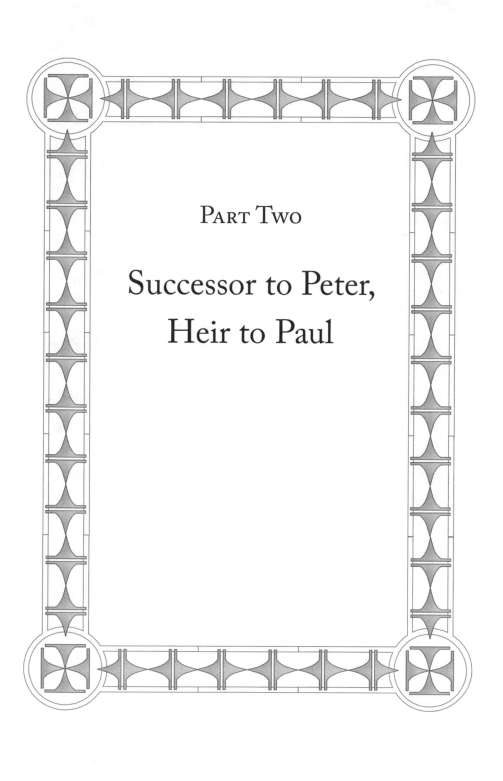

PART TWO

Successor to Peter,
Heir to Paul

The Days of Election

MAY JESUS CHRIST BE PRAISED. Dearest brothers and sisters, we are all still grieved after the death of our most beloved Pope John Paul I. And now the most eminent Cardinals have called a new Bishop of Rome. They have called him from a distant country, distant but always so close through the communion in the Christian faith and tradition. I was afraid to accept this nomination, but I did it in the spirit of obedience to our Lord Jesus Christ and of total confidence in his Mother, the most holy Madonna. I do not know whether I can explain myself well in your . . . *our* Italian language. If I make a mistake you will correct me. And so I present myself to you all to confess our common faith, our hope, our confidence in the Mother of Christ and of the Church, and also to start anew on this road of history and of the Church, with the help of God and with the help of men.[1]

> *Karol Wojtyła spontaneously spoke these words from the balcony of the Vatican Basilica. Only two hours had passed since his election as the 263rd successor of Saint Peter. The election happened around 5:15 P.M. on October 16, 1978.*

I lifted up my thoughts and sentiments to Christ the Redeemer after the canonical election last October 16; when I was asked, "Do you accept?" I answered, "Obedient in faith to Christ, my Lord, trusting in the Mother of Christ and of the Church, aware of the great difficulties, I accept." That answer of mine I want to make public to all today, without exception, showing thereby that the fundamental truth of the Incarnation is tied to the ministry that with the acceptance of the election as bishop of Rome and as successor of the Apostle Peter has become specifically my duty in his Chair.[2]

In autumn 1962 while he participated at the first session of Vatican Council II, he wrote a few verses dedicated to the first Pope, which clearly refer also to his successors.

Peter, you are the floor, that others
may walk over you (not knowing
where they go). You guide their steps
so that spaces can be one in their eyes,
and from them thought is born.
You want to serve their feet that pass
as rock serves the hooves of sheep.
The rock is a gigantic temple floor,
the cross a pasture.[3]

Now the role of the "rock" that must sustain the Catholic Church awaited him.

By the inscrutable design of Providence I had to leave the episcopal see of Saint Stanisłaus in Kraków and from October 16, 1978, I occupy that of Saint Peter in Rome. The choice of the Sacred College was for me an expression of the will of Christ himself. To this will I desire to remain always submissive and faithful. I desire furthermore to serve, with all my strength, the great cause to which I was called, that is, the proclaiming of the Gospel and the work of salvation.[4]

At this moment I can see before my eyes the figure of the Servant of God Cardinal Stefan Wyszyński, who, during the Conclave, on the feast day of Saint Hedwig of Silesia, came up to me and said: "If they elect you, I beg you not to refuse." I answered: "Thank you very much. God reward you, Cardinal." Comforted by the grace and words of the Primate of the Millennium[i] I was able to say my *fiat* to the inscrutable designs of Divine Providence.[5]

The Sistine Chapel is the place which contains the memory of a particular day in the life of every pope. For me, it was October 16, 1978.

---

i Stefan Cardinal Wyszyński (1901–1981), metropolitan archbishop of Gniezno and Warsaw, primate of Poland, was called Primate of the Millennium by Pope John Paul II because of his strong leadership, especially for his stand against Communism, including a three-year imprisonment.

Precisely here, in this holy place, the cardinals gather to await the manifestation of God's will as regards the Successor of Saint Peter. Here I heard from the mouth of my former rector, Maximilian de Fürstenberg, the significant words: *"Magister adest et vocat te"* (*The Master is here and calls you*). . . . And here, in a spirit of obedience to Christ and entrusting myself to his Mother, I accepted the election that came from the Conclave, declaring to the cardinal camerlengo, Jean Villot, my availability to serve the Church. Once again the Sistine Chapel became for the entire Catholic community the site of the action of the Holy Spirit who appoints bishops in the Church, and in particular the one who is to become Bishop of Rome and Successor of Peter.[6]

At the Conclave, through the College of Cardinals, Christ said to me, as he once said to Peter by the Lake of Genesareth: *"Tend my sheep"* (Jn 21:16). I heard echo in my soul the question he addressed to Peter at that moment: *"Do you love me? Do you love me more than these . . . ?"* (cf. Jn 21:15–16). Humanly speaking, how could I not have been apprehensive? How could so great a responsibility not burden me? I had to turn to Divine Mercy in order to answer the question: "Do you accept?" with confidence: "In the obedience of the faith, before Christ my Lord, entrusting myself to the Mother of Christ and of the Church, aware of the great difficulties, I accept."[7]

From the beginning of my pontificate, my thoughts, prayers and actions were motivated by one desire: to witness that Christ, the Good Shepherd, is present and active in his Church. He is constantly searching for every stray sheep, to lead it back to the sheepfold, to bind up its wounds; he tends the sheep that are weak and sickly and protects those that are strong. This is why, from the very first day, I have never ceased to urge people: "Do not be afraid to welcome Christ and accept his power!"[8]

We have all been brought together here by the memory of Pope John Paul I, who, after being elected to the See of Saint Peter, was the first to take the names of both his predecessors. We have been led here by the memory of the day of his election. It was exactly a year ago, on August 26, at about six o'clock in the evening after the conclusion of the voting, that Cardinal Albino Luciani, Patriarch of Venice, was asked by the cardinal camerlengo of the holy Roman Church, whether he accepted the election. He replied in a gentle voice: "I do." I remember that, while giving his reply, he smiled in his habitual manner. And the Church, which had been an orphan since the death of Paul VI, again had a Pope.[9]

I want to confide in you for a moment, a moment that is becoming characteristic of me, about the Conclave of August 1978, during which Albino Luciani, cardinal patriarch of Venice, was elected successor of Peter. When he accepted the election, the cardinal deacon asked him what name he intended to take, and he replied, "John Paul I." In that moment I thought to myself, "How well he has chosen!" None of the Popes before him had double names, but he wanted in this name to recall his two predecessors John and Paul, the two who opened a new epoch in the history of the Church and the story of the Church in our era. "How well he has chosen!" These were my thoughts on that afternoon of August 26, 1978. To tell you this does not violate the secrecy of the Conclave. I think that, choosing this name, he showed that he did not wish to detach himself from the rock, the rock that John and Paul had been for him, and that rock had been for him and for us all, Peter.[10]

At the end [of the Conclave], when everything had become clear, Cardinal Wyszyński approached me and said: "It would be desirable if you could take the name John Paul." I answered him: "Yes, I was thinking of doing so."[11]

I chose the same names as my beloved predecessor, John Paul I. In fact, on August 26, 1978, when he declared in the Sacred College his desire to be called John Paul—a double name of this kind was without precedent in the history of the papacy—I considered it a clear sign of grace for the new pontificate. Given the fact that his pontificate lasted only thirty-three days, it was for me not only to continue, but in a certain sense to take it back to the same point of departure. I confirmed this precisely by my own choice of those same two names. Choosing it, after the example of my venerated predecessor, I desired, as he did, to express my love for the unique heredity left to the Church by the pontiffs John XXIII and Paul VI, and to offer my personal availability to develop it with the help of God.[12]

Since the death in 1523 of Adrian VI of Holland, the last non-Italian Pope, 455 years had passed, and Pope Wojtyła proposed a reflection.

In the enclosure of the Conclave, after the election, I thought: what shall I say to the Romans when I, coming *from a distant country*, from Poland, present myself to them as their bishop? The figure of Saint Peter came to my mind. And this is what I thought: nearly two thousand years ago your ancestors accepted a newcomer; so now you, too, will welcome another: you will welcome John Paul II, as you once welcomed Peter of Galilee.[13]

On the evening of October 16, 1978, I appeared at the balcony of Saint Peter's Basilica to greet the people of Rome, and the pilgrims gathered on the piazza waiting for the result of the Conclave. I said that I came "from a far country." In fact, the geographical distance is not great. By air the journey takes barely two hours. In calling it a "far country" I intended to allude to the presence of the "iron curtain," which at that moment still existed. The Pope from behind the iron curtain truly came from afar, even if, in reality, he came from the very center of Europe. The geographical center of the continent is actually located on Polish territory.[14]

From this point of view, to summon a pope from Poland, from Kraków, could serve as an eloquent symbol. It was not simply the summons of an individual, but of the entire Church to which he belonged since birth; indirectly it was also a call to his nation. It seems to me that Cardinal Stefan Wyszyński saw and expressed this aspect of the event in a particularly profound way. Personally I have always been convinced that the election of a Polish pope can be explained in terms of all that the Primate of the Millennium had achieved, along with the rest of the episcopate and the Polish Church, despite the oppressive limitations and persecutions to which they were subjected in those difficult years.[15]

By electing a cardinal from Poland to the See of Rome, the Conclave was making a significant choice: it was as if they wanted to call upon the witness of the Church from which that Cardinal came—and to call upon it for the good of the Universal Church. In any case, their choice had a particular significance for Europe and for the world. By a tradition lasting almost five centuries, the responsibility of the See of Peter had devolved upon an Italian cardinal. The election of a Pole seemed like a revolution. It demonstrated that the Conclave, following the indications of the Council, was seeking to read the "signs of the times" and to ponder its decisions in the light of these.[16]

Italy! Rome! These names have always been dear to me. The history of Poland, the history of the Church in my country, are full of events which brought Rome and Italy close to me and made them dear to me, I would say made them mine. Kraków, the city from which I come, is often called "the Polish Rome." I hope that, coming from the "Polish Rome" I shall be able, as Bishop of Rome, to serve everyone, under the protection of the Mother of the Church and of your Patron Saints,[ii] but especially to serve this beloved land of yours and the people who have welcomed me with such goodwill.[17]

Having been elected by the Sacred College of Cardinals to be Successor of Saint Peter, I accepted this service with profound trepidation, considering it to be the will of our Lord Jesus Christ. When I thought about not being born here, but about being a foreigner to this land, there came to my mind the figure of Saint Peter, who was also a foreigner in Rome. And so, in the spirit of faith and out of obedience, I accepted this election, by virtue of which I have become Successor of Peter and Bishop of Rome.[18]

The crosier with the crucifix that I presently use is the replica of the crosier of Paul VI. I see in it a symbol of three duties: pastoral care, leadership, and responsibility. It is not a sign of authority in the common sense of the term, nor is it a sign of precedence or supremacy over others: it is a sign of service.[19]

A boy asked me how I decided to be the Vicar of Jesus; I did not choose this, the 120 cardinals gathered in Conclave made the choice. They, too, were only instruments. The one who really chose me was the Holy Spirit; it was Jesus. This is my faith; otherwise, it would not be possible for me to be the Pope.[20]

---

ii In this talk the Pope refers to the two patrons of Italy: Saint Francis of Assisi and Saint Catherine of Siena. The patron saints of the city of Rome are Saint Lawrence, Saint Martina, Saint Peter the Apostle, Saint Paul the Apostle, and Saint Philip Neri.

By virtue of God's inscrutable decree, called on October 16, 1978, by the votes of the College of Cardinals, I have assumed, after my great and beloved predecessors, the guidance of the Roman See of Saint Peter and together with it that ministry over the whole Church, as a result of which the Bishop of Rome has become, according to Saint Gregory's definition, "Servant of the Servants of God."[21]

Elected Bishop of Rome and heir of the Apostle Peter in the exercise of his office, the desire of the good of all the Church and that of all the human family will guide inseparably my efforts.[22]

With the eyes of the heart, however, he still saw, in the foreground, the sufferings of Poland.

Being the first in history of the Polish race, a son of the Polish land, to become the Successor of Peter, not only a Polish Pontiff but a Slav, I feel a particular debt to my fatherland, and therefore to all my countrymen. I think that the fatherland, its history, the history of the Church, the history of the nation, have prepared me in an exceptional way to be in solidarity with the diverse nations of the world. Not without reason have the Poles, throughout their history, sought alliances and united with their closest neighbors; not without reason, then, have they fought "for our freedom and yours." All this is part and parcel of the spiritual heritage of the Pope who has come from Poland. It is precisely due to this heritage that it is easy for me to feel a special solidarity toward those peoples, those nations that suffer, that in the great family of peoples are in any way discriminated against, oppressed, deprived of liberty, deprived of national sovereignty, deprived, in everyday life, or by reason of an entire system, of sufficient social justice; it is easy for me to be with them because I have learned ever since childhood to be in tune with our nation which did not have an easy history, and which has also a present that is not easy.[23]

Coming to Rome for the Conclave, I had no other desire than to come back among you [to Poland], to my beloved archdiocese and country. But Christ's will was different, therefore I remain and start the new mission he has entrusted to me. Such a high mission, but also such a difficult one, of such responsibility! If we think and reason with our mind, it exceeds human strength.[24]

Dear fellow countrymen, it is not easy to renounce returning to my country, "to these fields rich in varied flowers, silvered with wheat and gilded with rye," as Mickiewicz[iii] writes. To see once again these mountains and valleys, the lakes and rivers, the people loved so much, this royal city. But if such is Christ's will, it is necessary to accept it, and therefore I accept it. I pray only that this separation will unite us even more and strengthen us in true mutual charity. Do not forget me in prayer at Jasna Góra and in the whole country, in order that this Pope, who is blood of your blood and heart of your hearts, may serve the Church and the world well in the difficult times which precede the end of this second millennium.[25]

On October 22, the day of the solemn beginning of his ministry, there broke out from his lips the anguished invitation that would remain part of history.

I always remember, and preserve in my heart and memory, those moments, those days: October 16 and 22 (1978). Divine Providence and human weakness: those moments of most profound faith and hope. "Open wide the doors, open wide the doors": these are the first words I spoke to the Church of Rome and to the world.[26]

When, on October 22, 1978, I said the words, "Be not afraid!" in Saint Peter's Square, I could not fully know how far they would take me and the entire Church. Their meaning came more from the Holy Spirit, the Consoler promised by the Lord Jesus to his disciples, than from the man who spoke them. . . . Why should we have no fear? Because man has been redeemed by God. When pronouncing these words in Saint Peter's Square, I already knew that my first encyclical and my entire papacy would be tied to the truth of the Redemption.[27]

On November 12, 1978, with the "taking possession" of the Roman Cathedral of Saint John Lateran, came the conclusion of the canonical stage for the new pontificate.

I, the new Bishop of Rome, John Paul II, Polish by origin, stop on the threshold of this temple and I ask you to welcome me in the

---

iii Adam Mickiewicz (1798–1855) is honored as the national poet of Poland.

Lord's name. I beg you to welcome me as you welcomed my predecessors throughout the centuries. . . . I am not here by my own will. The Lord has elected me. In the Lord's name I beg you therefore: welcome me![28]

It has been asserted, that not without reason, the Pope, as Bishop of Rome, should belong to the nation of his diocese. I do not want to miss this opportunity of expressing my gratitude to the members of my Roman diocese, who have accepted this Pope from Poland as a son of their own country.[29]

And from this moment on, his Italianità (being Italian) and Romanità (being Roman) were indissolubly bound to his Polish roots.

A stranger like me, aware of the reality that makes up the history of his own nation, enters into the reality of your history with special respect and attentiveness. From its ancient roots how has the great human community called *Italy* grown? What binds the people who make up Italy today to the generations who lived in this land from the times of ancient Rome? The Successor of Peter, whose permanent seat has been in this land from the times of Imperial Rome, being witness of many changes and, at the same time, all the history of your land, has the right and the duty to ask such questions.[30]

The fact that I come from another country whose religious traditions are very vibrant, even though they are situated in a very different history, culture, and psychological makeup, makes me able to discover more each day, and appreciate with great emotion the new and ancient riches of Christian life in this country, which was chosen by the ineffable plan of God to host the See of Peter, to guard the relics of the apostles, to spread to the world the liberating Word of the Gospel.[31]

As bishop of this apostolic see and primate of Italy, in union of thought and heart with all the Italian bishops, I feel that I share the lot, the joys as well as the sufferings, of all the people of Italy. It is a concern which has been always constant in the Roman pontiffs. . . . In the wake of this tradition, I wish to express my profound affection for the Italian people, who daily attest to so many spiritual and moral values, confronting sorrowful events such as the unfortunately recurring earthquakes and economic and social situations which are not easy. I have also been able to have personal experience of these values, both during my various pastoral journeys along the peninsula, during which I always receive a warm and affectionate welcome, and during the meetings I have here in Rome with pilgrimages coming from dioceses and parishes from the various regions of Italy. They are values which are nourished by a Christian tradition which has deep roots in broad sections of the population.[32]

The Pope travels all over the world, but he always returns to Rome. Actually, he could not set out to visit the world if he did not come from Rome and return to Rome. Do you know why? No? But you must know why. It is because Rome is the See of Peter, to whom Jesus entrusted the special care of the whole church. So, the various countries of the world and the diverse local churches want to meet the Successor of Peter, because in his person the apostolic mission of Peter continues. So now you know better why the Pope, even if he travels to different parts of the world, always returns to Rome. Here at Rome is his Church; here, at Rome, he is the Successor of Peter.[33]

The *ad limina apostolorum*[iv] visits are a particular expression of collegiality. By principle, every five years (sometimes however, there are delays), all the bishops of the entire world (from more than two thousand dioceses) take turns to come to the Vatican. Now it is my turn to receive them. At the time of Paul VI, I was the one who was received by the Pope. I greatly appreciated my meetings with Paul VI, from whom I learned a great deal about how to carry out these visits. Eventually I created my own schema. First I receive every bishop personally, then I invite him to lunch with the group, and finally we celebrate the Holy Mass of the day together and have our general meeting together. I draw great profit from meeting bishops. I could simply say that from them I learn about the Church. I must continuously do this, because I am always learning new things. From speaking with them [the bishops] I learn about the situation of the Church in different parts of the world: in Europe, in Asia, in America, in Africa, and in Oceania.[34]

Called by the Lord to guide the universal Church, but aware that the foundation of this office is that of being Bishop of Rome, I cannot

---

iv Literally this means "to the threshold of the Apostle."

help repeating before you what I have already declared on other occasions: namely my readiness to do everything in my power for the complete development of Rome. The very visits that I pay, from week to week, to the various parishes, are with the primary intention of making a personal effort for a renewed and widespread evangelizing activity, so they aim at getting to know people and organizations, forces and capacities, but above all expectations and problems, as they occur in actual practice in the individual urban areas and outskirts.[35]

Within the limits of my other commitments, I have tried and am trying to visit the parishes as often as possible. In that way, I have already found my bearings to a certain extent in this field, which previously was almost completely unknown to me. I am learning to know Rome as the Pope's diocese, as my Church; and in these Sunday meetings with the various communities of the People of God and of the society of Rome, I am experiencing very deeply its needs, anxieties, and expectations.[36]

The Pontiff's Mission

"You are Peter, and upon this rock I will build my Church" (Mt 16:18). These words have a particular meaning for me. They express the heart of my mission as Peter's successor at the end of the twentieth century. Jesus Christ is the center of the universe and of history. He alone is the Redeemer of every human person. In the inscrutable Providence of God, I was chosen to continue the mission of Peter and to repeat with the same conviction: "You are the Messiah—the Christ—the Son of the Living God" (Mt 16:16). Nothing in my life and ministry can take precedence over this mission: to proclaim Christ to the nations, to speak about his marvelous goodness, to manifest his saving power, and to assure every man and woman that whoever hopes in Christ will never die, but will have eternal life.[37]

The new Successor of Peter in the See of Rome today makes a fervent, humble, and trusting prayer: Christ, make me become and remain the servant of your unique power, the servant of your sweet power, the servant of your power that knows no eventide. Make me be a servant. Indeed, the servant of your servants.[38]

My eyes see your salvation. I see in you the salvation of man and of the world, Jesus Christ, born at Bethlehem, Redeemer of man and of the world. You are the whole hope of my life, just as you were the hope of Israel's generations. For you I have lived until now—and for you I want to live from this moment on. You are the faith, the hope, the love of my heart, of all my deeds, aspirations, and desires.[39]

You asked me if I am happy to be Pope. Of course I am happy, above all because I am able to welcome you like this: "Praised be Jesus Christ." I am happy to know Christ, and to carry his word and his holy name, in which there is salvation for every person.[40]

All of us here present, including the Pope, are students in the school of Jesus Christ. And we have been enrolled at this school from the beginning of our life, from the moment of our Baptism. This enrollment is also preserved in our parish, but above all, it is made in our hearts. Each of us carries it with us as an indelible sign. You attend this school because your parish is the school of Jesus Christ. In this school Christ's disciples—the priests, the sisters, the laity, your parents, everyone—studies. All the people in your parish study in this school, as does the cardinal vicar, and even the Pope.[41]

This [service of Successor of Peter] I see above all as a maturity in the priesthood and as the permanence in prayer with Mary, the Mother of Christ, in the same way as the apostles were assiduous in prayer, in the upper room in Jerusalem when they received the Holy Spirit. . . . The service of the bishop, and in particular that of the Pope, is bound up with a special responsibility through which the Spirit speaks: it is bound in all that regards the faith of the Church and Christian morality. In fact, it is this Faith and this morality that they, the bishops with the Pope, must teach in the Church, watching by the light of the ever-living tradition over their conformity with the revealed Word of God.[42]

The Pope knows that the episcopal ministry brings with it thorns and crosses that often remain hidden in the secrecy of the heart. But he also knows, as do you, that in the mysterious design of Providence, these sufferings are the guarantee of fruitfulness of an apostolate that, with God's help, will produce abundant results.[43]

I, too, who am speaking to you, I the Pope, what must I do to act prudently? There comes to my mind the "letters to Saint Bernard" of Albino Luciani, then patriarch of Venice. In his answer to Cardinal Luciani, the Abbot of Clairvaux—a Doctor of the Church—recalls emphatically that he who governs must be "prudent." What, then, must the new Pope do in order to operate prudently? Certainly he must do a great deal in this direction. He must always learn and always meditate on these problems. But in addition to this, what can he do? He must pray and endeavor to have that gift of the Holy Spirit which is called the gift of counsel. And let all those who wish the new Pope to be a prudent pastor of the Church, implore for him the gift of counsel. And for themselves, let them also ask for this gift through the special intercession of the Mother of Good Counsel.[44]

The Pope has come to encourage you, to bid you not to lose heart but to look ahead with trust. Sustained by the convictions of hope, each performs courageously his or her daily duty, knowing that this attitude draws the abundant gifts and comforts of the divine assistance.[45]

The Pope would like to be able to cross the threshold of all homes, especially those in which poverty, illness, and loneliness make their weight felt—including hospitals and prisons—and bring everywhere a word of comfort, encouragement, and hope.[46]

From the time of my election to the Chair of Peter, I have considered it to be my duty to continue the work of the Second Vatican Council. In order to fulfill this task I have felt the need to call attention to the Church's understanding of her own nature and mission, as set out in the *magna carta* of the Council, the Dogmatic Constitution on the Church, *Lumen Gentium*. Again and again we need to ponder the mystery of the Church, striving to appreciate ever more keenly this visible communion of faith, hope, and charity through which Christ communicates truth and grace to all men and women.[47]

It is said—and it is true—that the Pope is the Vicar of Christ. It is true, and I accept this in humility. I accept it more easily after Vatican II, because in the documents of the Council, this same definition of

Vicar of Christ is applied to all the bishops: each bishop is the Vicar of Christ for his church. The Pope is the Vicar of Christ for the Church of Rome by vocation, and because of the characteristics of this Church of Rome, he is also the Vicar of Christ for the worldwide Church. We here speak of a title, a word that makes me tremble. I confess that I prefer not to abuse this word, and I use it rarely. I prefer the term "Successor of Peter," yes, but I prefer even more the title "Bishop of Rome." That other title needs to be reserved for more solemn moments, when the Church presents itself in its Christological dimension and identity as the Body of Christ. It is in this circumstance, this context, that the term "Vicar of Christ" is justified.[48]

[The mission of the Pope] is a bit the mission of each of you. All Christians, each one of us, have a mission: we all share in the mission of Christ. There are many ways of sharing in this mission, but every one of us is involved. If the Lord calls us to carry out a mission, we know and believe that he will give us the grace that enables us to complete it. This is certain. Naturally, I feel very much helped by the prayers of so many people throughout the world. And not only prayers, but sacrifices, many sacrifices that are offered for the mission of the Pope and of the Church. For this, I am greatly indebted. The problems I hold in my heart are many and varied. I guess I feel in a particular way for those people who cannot profess their faith, who do not have freedom. This appears to me to be a great injustice against the rights of man and the rights of Christ, against the rights of God in human life and society. But there are many other [preoccupations]; for example, I cannot help but suffer together with the many hungry people, and those who meet their deaths by violence.[49]

Throughout my ministry as pastor of the Universal Church, I have paid special attention to the protection and promotion of the dignity of the person and of his rights, in all the phases of his life and in every political, social, economic, or cultural circumstance.[50]

Participating fully in the preoccupations for peace, in the problems posed by growth and by poverty, in a word, in the problems of man, I feel a profound joy. The origin of this joy is seeing that, in the course of recent years, numerous populations have claimed national sovereignty, often at the end of a delicate process, but one that has the power to take that choice into their own future. This is a phenomenon which I understand very well, if only through my personal origins. I know because I have seen the efforts made by my people for their sovereignty. I know what it means to claim the right to self-determination, in the name of justice and national dignity.[51]

The Pope is with you, at your side, whenever one speaks of defending violated justice, of scattering the threats brought against peace, and of promoting the just rights of every person and the common good of all.[52]

As one whose ministry is void of meaning except insofar as he is the faithful Vicar of Christ on earth, I now take leave of you with the words of the one whom I represent, of Jesus Christ himself: "Peace I leave with you, my peace I give to you" (Jn 14:27). My constant prayer for all of you is this: that there may be peace in justice and in love. May the prayerful voices of all those who believe in God—Christians and non-Christians alike—bring it about that the moral resources present in the hearts of men and women of good will be united for the common good, and call down from heaven that peace which human efforts alone cannot effect.[53]

To Farthest Boundaries

The service of the Church and of man expands more and more and demands that the Pope be present wherever the requirements of faith and the affirmation of true human values call him. It is to strengthen this Christian faith and to promote these true human values that the Pope sets out along the ways of the world.[54]

If God permits, I will accept most of the invitations I have received.[55]

As for my journeys—made in the context of my apostolic ministry—this is the position. First of all, it was not I who started this practice. It was started by my two great predecessors, the popes of Vatican II, especially by Paul VI. But John XXIII had already let it be understood that the pope must not only be visited by the Church but that he himself must visit the Church. In spite of his eighty years he had taken the first step in this direction with the pilgrimage to the shrine of Our Lady of Loreto before the opening of the Council. As for Paul VI, traveling was part of the program of his whole pontificate. I can still remember with what enthusiasm the Council Fathers learned of his plan to make a pilgrimage to the Holy Land, at the end of the second session of the assembly. He could not have made a better start. So I found this chapter in the history of the pontifical ministry already started. I was soon convinced that it was necessary to carry on with it. How could a relatively young pope who in general enjoyed good health not have taken over this duty and followed the example of an octogenarian pope and a Paul VI of advanced years and delicate health?[56]

Visiting various other places of the earth, Paul VI would begin his visit with a kiss to the ground of that country as soon as he left the plane. I took this from him, and I observe it faithfully.[57]

[The trips are] the application on a universal scale of the charism[v] of Peter.[58]

Like Peter, the Pope is called to be a rock, to confirm his brothers in the faith, notwithstanding his own personal weakness. This is why the Pope visits his brothers all over the world.[59]

Some in Europe feel that the Pope does not need to travel, that he should stay in Rome, as popes always had done. I read this in the newspaper, and I receive counsel along these lines. Instead, I say that it is a grace of God to have come, because by coming I can get to know you. How can I know who you are, how you live, and your history otherwise? And this strengthens my conviction that the time has come for the bishops of Rome—that is, the popes—to cease to consider themselves only the Successors of Peter, but also as Heirs of Paul, who, we well know, never stayed still, but was always on a journey. And what is true for him (the pope) would also be true for those who work with him in Rome.[60]

How many times we heard it said: If Paul were living in our times, how he would use the periodicals, the newspapers, radio, the telephone; he would journey with airplanes. . . . The Pope is trying to do just that.[61]

---

v *Charism* comes from the writings of Saint Paul (1 Cor 12:7, 11) in which he refers to special gifts given by the Holy Spirit to individuals or groups. In the case of the papacy, the charism is to represent the Person and the authority of Christ for the whole Church.

In its own way, every nation, every city, every parish, every person that I have visited on the different continents has moved me, and with this emotion, I have grasped the mystery, the secret of each country, each people, each city, each group.[62]

The Lord has given me the necessary strength to be able to visit many of these countries, in fact a majority of them. This is very important, because to personally spend some time in a country, even a brief amount of time, permits one to see all sorts of things. Besides, such meetings permit me to enter into direct contact with the people, and this has enormous value both at the interpersonal and at the ecclesial level. Thus it was for Saint Paul, who was unceasingly on the road. Precisely because of this, when we read his letters to the various communities, we sense that he had spent time with them, and that he knew the people of each locality and their problems. The same is true in every age, even in our own time. I have always enjoyed traveling, and it is very clear for me that this duty was given, in a certain sense, to the Pope by Christ himself. Even while I was a diocesan bishop I enjoyed pastoral visitations, and I felt that it was very important to know what was happening in the parishes, to know the people and to meet them directly. What now constitutes a canonical norm (these pastoral visits) is already dictated by the experiences of the past, which are sufficient to recommend them. Saint Paul is the model here. Peter too, but Paul first and foremost.[63]

People tell me that the Pope travels too much, and schedules the journeys too close to each other. I think that, humanly speaking, they would have a valid point. But it is Providence that shows us the way, and sometimes suggests that we be excessive.[64]

The Lord, Master of history and of our destinies, has established that my pontificate should be that of a pilgrim pope of evangelization, so as to travel the paths of the world carrying the message of salvation everywhere.[65]

Today a young boy asked me why the Pope travels. I started teasing him a bit, but then I responded: the Pope travels because Jesus said, "Go into the whole world." This is the answer.[66]

Many people ask me why the Pope travels; some have accusations and some also use strongly opposing words about the way he travels.

The Pope travels to give courage to others, but also to receive from others their encouragement. This is how I always interpret those words that Jesus spoke to Peter: after your conversion you must comfort and confirm your brothers. This is good, but I say this: I also need to be confirmed by my brothers; by my brothers and my sisters.[67]

Becoming the bishop of Rome and Pope during this epoch of itinerants, I need to be an itinerant also. There is a sort of parallel, a coincidence here. But I must say that the travels I make are not very strict. Yes, it is true that these ask a lot from us and that the daily program is demanding enough, but still, I am not traveling by foot.[68]

The Pope also tries to be more on the move, even if I do it with more "sophisticated" means and, because of that they are perhaps less authentic than yours, because you are the itinerant poor, who travel without airplanes. But I do wish for us all, the Pope included, that we always and with every means possible be itinerants of the Gospel, that is, itinerants of the mystery that was revealed by the birth of Jesus, by the incarnation of the Son of God; and then, by his mission, by his death on the cross, and by his resurrection.[69]

With regard to my trips, thank God, I don't tire easily, but there is always some fatigue. One could not live without getting tired, and so also the Pope must tire a bit so as to be alive.[70]

Every trip the Pope makes is an "authentic pilgrimage to the living sanctuary of the people of God." Seen this way, the Pope travels sustained, as Peter was, by the prayers of the entire Church, in order to announce the Gospel, to "confirm the brothers" in their faith, to console the Church, to meet humanity. They are journeys of faith, of prayer, and they are always centered on the meditation and proclamation of the Word of God, the Eucharistic celebration, invocations to Mary. They are occasions for an itinerant catechesis, for a prolonged announcement of the Gospel to all latitudes, the Gospel and the apostolic teaching expanded today all over the planet. They are journeys of love, of peace, of universal brotherhood.[71]

From my youth I cultivated the Christian practice of the pilgrimage; and during my apostolic journeys as the Successor of Peter, I visit Marian sanctuaries as a pilgrim. These visits, from a personal point of view, are among the high points of my visits to the People of God spread throughout the earth, my brothers and sisters of the great human family. And I always feel the same emotion as I did the first time, when I placed into the hands of Mary most holy all the good that I had been able to do and all that I could do at the service of the holy Church.[72]

In the exercise of the mission that by the mysterious plan of Divine Providence was entrusted to me, during the apostolic pilgrimages that I make around the world, the desire to be the bearer of a message and to collaborate as long as I can animates me. As long as an authentic sense of humanity prevails in minds and hearts as a point of encounter among all those who have good will, then in the limits of my possibilities, I can help to build a world always more worthy of the human person.[73]

When persons meet for the first time and want to make friends, they usually introduce themselves. Is it necessary to do so? You already know my name and possess some facts about my person. But since I intend to make friends with you, I will introduce myself: I come to you as a missionary sent by the Father and by Jesus to continue to proclaim the kingdom of God which begins in this world but is realized only in eternity, in order to consolidate the faith of my brothers, to create a deep communion among all sons of the same Church. I come as minister and unworthy Vicar of Christ to watch over his Church; as the humble Successor of the Apostle Peter, the Bishop of Rome, and Pastor of the universal Church.[74]

The Pope must live the Church. He needs to know the Church not only through statistics and information, but as much as is possible through experience, he must live the Church in its various areas. Then, there are the continual requests; the Church also wants to meet the Pope in their diverse places. They want the Pope to come, to be with them. This is a sign of the times, of this moment in history.[75]

The various journeys that the Providence of the Lord has permitted me to complete this year have also clearly indicated this dimension, this primary vocation of the Church in the contemporary world. It is not just a question, in fact, of contacts with the People of God, with this magnificent reality which constitutes and prolongs on earth the kingdom of heaven and prepares its glorious finale; but those pilgrimages in nations and to peoples so different in tradition, culture, intellectual and social formation, sociopolitical character, and form of government afforded the opportunity to greet the illustrious representatives of those numerous states at meetings rich in warmth and human and social significance. It was an absolutely positive expression, which, better than any words, served to create a real and concrete rapprochement, indeed a universal brotherhood among peoples, and to drive back further and further all the kinds of barriers which divide the various systems from one another.[76]

You ask me, in the first place, why I have just spoken in Japanese. I have done so, and I mean to continue to do so in certain circumstances, in order to show my respect for your culture, which, like the culture of every nation, is expressed partly (in fact primarily) in its language. Language is a form that we give to our thoughts. It is, as it were, the clothes that we put on those thoughts. A language displays a particular characteristic of the identity of a people or a nation. In a sense, a language is a nation's heartbeat, because it is in that language, in his own language, that expression is given to the essence of a person's life in the community of the family, of the nation, and of history.[77]

The problem that is always present in the Church is the spread of the reign of God to the non-Christian nations. I have pointed it out since the inauguration of my ministry as universal pastor of the Church. This inauguration took place; I would say providentially, on October 22, 1978, World Missionary Day for that year. Because of this, in many circumstances, I have made myself, from year to year, a "traveling catechist" in order to meet the many people who still do not know Christ. I shared with them the spiritual riches of the young churches, as also the sufferings borne and the needs to be met, and their efforts to root the Christian faith ever deeper into their culture. I encouraged all those in the vanguard of the immense work of evangelizing, that they would always give credible witness with their lives, above all to young people, of the Gospel message they announce.[78]

I always thought that the Romans, especially the children, would be angry with the Pope because he goes away to travel to other countries, other continents, other cities. Instead, your colleagues have encouraged me, at least it seems that way.... One could also interpret this greeting in another way: the Romans are happy if the Pope stays away from Rome![79]

The Pope is the bishop of Rome, as Successor to Peter, and not to Paul. If he were the successor of Paul, it would be easier to explain his many journeys, his being away from Rome. As Successor to Peter, my absences thus seem less excusable. That child was right, then, who said that the Romans, and every parish of Rome, had more of a right to have the Pope in their midst.... On the other hand, if Divine Providence and Christ himself have given to the Church of Rome these two apostles, Peter and Paul, for the good of this Church, of each parish, then it is useful, even necessary, that the Pope makes pastoral visits outside Rome. . . . It is due to this title of Successor to Peter and Bishop of Rome, that they invite him and insist that he come to them. In this way, the Church of Rome and every parish of Rome will gain by the absence of the Pope, by his journeys.[80]

I carry out pastoral visits outside Rome, in Italy and the various continents. The churches from all parts of the world invite me, and I thank God that I am able to do this. But my first duty is to be Bishop of Rome. I am a man from far away who has become Bishop of Rome.[81]

Since the Pope cannot do everything, what should his first priority be? I think that his first task is to gather the people of God in unity. The experience I acquired in Kraków has taught me that it is important to visit the communities personally, starting with the parishes. Of course, this is not an exclusive duty, but I consider it of the first importance. Twenty years of experience has made me realize that thanks to the bishop's visits, a parish comes to be all the more closely integrated in the architecture of the Church and thus adheres more closely to Christ. My visits to the Roman parishes are necessarily shorter, and I have had to give up the sort of program I used to follow at Kraków. This vaster and more detailed program falls to the lot of the auxiliary bishops.[82]

It is a custom to greet guests with the words "We wish you well." Every time I hear these words, I want to answer, "I wish you well." I greet all of you parishioners, all those present and those who are not able to be here, all your families, all the generations, from the oldest to the youngest ones. In the name of Jesus Christ, I wish you well.[83]

Happy Among the Young

The Pope wishes well to everyone, to each man and to all men, but he has a preference for the youngest, because they had a preferential place in the heart of Christ, who wished to remain with the children (Mk 10:14; Lk 18:16) and to talk to the young. He addressed his call to the young particularly (Mt 19:21); and John, the youngest Apostle, was his favorite.[84]

Now, as I think back to the past with gratitude, I turn my gaze on the young people with whom I have built up a preferential dialogue since the very beginning of my Petrine ministry. I recall that at the end of that first Angelus I added a special greeting to them, saying, "You are the future of the world, the hope of the Church. You are my hope!" I must recognize that their response was truly encouraging. Today I would like to thank them for having been constantly close to me in these years, and I would like them to know that I continue to count on them.[85]

I am happy to be here with the kindergarteners, those of the pre-school level. I heard good presentations and I learned some things. For example, they told me that they watch the Pope on television often. I must say that I watch very little. But this gives me some consolation. If you see it, this is enough for me. I am dispensed![86]

The Pope loves you; he loves you very much! He loves you because he is an apostle of Jesus. Jesus loves you, so his apostle also loves you. The Successor of Peter cannot fail to love you, he loves you a lot and remains with you with great joy looking into your eyes, and he is happy to meet you.[87]

Friendship indicates sincere love, a two-way love that wishes all good things for the other person—a love that brings about union and happiness. It is no secret that the Pope loves young people like you, and that he feels immensely happy in your company.[88]

Returning to your homes, your schools, and your associations, tell everyone that the Pope counts a great deal on the young. Tell them that the young are the comfort and the strength of the Pope, who wishes to see them all, to let them hear his voice of encouragement in the midst of all the difficulties that insertion in society involves.[89]

You will ask, dearest young people, why the Pope always has some words especially for you in his speeches. The answer is simple: he has an unbreakable commitment to bring you as close as possible to the humanity of Jesus, who, being God made man, is eternally young, and can bring forth from you many generous initiatives and programs of life. You are searching for what will respond to your legitimate desires and fully satisfy you, so that you also can be givers of joy and consolation to others. You have in Jesus an incomparable model.[90]

Here, "we are awaiting your word." To tell you the truth, your word was rather short, so also mine must not be too long. Your word, being brief, was pretty condensed, especially that "performance": you have become masters of the art of "condensed" performances! When I was young (that was decades ago), I also liked performances, but they were of a different style.[91]

Now, if they ask you what the Pope said, you can answer: the Pope read his talk, and after that he gave another talk on what he just read.[92]

Our dear Cardinal has wished to thank me for the words I said; I think he should thank me for the abbreviated version; the actual prepared text was a bit longer, but I believe in brief homilies, since it is one thing to read them and another to have to listen to them. So, many thanks to His Eminence for his thanks![93]

Dear friends, I know from my experience as a university professor that you like a synthesis to be concrete. The synthesis program that I have prepared for you is very simple; it is limited to a no and a yes: *no* to egoism; *no* to injustice; *no* to pleasure without moral responsibility; *no* to desperation; *no* to hate and to violence; *no* to a life without God; *no* to irresponsibility and mediocrity. *Yes* to God, to Jesus Christ, to the Church; *yes* to faith and to the commitment it contains; *yes* to respect for the dignity, liberty, and rights of every person; *yes* to efforts to elevate each person and bring them to God; *yes* to justice, to love, to peace, to solidarity with all, especially those who are most needy; *yes* to hope; *yes* to your duty to build a better society.[94]

The Cardinal Vicar has been very understanding toward me. He has not rung that bell. Maybe he should have. But there is another system of alert, one less official: applause. That system did not work well, either. So, I have talked too much and taken too long; but neither the bell nor the applause has the responsibility for this.[95]

Here are some phrases written in Romanesco, the Roman dialect: *Dàmose da fà!* (Let us keep busy), *Volèmose bene!* (Let us love one another), *Semo Romani!* (We are Romans). I never learned Romanesco: does that mean that I am not a good Bishop of Rome?[96]

I don't mind your applause because when you applaud—the Pope can rest a bit![97]

Entering this house, I asked until what age a person can consider oneself to be young. Someone answered "until 40 years old." So I answered, "Well, then, I'm finished!" But in spite of all that, I always begin again, and up to today, I still have not been rejected by young people.[98]

It is a continual surprise for me to receive this type of welcome from young people who always tell me: "You are young." So I cannot be otherwise: more or less I pretend to still be young. It's true that the body has its rights, but there is always the spirit that can be rejuvenated, and it can rejuvenate the body as well.[99]

When I enter an encounter with young people, many reach a hand out to me. And I observed: when they give me a hand, they look at the photographer, thinking they will get a picture of themselves with the Pope! [100]

"Take us with you." It's obvious I have no air tickets for you, or any other kind. But from the beginning [of my ministry] in 1978, I have taken you with me everywhere I go. Not a day goes by without my feeling your presence near. Young people all over the world have the custom, which you most likely have learned already, to get ahead of the crowd to the place where the Pope will stop. I am really happy, and I see this as a continuance of your "take us with you." If I had not already learned to be "with you," something so beautiful and difficult that I learned a long, long time ago, most probably I would not have been able to do this, and you would not reach out to grasp my robes as you do, as you say, "Come!" "Stay with us!"[101]

I have one more thing to say, a thought that accompanied me during this talk. When I came in, I saw you all in the sunlight and the Pope here in the shadow, the shadow of Wisdom, yes, but still, the shadow. I thought that at the end of this encounter the sunlight of the young people would reach me. I awaited the sunlight that is in you, which you symbolize, that speaks about you. And I have to say that I did succeed in this: finally the sunlight came from your side over to me. What to do? We need to thank the Lord, and we need to thank you for this "solar" success that you have had even with the aged Wisdom from Rome.[102]

I would like to add—maybe it is not good to joke, but sometimes one can—that this visit could not be carried out without rain, without water, because the Lord said to us that we must all be reborn of water and of the Holy Spirit: and this is what one does in Baptism. And look, the parish of the Baptism of our most dear Cardinal Agostino Casaroli welcomes us with the sign of Baptism, with the external sign, with water, with rain. Thank you for this water![103]

I don't know who is responsible for this rain. It may be the Pope, but it also could be everyone present, the children. I would say that this rain is a good sign, because we know how well it serves to fertilize the fields. And school is like a great field that needs to be cultivated: the field of the human personality, of youthful humanity. Then this rain can be seen as a symbol of fertility, of all the good of the ethical order, of the spiritual order, of a good character, a good education, a well-rounded intelligence, of all those things that are sought in the schools and that we wish for the schools. In the name of this rain, my wish for you is spiritual fertility, as also for your great school at its various levels, beginning with the youngest students and passing on to middle and higher school.[104]

People sometimes ask me: "What do you enjoy most about young people? Why do you so often meet them? Why did you write an Apostolic Letter to Youth, and why did you establish the World Youth Day to be celebrated on Passion Sunday each year?" My answer is very simple: I have confidence in young people. I see in them the future of the world, the future of the Church. I believe that the youth of today want to build a world of justice, truth, and love; and with God's help they can do so.[105]

From the first day of my pontificate, I have said that youth are the hope of the Church; I repeat this always and everywhere. But I repeat it not just with my lips, but with my deepest conviction, with my whole life. I am convinced that the Church in the world of today must be built on the commitment of youth. They are the generation that holds the future within.[106]

From the beginning of my pontificate I have made a "preferential option for youth." The encounters with young people at Rome and in many other countries of the world have been many and brought enrichment. I have flung open, and will continue to open the doors of my heart to young people and ask them to open their hearts to Christ. I began the annual World Youth Days in the Church and cannot but remember with emotion these great global encounters.[107]

I have always loved young people very much: when I was your age, but also in my priestly and episcopal ministry, and even now that the Lord asked me to serve as head of the Church. I love the youth, because they are like the spring that rises on the world and on each nation in particular, with its light and its rich promises. The youth that I have met gave me the certitude that our world has a future thanks to them.[108]

I thank you for the ardor that is revealed by your words and also by your screams. We say always that we love you, young people; we love you. But the Pope knows that true love is always strict. So, the Pope must comport himself well since he is loved so ardently, with such enthusiasm. I thank you for this love, because it spurs me on, and makes clear to me the requirements of my ministry at Rome, as Bishop of Rome, but also my Petrine role, in Africa and wherever Providence sends me.[109]

I am also indebted to young people, because they offer me their freshness and their availability to be together, and together as optimists. And I have to tell you that even the Pope needs this help. He needs it because even he encounters difficulties.[110]

You just sang "the sun has already gone down": this is a sign for a person who lives a normal schedule, the solar schedule; it is a sign;

when the sun goes down, people also need to think of descending into sleep. But the young are always different; because of this I said: for them when the sun goes down it means the songfest begins. I have no objection to this program; if it is good for you, it is good for me, too. But I repeat again that there is a difference between *giovani* (the young) and *Giovanni* (John), even if John Paul is that difference. If for you young people the sunset means the beginning of a night of song, for me, John Paul, the setting sun says to rest a bit.[111]

The Pope confides in you, young people, to give newness once again to the Christian face of old Europe. Engage yourselves in personal witness. You are a "letter of Christ," his calling card! Those who meet you must be certain of having found the correct address.[112]

I am used to receiving requests. For some years young people have been giving me a "test." But I will try to come out on top, to overcome the difficulty, because young people are good. They encourage me, for example when they call out: "Long live the Pope!" They are telling me: you must live, you must be strong. So now, I must obey.[113]

At the beginning I wanted to say: "Long live the Pope!" Thank God, the Pope is still alive on this earth, but above all he lives with hope in eternal life.[114]

Improvising, on different occasions, John Paul II said humorous things about himself or regarding the situation in which he found himself.

When the Pope finds himself surrounded by little "wolves," he could be afraid that they will want to devour him, to eat something ... but these are good little wolves, they will not eat anything. In the parishes, I have already met many little wolves, but they never ate me, because they are good.[115]

I ask you to accompany me with your prayers on my forthcoming apostolic visit to Cuba. Many thanks for your contribution. Let us really hope that with your prayers I can not only go to Cuba but also return.[116]

[To the journalists who asked him if he felt up to a trip to Cuba:] Certainly I am older than I was in 1979, but up to now Providence has maintained me. And then, if you want to know something about my health and my illnesses, you must follow the news![117]

I would ask all of you: why does the Pope carry a cane? I thought that you would respond: because he is old! Instead you gave the right answer: because he is a "shepherd!" The shepherd carries a cane to prop himself up, as well as to organize a bit the sheep.[118]

To the French Cardinal Albert Decourtray, when he spoke about *The Prophecies* [vi] of Nostradamus that would have predicted as unlucky his journey to Lyons in October 1986: "I assure you, Your Eminence, that no place is as dangerous as Saint Peter's Square!"[119]

At the end of the Mass on the day of his seventy-ninth birthday, the Pope greeted the bishops who were present, and then joking about the fact that he was entering his eightieth year, said: "Octogesima adveniens," (the title of the encyclical written by Paul VI eighty years after Pope Leo XIII wrote the document Rerum Novarum*). One of the bishops responded: "Centesimus annus," (the title of the encyclical written by John Paul II in 1991, on the hundredth anniversary of the first encyclical on social doctrine).*

Prayer and Suffering

At the beginning of my pontificate, I said that for me prayer is the first duty and almost the first announcement, since it is the first condition for my service in the Church and the world. It needs to be reconfirmed that prayer, for every person consecrated to the priestly ministry or the religious life, as well as for every believer, must always be held as the essential and irreplaceable duty of one's own vocation.[120]

When you ask me how the Pope prays, I answer you: like every Christian, he speaks and he listens. Sometimes, he prays without words, and then he listens all the more. The most important thing is precisely what he "hears." And he also tries to unite prayer with his obligations, his activities, his work, and to unite his work with prayer. In this way,

---

vi *The Prophecies* (1555) was a series of rhyming predictions, one per year until the end of the millennium, written by the French scientist and seer Michel de Nostredame, known as Nostradamus (1503–1566).

day after day, he tries to carry out his "service," his "ministry," which comes to him from the will of Christ and from the living tradition of the Church.[121]

The rosary is my favorite prayer. A marvelous prayer! It is marvelous in its simplicity and in its depth. In this prayer we repeat many times the words that the Virgin Mary heard from the Archangel, and from her kinswoman Elizabeth. The whole Church joins in these words.... Against the background of the words "Ave Maria," there pass before the eyes of the soul the main episodes in the life of Jesus Christ. They are composed altogether of the joyful, sorrowful, and glorious mysteries, and they put us in living communion with Jesus through—we could say—his Mother's heart. At the same time our heart can enclose in these decades of the rosary all the facts that make up the life of the individual, the family, the nation, the Church, and mankind; personal matters and those of one's neighbor, and particularly of those who are closest to us, who are dearest to us. Thus in the simple prayer of the rosary beat the rhythms of human life.[122]

In Rome there is a beautiful custom that on every Sunday and holy day the Pope recites the Angelus with the faithful gathered in Saint Peter's Square. I inherited this custom from my venerable predecessors and I continue it with great joy. The prayer is preceded by a short meditation and a mention of certain events which need to be particularly recommended to God in prayer, and we conclude with a blessing. . . . Through the Angelus we are spiritually linked together, we remember each other and we share the mystery of salvation and our hearts also.[123]

I address especially the boys and girls who have come to Saint Peter's Square with a statue of the Infant Jesus to be blessed by the Pope before being laid in the crèche prepared at home. Take home, with great care, the little statue of the Infant Jesus, also as a sign of the Pope's love. Place it in your crèche with intense faith, with that faith with which Mary, most holy, the Mother of God, laid the newborn Jesus in the manger. Invite your whole family to gather around the crèche in these days of the Christmas Novena, to recite together the prayers learned at your mother's knee, to sing the sweet, familiar carols, so full of human and Christian sentiment.[124]

The Pope prays as the Holy Spirit permits him to pray. I think he has to pray in a way in which, deepening the mystery revealed in Christ, he can better fulfill his ministry. . . . The subject of the Pope's prayer is the phrase that begins the last document of the Second Vatican Council, the Pastoral Constitution on the Church in the Modern World: *Gaudium et spes, luctus et angor hominum huius temporis*: The joy and the hope, the grief and the anguish of the people of our time.[125]

I have a special devotion to my guardian angel. Ever since I was a child, probably like all children, I would often pray: *"Angel of God, you who are my guardian: enlighten, guard, support and govern me . . . ."* My guardian angel knows what I am doing. My trust in him, in his protective presence, is continuously being deepened in me. Saint Michael, Saint Gabriel, and Saint Raphael are the archangels I frequently invoke in my prayer.[126]

In his concern for all the churches, every day the pontiff must open his prayer, his thought, his heart to the entire world. Thus a kind of geography of the Pope's prayer is sketched out. It is a geography of communities, churches, societies, and also of the problems that trouble the world today.[127]

I simply pray for everyone every day. Whenever I meet a person, I pray for them, and this always helps me in my relationships. It is difficult for me to explain how others perceive this. You would have to ask them. However, I follow the principle of accepting each one as a person whom the Lord sends to me, and at the same time entrusts to me.[128]

You are remembered in my prayers; you are in my heart. We are all pilgrims on our way home to our heavenly Father. Let us walk in the way of love. Let us walk with faith. Let us walk in Christ Jesus.[129]

The Pope, as the Vicar of Christ on earth, wishes in the first place to unite with all those who strain toward union with Christ in prayer, wherever they may be: as a Bedouin in the steppe, or the Carmelites or Cistercians in deep enclosure, or the sick on a hospital bed in the sufferings of the death agony, or a person in activity, in the fullness of life, or oppressed and humiliated individuals . . . everywhere.[130]

The problems are truly many and I try to follow them as best I can, above all with my prayers. I must confess that the people and communities that ask for my prayers are never lacking. I always make a list so

I will remember them all at the altar and during the Eucharistic Celebration.[131]

I think of the great number of requests, of intentions for prayers that are presented to us constantly by various people. I make notes of the requests from people all over the world and their intentions and I keep them at the kneeler in my chapel, so they will be present to me at all times, even when I am not able to repeat the names every day. They remain there, and I can assure you that the Lord Jesus is familiar with them all, because he sees them in the notes I have taken, and also in my heart.[132]

The Pope prays for everyone: pray also for him.[133]

I count a great deal on the prayer of the sick, on the intercession with God of those who are suffering. They are so close to Christ! And I approach them, aware that Christ is present in them.[134]

In effect, every day I have experienced that my ministry is supported by the unceasing prayer of the People of God: of so many persons unknown to me but close to my heart, who offer to the Lord their prayers and sacrifices according to the intentions of the Holy Father. In moments of greater difficulty and suffering, this spiritual force is a valid help and intimate comfort. I always need your prayer, dear faithful of Rome and of the whole world. In fact, without it, how could I respond to the word of the Lord, who commands Simon Peter, *"Duc in altum"*; "Put out into the deep."[135]

Speaking from experience, I can tell you that as an adolescent, I was above all *intimidated* by human suffering. There was a time when I was afraid to approach those who were ill: I felt a sort of remorse when confronted with this suffering that I had been spared. In addition, I felt embarrassed; I thought that all I could say to the sick was like a "bounced check"; or rather a check drawn on *their* account, for it was they who were suffering, not I. . . . The pastoral ministry, by leading me more and more often to meet the sick, has enabled me to emerge from this period of timidity. I must add at this point that I have emerged from it mainly because the sick themselves have helped me to do so. Through visiting them, I came to realize, at first gradually, then in a way that banished all doubt, that quite unexpected connections developed between their suffering and their consciousness of it.[136]

I have always had the clear awareness of the fundamental contribution that those who suffer bring to the life of the Church. I remember that initially the sick intimidated me. I needed a good deal of courage to stand before a sick person and to enter, so to speak, into their physical and spiritual pain, without being conditioned by discomfort, and to show at least a bit of loving compassion. Only later did the profound meaning of the mystery of human suffering begin to awaken in me. In the weakness of the sick, I saw emerging ever more clearly a new strength—the strength of mercy. In a certain way, the sick "provoke" mercy. Through their prayer and sacrifice, they not only beseech mercy but they constitute a "space for mercy," or better they "open up spaces" for mercy. Through their infirmity and suffering they call forth acts of mercy and they create the possibility to accomplish them. I would often entrust the needs of the Church to the prayers of the sick, and the results were always positive.[137]

The day after my unforeseen election to the pontificate, October 17, 1978, I went to the Gemelli Hospital to visit my friend Monsignor Andrzej Maria Deskur[vii]; I was obeying an impulse of my heart. But I also wanted to give even then a clear indication of what I understood, and still do understand, to be the formidable ministry of the Successor of Peter. In that situation, I told the patients that I counted very much on them: on their prayers and above all on the offering of their sufferings from which I would draw a special strength, which for me was and still is necessary in order to carry out less unworthily my grave responsibilities in the heart of the Church of Christ.[138]

Andrzej Maria Deskur has often helped me since the beginning of my pontificate, especially through his suffering, but also with his wise counsel.[139]

The Pope addresses himself to all people, and if he meets above all with the spiritual and civil leaders, it is because their responsibilities are broader, directed to the good of a great number of persons. But I would fail in my mission if I did not spend quality time with those for whom

---

[vii] Andrzej Maria Deskur, the Pope's friend since they were young men, had suffered a serious stroke October 13 while serving as president of the Pontifical Commission for Social Communications.

Jesus had a special esteem because of their infirmities, because they needed comfort, relief, healing, and hope.[140]

When I passed through the nave of this church, I extended my arms to all those who press against the barricades. Then through them this gesture will extend further, to all. This is a significant sign: I have extended my hands to you to show you that we are united and to manifest my desire that we will be always more so. I desire very much to be united to those who are suffering; it is my strength, since my strength comes from the Cross of Christ and is present in your sufferings.[141]

The efficacy of my ministry as successor to Peter, for the fidelity and unity of the whole church, is very indebted to the prayers and offerings of the sick. I count on them. And you all have a great place in my heart and in my prayer.[142]

The Pope counts greatly on the value of your prayers and of your sufferings: offer them for the Church and for the world; offer them also for me and for my mission as universal Pastor of the Christian people.[143]

I always feel the need of your help before the Lord, so as to fulfill the mission that Jesus has entrusted to me. Every year the season of Lent reminds us of a fundamental truth: we cannot enter into eternal life without carrying our cross in union with Christ.[144]

Times change, circumstances change, but there are always in our midst those who need the voice of the Church and that of the Pope, to give expression to their anxiety, pain, and misery. They must not be disappointed. They must know that the Church was and is with them, that the Pope is with them; that he embraces with his heart and with his prayer all who are affected by suffering.[145]

Suffering is a great mystery within God's design. I remember very well my address during the Year of Redemption to all those who suffer. It was the apostolic letter *Salvifici Doloris*. Suffering is a great mystery of human destiny.[146]

Suffering is something that directly touched John Paul II many times, and he always lived this reality with a supernatural vision.

God has allowed me to experience suffering in the past months; he has allowed me to experience the danger of losing my life. During this time, he has enabled me to understand clearly and profoundly that this is his special grace for me as a person, and at the same time—considering the service I carry out as Bishop of Rome and Successor to Peter—for the entire Church.[147]

I want to express, through Mary, my gratitude for this new gift of suffering,[viii] joined as it is to the Marian month of May. I am grateful, and at the same time, I understand that this is a necessary gift. The Pope has found himself in the Gemelli Hospital and has had to suffer being absent for four weeks from the weekly Sunday meeting at this window [in the Vatican]. As I had to suffer thirteen years ago, so also again this year.[148]

In these days of my illness,[ix] I have the opportunity to understand always more the value of the service that the Lord has called me to carry out in the Church as priest, as bishop, as successor of Peter: this, too, passes through the gift of suffering.[149]

I cordially greet all those gathered in this, shall I say, "Vatican III," because "Vatican I" is Saint Peter's Square. And "II" is Castel Gandolfo. "Vatican III" has become Gemelli Hospital. As in 1981, and now fifteen years later in 1996, we confirm "Vatican III."[150]

The condition of his health[x] caused some commentators, on different occasions, to presuppose that he would retire voluntarily. But, on many occasions, Pope Wojtyła gave a clear-cut answer to this type of indiscretion.

Following the example of the Servant of God, I can—as long as it pleases God—remain a faithful and humble servant of this mission to the entire Church, and I feel, remember, and repeat only this: that I am a useless servant.[151]

When I first visited this shrine of Our Lady of Kalwaria in 1979, I asked you to pray for me, while I am alive and after my death. Today I thank you and all the pilgrims of Kalwaria for these prayers, for the

---

viii This hospitalization was for a broken femur and, consequently, a hip replacement.

ix From October 6 to 15, 1996, he was in the hospital for an appendectomy.

x In addition to numerous illnesses and hospitalizations, in 1993 the Pope was diagnosed with Parkinson's disease.

spiritual support I continually receive. I continue to ask you, do not stop praying—once again I repeat it—as long as I am alive and after my death. As always, I will repay your kindness by recommending all of you to the merciful Christ and to his Mother.[152]

Most Holy Mother, Our Lady of Calvary, obtain also for me strength in body and spirit that I may carry out to the end the mission given me by the Risen Lord. To you I give back all the fruits of my life and my ministry; to you I entrust the future of the Church; to you I offer my nation; in you do I trust and once more to you I declare: *Totus tuus, Maria!* I am all yours, Mary![153]

I repeat here today the motto of my episcopal and pontifical service: "*Totus tuus.*" I always experienced in my life the loving and efficacious presence of the Mother of the Lord. Mary accompanies me each day in the fulfillment of the mission of Successor to Peter.[154]

> *Even with the passing of years and fatigue, the Pope valued the mature years which "from a biblical point of view, are a sign of benevolent blessing from the Most High. Longevity is thus seen as a special divine gift."*

If aging, with its inevitable limitations, is accepted serenely in the light of faith, it can become a precious opportunity to understand better the mystery of the Cross, which gives meaning to human existence. . . . The abundant free time available during this stage of life offers the elderly person the opportunity to confront the deep questions that perhaps were left to one side because of urgent situations or priority concerns. The awareness of coming near to the final goal leads the aged to concentrate on what is essential, giving importance to that which time cannot destroy.[155]

> *Having arrived at the threshold of the twenty-fifth anniversary as pontiff, his thoughts moved toward the one who would succeed him on the Chair of Peter.*

Those entrusted with the legacy of the keys
gather here, letting themselves be enfolded
by the Sistine's colors,

by the vision left to us by Michelangelo—
So it was in August, and again in October,
in the memorable year of the two Conclaves,
and so it will be once more, when the time comes,
after my death.
Michelangelo's vision must then speak to them.
"Con-clave"[xi]: a shared concern for the legacy of the keys,
the keys of the Kingdom.
Lo, they see themselves in the midst of the
Beginning and the End,
between the Day of Creation and the Day of Judgment . . .
It is granted man once to die, and thereafter, the Judgment![156]

Finally the Holy Father, responding to the many young people who were crying out: "Long live the Pope!" said:

"With these greetings it will be difficult for me to die, but that moment will come."[157]

I often think of that day of vision:
it will be filled with amazement
at the Simplicity
that can hold
the world.
And the world dwells in it, untouched
until now, and beyond.
And then the simple necessity grows
to a still greater yearning
for that one day
embracing all things
with the immeasurable Simplicity
that love's breathing can bring.[158]

[xi] Conclave (con-clave: "with key"), refers to a room that can be locked. In the Church it refers to the secret and secluded meeting of the College of Cardinals to elect a new pope.

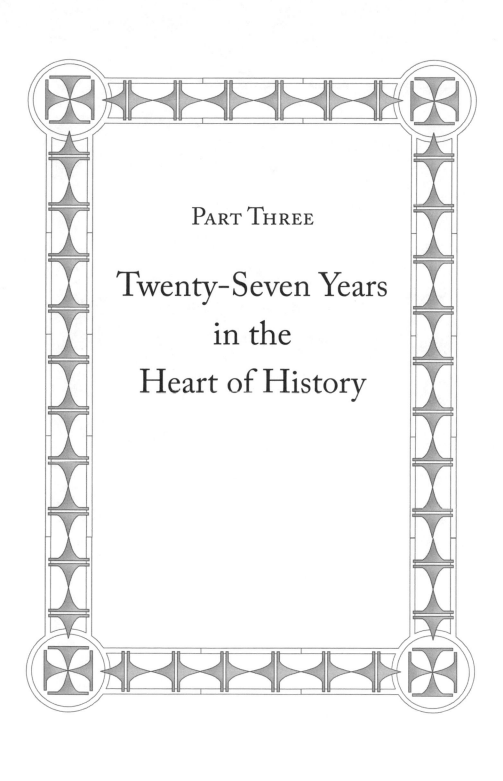

PART THREE

Twenty-Seven Years
in the
Heart of History

1978: The 264th Pontiff

I ASK THE LORD FOR the strength and assistance to continue on the way laid out by my unforgettable predecessors: [from the] patience and heroic firmness and farsightedness of Paul VI, who will shine forever for what he accomplished in the Church toward the implementation of the Second Vatican Council; to the smile of John Paul I, who in his swift passing left a profound impression, reminding us once again that "the ways of God are not our ways" (cf. Is 55:8).[1]

On October 25 Pope Wojtyła held his first Wednesday general audience, which was repeated eleven hundred times during his papacy, with the participation of almost 18 million people from every part of the world.

When the Holy Father John Paul I spoke to participants in the general audience on Wednesday, September 27, no one could imagine that it was for the last time. . . . Today John Paul II presents himself to you, for the first time. Four weeks after that general audience, he wishes to greet you and speak to you.[2]

On October 29 he carried out his first pastoral visit, which brought him to the crowds of Rome and to the mountain of Mentorella, as he himself noted. In almost twenty-seven years, he carried out 146 trips throughout Italy, 259 to different locations, 279 days in all. On November 5 he made a pilgrimage to the patron saints of Italy, both in Assisi and Rome.

During my stays in Rome, I often visited the Sanctuary of the Madonna of Mentorella. This place, hidden among the mountains, has fascinated me in a particular way. Its view of the Italian landscape is sweeping and magnificent. I came here a few days before the last Conclave. . . . During my stays in Rome this place was helpful to my prayer. And so I also wanted to come here today. Prayer, which in various ways expresses the relationship of man with the living God, is also the first task and almost the first announcement of the Pope, just as it is the first condition of his service in the Church and in the world.[3]

I wish to respond to your welcome in a special way. For this reason I am going to your patron saints, to Assisi, the city of Saint Francis, and to the tomb of Saint Catherine of Siena, which is, as you know, in the Basilica of Santa Maria sopra Minerva[i] in Rome. Unfortunately, sunset in the month of November does not permit me to go also to Siena on the same day, as I would have so much liked. In this way John Paul II intends to take his place in the history of salvation, imprinted, so eloquently and abundantly, on the history of Italy and on various places in this country.[4]

On December 3 he carried out his first parish visit in the diocese of Rome, going to Saint Francis Xavier in Garbatella. He would visit 301 of the 334 parishes in the diocese of Rome. (At the beginning of his pontificate there were 296 parishes.)

This is my first visit to a parish in the diocese of Rome, entrusted to me by Christ through my election as Bishop of Rome. . . . It is a great joy for me to be able to visit as the first Roman parish precisely yours, to which I am linked by a special memory. In fact, in the years of the immediate postwar period, as a student in Rome, I used to go nearly every Sunday to Garbatella, to help in the pastoral service. Some moments of that period are still alive in my memory, although it seems to me that in the course of over thirty years many things have changed enormously here.[5]

On December 22 he initiated the practice of meeting before Christmas with the College of Cardinals, a practice later enlarged to include the members of the Roman Curia. Here he would propose some brief reflections on the year that was about to end.

---

i The Basilica of Saint Mary on Minerva, the present-day gothic structure near the Pantheon, is the site of the eighth-century basilica Pope Zacharias built on top of the ancient temple of Minerva, goddess of wisdom and war.

You, Lord Cardinals, have extended the circle of my family and you have become by a very special title "my relatives," by means of that transcendent but very real communion created by bonds as firm as those of any human family, which is called, and is, ecclesial life. . . . I know well how my predecessor, Paul VI of venerable memory, during the course of similar gatherings which took place in this hall during the busy yet bright span of his fifteen-year pontificate, would always like to extend his gaze to the duties of his pastoral mission. He would recall the salient facts of the Church and of the world, not just to give a precise content to the meeting with his most qualified collaborators, but also to take stock of the situation through a careful examination of the most recent events. An opportunity like that presents itself to me today, in a form similar and at the same time diverse, but perhaps a bit easier.[6]

After a look at the Church, one's thoughts turn quite naturally—as Paul VI's thoughts used to turn—to the surrounding world. How has human society progressed during this year which has just come to an end? How is it faring just now? Beyond the facts of which we take note, we must look at the connections between them, in order to grasp—as far as possible—their sense and direction. For example, we may ask: is the cause of peace among men progressing or stagnating? And the answer can make one anxious and uncertain when we discover, in different countries, persistent virulent tensions that both root and give rise to furious outbreaks of violence. . . . Just how urgent the need is to pledge oneself to the cause of peace has been confirmed by the sad news coming recently from the South American continent. The dispute between Argentina and Chile has become all the more acute in these recent days, notwithstanding the lively appeal for peace sent to the authorities by the bishops of both countries, and vigorously upheld and reiterated by my predecessor, Pope John Paul I. This is a cause for deep sorrow and personal anxiety.[7]

Toward the middle of January 1979 a similar practice could be observed. Meeting with the diplomatic representatives accredited to the Holy See, John Paul II produced an assessment of the past year.

Is not this participation in the most important events of the life of the Church, by the representatives of those who wield political responsibilities, a way of emphasizing the presence of the Church within the modern world, and in particular of recognizing the importance of her mission—especially the mission of the Apostolic See? The mission, while being strictly religious, also fits into the general pattern of the principles of morality, which are indissolubly bound up with it.[8]

It is the common good that inspires not only the social teaching of the Apostolic See but also the initiatives which are possible for it in the framework of its own specific field. This is the case, a very topical one, of Lebanon. In a country upset by hatred and destruction, with innumerable victims, what possibility remains of reestablishing relations of common life between Christians of various tendencies and Muslims, between Lebanese and Palestinians, if not in a loyal and generous effort which respects the identity and vital requirements of all, without the vexation of any? . . . My thought and my prayer also turn to so many other problems that, these days in particular, are seriously troubling the life of the world, and which are again causing so many deaths, so much destruction and rancor in countries which contain few Catholics but which are equally dear to the Apostolic See. We are following the dramatic events in Iran and are very attentive to the news reaching us with regard to the Khmer country [Cambodia] and all the peoples of this, already so sorely tried, Southeast Asia. We see clearly that humanity is divided in a great many ways. It is a question also and perhaps above all, of ideological divisions bound up with the different state systems. The search for solutions that will permit human societies to carry out their own tasks and to live in justice, is perhaps the main sign of our time.[9]

1979: The Encyclical on the Redeemer

With his pastoral visit from January 25 to February 1, which led him to the Dominican Republic, Mexico, and the Bahamas, John Paul II initiated a chain of international trips that in the almost twenty-seven years of his pontificate reached 104, in 129 nations, totaling 543 days. During

*his flight from Rome to Santo Domingo, he began the tradition of offer-
ing consecutive interviews in the airplane with one reporter after
another. This practice continued almost until the end of his pontificate.*

I visited the sanctuary of Guadalupe in January 1979 during my
first apostolic pilgrimage. The decision to undertake this trip was made
in response to an invitation to participate in the assembly of the
Conference of Bishops of Latin America at Puebla de los Angeles.
That pilgrimage to some degree inspired and gave direction to the succeeding years of my pontificate. First I stopped in Santo Domingo,
after which I went on to Mexico. While we were on our way to our
lodging, something absolutely extraordinary and moving happened as
we passed through the streets packed with people: in a sense we could
touch with our hands the devotion of these numberless crowds. When
we finally reached the place where we were to spend the night, the
people just kept on singing—and it was already midnight. Then Father
Stanisław Dziwisz[ii] felt like he needed to go out and silence the crowd,
explaining to them that the Pope had to get some sleep. Only then did
they quiet down.[10]

The purpose of the journey was—in addition to participating in the
opening of the Puebla Conference—that of strengthening the spiritual
ties which unite in Christ's one Church, men of different nations,
countries, islands, races, and continents: bonds which made them all
not a mere aggregation, but a community which, extraordinarily com-
posite though it is, constitutes a marvelous unity in Christ Jesus (cf.
Gal 3:28). I think that these ties have really been deepened and con-
solidated. I humbly thank the Lord for this, well aware that their
strengthening is the peculiar mission and responsibility of the Bishop
of Rome as the Successor of Peter.[11]

I wish to refer to the subject of the third Conference of the Latin-
American Episcopate: to evangelization. It is a fundamental subject,
a subject that is always topical. The conference, which ended its work
at Puebla on February 13, bears witness to this. It is, moreover, the

---

ii Stanisław Dziwisz, now cardinal archbishop of Kraków, was for many years the
Pope's secretary and adviser.

subject "of the future," the subject that the Church must live continually and prolong in the future. The subject, therefore, constitutes the
permanent perspective of the Church's mission. To evangelize means
making Christ present in the life of man as a person, and at the same
time in the life of society. To evangelize means doing everything possible, according to our capacities, in order that man "may believe," in
order that man may find himself again in Christ, in order that he may
find again in him the meaning and the adequate dimension of his
own life.[12]

On March 4 Pope Wojtyła published his first encyclical, Redemptor
Hominis, *with March 15 as the official release date.*

Everything I said in the encyclical *Redemptor Hominis*, I brought
with me from Poland.[13]

I tried to express in it what has animated and continually animates
my thoughts and my heart since the beginning of the pontificate which,
through the inscrutable plan of Providence, I had to assume on October
16 of last year. The encyclical contains those thoughts which then, at
the beginning of this new life, were pressing with particular forceful-
ness in my mind and which, certainly, had already been maturing in me
previously, during the years of my service as a priest, and then as a
bishop. I am of the opinion that, if Christ called me in this way, with
such thoughts . . . , with such sentiments, it was because he wanted
these calls of the intellect and of the heart, these expressions of faith,
hope, and charity, to ring out in my new and universal ministry, right
from its beginning. Therefore, as I see and feel the relationship between
the mystery of the Redemption in Christ Jesus and the dignity of man,
so I would like so much to unite the mission of the Church with service of man in this his impenetrable mystery. I see in that the central
task of my new ecclesial service.[14]

His words often expressed a reference to the present reality.

In Vienna tomorrow, Monday, June 18, the highest authorities of
the major nuclear powers will sign the second accord, called Salt II, on
the limitation of strategic armaments. The agreement is not yet a

reduction of armaments or even, as would be desired, a disarmament proviso, but it is not without significance that the measures presented are a sign of the willingness to pursue a dialogue, without which all hope of working effectively for peace would disappear.[15]

From June 2 to 10 Poland welcomed, with a warm embrace, a brief return visit of John Paul II, who responded as completely as is possible.

I am coming to you as a son of this land, of this nation, and also, by the inscrutable designs of Providence, as a Successor of Saint Peter in the See of Rome. I thank you for not having forgotten me and for not having ceased, from the day of my election, to help me with your prayers and to show me also such kindly benevolence.[16]

I am happy to be able to express at this moment the profound happiness in my heart at having been able to take part in the centenary celebrations of the martyrdom of Saint Stanisław. Warsaw, Gniezno, Częstochowa, and Kraków, the stopping-places of my pilgrimage, have been moments of joyous communion, friendship, constructive talks, and especially of prayer. The deep and intimate emotions of the various meetings have blended together in my soul, and have enriched it with a new and gratifying experience that is a pure grace of the Most High.[17]

On June 30 he celebrated his first consistory, with the nomination of fifteen of the 231 cardinals who would be part of nine consistories during his almost twenty-seven-year pontificate.

We have had the fortune to solemnly introduce into the College of Cardinals of the Roman Church fifteen men. Of these, one remains "in pectore,"[iii] in expectation of the decisions of Divine Providence that one day we may be permitted to reveal his name; the others are already commonly known to everyone. In this sublime rite there was renewed the thousand-year-old tradition of the Roman Church, which has a

---

iii This term means "in the heart," or in secret. The name of the fifteenth cardinal was revealed twelve years later when he was solemnly invested during the fifth consistory of John Paul II's pontificate: Ignatius Cardinal Kung (Gong) Pin-Mei (1901–2000), the bishop of Shanghai (who was serving a life sentence in prison at the time).

great significance not only for the subsequent stability of the Church, but also for adequate understanding of her character which is twofold: local and, at the same time, universal.[18]

A prominent appointment on October 2 with the General Assembly of the United Nations took place during a pastoral visit to Ireland and the United States from September 29 to October 8.

The words spoken before the United Nations Organization became a particular fruit of my pilgrimage during these important steps in the history of the whole Church and of Christianity. What else could I say before that supreme *forum of* political character, if not that which constitutes the very core of the Gospel message: the words of a great love for man, which lives in the communities of so many peoples and nations, within the frontiers of so many states and political systems. If political activity, in the dimensions of the single states and in international dimensions, must ensure a real primacy of man on earth, if it must serve his real dignity, the witness of the spirit and of truth borne by Christianity and the Church is necessary.[19]

On my way to the United Nations, I felt equally called to visit Ireland, for two reasons. The Church and Christendom owe so much to the Irish people for its historic contribution and its present vigor, and I had to strengthen these brothers and these sons in their faith and encourage them in their Christian identity. Moreover, the present situation was at once a challenge and a cry that drew me to the spot in order to utter forceful exhortations to peace, forgiveness, and brotherly collaboration in justice.[20]

On October 21 he visited Pompeii and Naples.

I have come to this shrine, in the spirit of a fervent and humble pilgrimage, to venerate the Blessed Virgin and fulfill as it were a secret vow of mine, of piety, gratitude, and love. I greeted in the first place her, the Blessed Virgin, who, from the venerated and miraculous effigy, unites us all with the "sweet chain" which is the holy rosary. She offers it to us, proposes it to us, and commends it to us as a simple, humble, but rich and efficacious means of Christian prayer.[21]

The appeal that I address, in the first place, to sons of the Church, but then also to all men of goodwill, and to the religious and civil authorities, is to double their efforts in order that certain situations of want and hardship, which unjustly befall so many brothers, making them suffer, may be happily overcome in a spirit of harmony and collaboration. In proposing to you such a commitment of active solidarity as your immediate and primary aim, I want to confide in you that I was thinking precisely of this on accepting your invitation, and that I will consider it, therefore, the most consoling fruit of my visit to have contributed—even to a modest extent—to encouraging and supporting the necessary initiatives to be undertaken. Naples, in fact, deserves this special interest; Naples calls for direct solicitude; Naples needs to hope: I am speaking of hope in its existence, in its future. I am speaking of hope also in the human and civil sense, which—like the dual concept justice and charity, as we have seen—is inseparable from the higher hope that smiles, in the light of God, on Christian life.[22]

A moving visit was the trip to Turkey from November 28 to 30, almost a pilgrimage of memory in the footsteps of Paul VI.

I wish to thank Divine Providence for this visit, which I desired so much and which—under a special inspiration of that eternal Wisdom, worshiped for so many centuries in the Church on the Bosphorus, Hagia Sophia—has brought about a mutual strengthening along those ways on which Patriarch Athenagoras I and my great predecessors, Popes John XXIII and Paul VI, had started. . . . I consider the meeting with Patriarch Dimitrios I a fruit of the particular action of the Spirit of Christ, who is the Spirit of unity and love. That meeting took place precisely in this spirit and bore witness to this spirit.[23]

At the conclusion of the year he recounted his experience with deep emotion.

In this year of my pontificate, "the daily pressure upon me of my anxiety for all the churches" (2 Cor 11:28) was solely that of meeting man, in order to let man meet Christ. The crowds that thronged to the Wednesday audiences week after week, the people I met on my pilgrimages, the weekly visits to the parishes of my Roman diocese, have given me the privilege of establishing this living contact, permitting a constant catechesis of the magisterium, the lines of which I have laid down in the recent document *Catechesi Tradendae*, which sums up the wishes expressed at the Synod of Bishops. It was a direct relationship with everyone. . . . At the same time there was a meeting with the Church. She was instituted, in fact, by Christ for the salvation of man, every man, in the concrete situations of life. The Church today knows a really exciting moment of vitality, and is the center of orientation and interest for the whole world.[24]

And therefore he proposed a snapshot of the world's problems.

I cannot fail to recall the points of greatest danger in some parts of the world: the persistent crisis in the Middle East; the situation in South Africa; the strife in the Indo-Chinese peninsula: and here again one thinks of the miserable human caravans, wandering over the wide seas or in search of asylum, of political refugees, of the exiles, of prisoners, whose situation is, and remains, very painful owing to lack of food, clothes, housing, work, and above all, of any security for the future.[25]

1980: The Embrace of Those Shaken by Tragedy

On March 26 he expressed his sorrow at the assassination of Archbishop Oscar Romero in San Salvador, killed the day before while celebrating Mass.

He was struck down precisely at the most sacred moment, during the highest, most divine service. Words fail us all, in the face of such violence, which did not stop even before the threshold of a church to carry out its blind program of death. . . . Where, where is the world going? I repeat it again today. Where are we going? It is not with barbarity that society is improved, conflicts eliminated, and the future constructed. Violence destroys, nothing else. It does not replace values, but runs along the edge of an abyss: the bottomless abyss of hatred. Only love builds up, only love saves![26]

On April 13 he visited Turin.

The Pope has come among you to recall to the world of the city and of modern labor this decisive and irreplaceable presence, strong and gentle, which poses stringent questions to our quiet lives, but out of which comes certain effective and lasting solutions to crises which the world is going through. In your midst the Pope is the bearer of Christ's liberating message: while he feels unequal to the tremendous task, and is therefore meeting you with the defenseless humility of his exclusively spiritual mission, he is at the same time aware of the value of his witness, which aims to adapt itself to your expectations at this moment.[27]

From May 2 to 12 he carried out his pastoral visit to Zaire, Republic of Congo, Kenya, Ghana, Upper Volta (now Burkina Faso), and Ivory Coast.

In Africa I spoke to the various African ethnic groups and populations of the problems pressing upon their conscience, at the individual and collective level: possible use, in the framework of the specific characteristics of Catholicism, which is by definition "universal," of the specific elements of those particular cultures was encouraged; esteem for those special values that Africa has to offer the world was expressed; the necessity of safeguarding the spiritual heritage, the extraordinary richness of sensitivity to religious realities was affirmed, as well as the need to protect deeply rooted family traditions with all their African warmth and identity; attention was drawn once more to the tragedy of the areas suffering from drought, hunger, and illiteracy, which carries off populations and undermines their continuity, as I cried, with a lump in my throat, in my appeal for Sahel.[iv] [28]

---

iv The Sahel is the fertile grassland extending through several African nations bordering the Sahara Desert. Over the last three decades the Sahara has been claiming more of this land as desert.

From May 30 to June 2 he carried out his pastoral visit in France. During this time he spoke to UNESCO, the United Nations Educational, Scientific and Cultural Organization.

My visit to the headquarters of UNESCO . . . created a special occasion to highlight that relationship of the Church with culture, which found its expression in the teaching of the Second Vatican Council, and particularly in the constitution *Gaudium et Spes.* This visit was also the occasion to recall, by means of a special appeal to scientists of the whole world, the great cause of peace. Paris remains the city particularly suited to act as host to the headquarters of UNESCO. Thanks to the initiative of the archbishop of Paris, Cardinal Marty, the visit to the headquarters of that organization had at the same time a fully pastoral character in regard to the Church in France. . . . It is a Church that has great merits both as regards the emergence of forms of consciousness and of Christian spirituality, and for the carrying out of missionary activity. The visit to Lisieux, therefore, seemed very justified in order to honor Saint Thérèse, who from the Carmelite convent of that city indicated to many contemporaries a special interior way to God—and who at the same time the Church has recognized as the patron saint of missions in the whole world.[29]

From June 30 to July 12 was his pastoral visit in Brazil.

In Brazil the Church is in contact with a particular social situation which is waiting for vigilant attention and concrete measures on the part of the rulers; I cannot forget the meetings with the *favelados*[v] of Rio de Janeiro, with the workers of São Paolo, with the farmworkers in Recife, with the peoples of Amazonia. It was a unique opportunity to proclaim once more not only to those populations, but before the whole world, that "the Church, when she proclaims the Gospel, without abandoning her specific task of evangelization, tries to obtain that all aspects of social life in which injustice is manifested should undergo a transformation toward justice."[30]

---

[v] *Favelados* is the pejorative term for the poor who live in the slums, or favelas, of Brazil, particularly on hillsides around Rio de Janeiro and São Paulo.

The outbreak of the war between Iran and Iraq on September 22 pressed the Pope to speak out strongly.

The news of the fighting that has broken out between the armies of Iraq and Iran, who are engaged in battle with vast means of destruction and death, arouses deep concern and sorrow. My thoughts turn to the victims, already numerous, not only among the fighting forces, but also among the civilian populations; I am thinking of the mourning families, of the people living in the nightmare of a catastrophe that might sweep down upon their own homes and on the nations; not to mention the destruction and damage to the resources of the two countries, from which the populations hope for improvements of their standard of living, and the rekindling of the feelings of hostility and hatred that war causes. In the region of the Middle East, already swept by tensions, shocks, and chronic insecurity, and armed conflict such as the one that has sprung up between Iraq and Iran might have—God forbid!—even wider and more devastating consequences.[31]

From November 15 to 19 he made a pastoral visit in the Federal Republic of Germany.

The Church in Germany is faced with the major tasks of evangelization connected with the situation of a society divided, as a result of the Second World War, into two separate German states. These are the typical tasks of a highly industrialized society in the areas of economy and civilization, and at the same time, subject to intense processes of secularization. In such circumstances, the mission of the Church, not an easy one, requires a particular maturity of the truth preached, and a love that is capable of overcoming indifference and the absence of many people from the community of believers.[32]

On November 25 the Pope made the spontaneous decision to go to Campania and Basilicata to comfort the people who were hit by a strong earthquake that left thousands of victims.

The Church is the leaven of the world; she participates in the hopes, the conquests, as well as in the anxieties, the sorrows, the fears, the setbacks, the tragedies of man. I was thinking of this against the terrible background of the ruins of Campania and Basilicata, among the remains of the cataclysm which had just exterminated so many human lives and destroyed villages and houses, while I was speaking to those brothers and sisters and gazing into their sorrowful eyes turned to me amid tears, but with so much faith.[33]

On December 2 the encyclical Dives in Misericordia *(dated November 30) was released to the public.*

It was my great desire that the announcement of the encyclical *Dives in Misericordia* should be connected with the first Sunday of Advent. Its main purpose is to recall the Father's love, revealed in the whole Messianic mission of Christ, beginning with his coming into the world up to the paschal mystery of his cross and resurrection. This encyclical . . . has as its subject God's mercy. The Church and the world need mercy, which expresses love stronger than sin and every evil in which man and his earthly existence is involved.[34]

The reflections offered in *Dives in Misericordia* were the fruit of my pastoral experience in Poland, especially in Kraków. That is where Saint Faustina Kowalska is buried, she who was chosen by Christ to be a particularly enlightened interpreter of the truth of Divine Mercy. For Sister Faustina this truth led to an extraordinarily rich mystical life. She was a simple, uneducated person, and yet those who read the *Diary* of her revelations are astounded by the depth of her mystical experience. I mentioned Sister Faustina because her revelations, focused on the mystery of Divine Mercy, occurred during the period preceding the Second World War. This was precisely the time when those ideologies of evil, Nazism and Communism, were taking shape. Sister Faustina became the herald of the one message capable of offsetting the evil of those ideologies, the fact that God is Mercy—the truth of the merciful Christ. And for this reason, when I was called to the See of Peter, I felt impelled to pass on those experiences of a fellow Pole that deserve a place in the treasury of the universal Church.[35]

In closing the year, a particular thought was given to the tragedy of terrorism.

Unfortunately, in some nations, such as Spain, Italy, Ireland, and elsewhere, there is still a very serious danger of terrorism and violence, this real war waged against defenseless people and institutions, moved by obscure centers of power, which do not realize the order which they hope to reach through violence cannot but call further violence. . . . I beg the men of violence, who are also my brothers, to desist from their path of death; I call upon the young not to let themselves be swept away by the perverse ideology of destruction and hatred, but to collaborate with all generous forces existing in the various nations, to construct a world "in the dimension of man"; only in this way will it be possible to ensure a really positive future, in the impetus of industrious progress from which the humble, the excluded, and poor must benefit particularly. And I again raise my thought, my prayer, for the many unknowing victims of terrorism, as I did with great sorrow last February after the tragic end of the dear, good, and unforgettable Professor Bachelet,[vi] and as I did in August at the barbarous slaughter in Bologna.[vii] [36]

1981: The Attempt on His Life in the Vatican

On January 11, John Paul II baptized nine infants in the Vatican, thus beginning a custom that would last for years to come. During his entire pontificate, he performed almost fourteen hundred Baptisms. A few days later, he rejoiced over a happy outcome of a dramatic event in Iran.

The freeing of the American hostages held for over fourteen months in Teheran[viii] is something that I greet with deep satisfaction. I am

---

vi Vittorio Bachelet (1926–1980), Italian politician, lawyer and professor, Catholic Action leader, and member of the Pontifical Council for the Family, was assassinated on February 12, 1980, by the Red Brigades.

vii The Bologna massacre (August 2, 1980) was a terrorist bombing at the Central Station, perpetrated by members of the Nuclei Armati Rivoluzionari, in which eighty-five people were killed and more than two hundred injured.

viii On November 4, 1979, militant Islamic students stormed the U.S. Embassy in Teheran, demanding the extradition of Shah Reza Pahlavi, who had fled to the United States after the Iranian revolution. Of the ninety hostages taken, fifty-two remained in captivity through January 21, 1981.

profoundly pleased that it was possible, after a long and difficult negotiation, to reach an agreement between the two countries on this subject. During all this period I have followed with constant interest and
concern the developments of their situation. I have shared the grief
and the anxiety of their families. I have done what I could by word and
by continued fervent prayer to hasten a solution.[37]

*From February 16 to 27 he carried out his pastoral visit in the countries
of Pakistan, Japan, and the Philippines, with a brief stop also in the
United States.*

That Eastern journey was an experience that made a great impact
on me. After Paul VI, who had already visited the Philippines, it was
the first time that a Successor of Peter had set foot on those distant
shores (and I have in mind especially the ancient and noble country of
Japan), thus bringing out the continuity of the evangelical mandate,
which down the centuries has inspired the apostles and their successors, the missionaries, to bring the good news to all people according
to Christ's command (cf. Mk 16:15). On February 21 I was able to
address, from the auditorium of "Radio Veritas" in Manila, a message
to all the peoples of Asia; a vast continent with immense resources of
civilization, culture, work, human spontaneity, and kindness, which
make a very special contribution to international life. On February 17
I had dedicated these same peoples to the Virgin of Perpetual Help,
venerated at Baclaran.[38]

*At 5:19 P.M. on Wednesday, May 13—while he greeted the faithful who
were gathered in Saint Peter's Square for the audience—Pope John Paul
II was shot by Ali Agca.[ix] Following emergency surgery and a 22–day
stay at Gemelli Hospital, the Pope returned to the Vatican on June 3. A
viral infection impelled him on June 20 to return to the hospital. After
undergoing another surgical procedure on August 5, he was finally
released on August 14.*

---

ix The total story behind the attempted assassination of the Holy Father by the young
Turk Mehmet Ali Agca has never come to light. It is unknown whether he acted alone,
was part of a fanatical group, or was an agent of the Soviet Union. He was extradicted to
Turkey in 2005 to serve another prison sentence.

The attempt on my life on May 13, 1981, in some way had confirmed the full meaning of the words written at the time of my spiritual exercises in 1980. I feel even more deeply that I am totally in the hands of God—and I continually remain at the disposition of my Lord, entrusting myself to him through his Immaculate Mother (*Totus tuus*—I am all yours).[39]

We all remember the hour that afternoon, when some shots from a pistol were fired at the Pope with the intent to kill him. The bullet which entered his abdomen is now found in the Sanctuary of Fatima; and the sash pierced by the shell is in the Sanctuary of Jasna Góra. It was a maternal hand that guided the path of the bullet. The seriously injured Pope was transported to Gemelli Hospital where he remained on the threshold of death.[40]

I am particularly close to the two persons who together with me were wounded. I pray for the brother who shot me, and whom I have sincerely forgiven. United to Christ, priest and victim, I offer my sufferings for the Church and for the world.[41]

In the days that followed May 13, and during the course of my long convalescence, I often meditated on the mystery of evil, of its expansion, which seems contagious; yet at the same time—having received and been helped by innumerable demonstrations of kindness—I meditated on the even more pronounced mystery of the solidarity of people in doing good, in the construction and reconstruction of a society and of a civilization founded on love and sharing.[42]

The Pope recounted that he never doubted that he would survive this attempt on his life; instead, he meditated continually on the story of what had happened to him and on the apparitions of Fatima.[x]

The very instant that I fell in Saint Peter's Square I had a clear premonition that I would be saved. This certitude never left me, not even during the worst moments: neither after the first operation nor during the viral sickness.[43]

---

[x] The Third Secret of Fatima, revealed by the Holy Father on May 13, 2000, relates a symbolic vision of Christian suffering and death, first of the Holy Father and then of bishops, priests, religious, and the laypeople. This results from refusal to heed Our Lady's plea to pray and do penance for the conversion of Russia from atheistic Communism to Christianity. For the full document see the Vatican Web site: http://www.vatican.va.

Could I forget that the event in Saint Peter's Square took place on the day and at the hour at which for more than sixty years is recalled the first appearance of the Mother of Christ to the poor little peasants at Fatima in Portugal? For, in all that happened to me that same day, I sensed that extraordinary motherly protection and care which showed itself stronger than the deadly bullet.[44]

In the event that befell me, I cannot help recalling a parallel with the holy Archbishop Charles, whose name I bear. The chronicles relate that on October 26 of the year 1569, while he was praying in his private chapel, and in opposition to a reform proposed by him, a shot from an harquebus[xi] was fired at him but left him miraculously unharmed (cf. *Bibliotheca Santorum*, vol. III, Rome: 1963, col. 830). In spite of the different circumstances, I too must humbly thank the Lord for having wished my life to be saved, so that I could spend it further in the service of the Holy Church.[45]

On September 14 his encyclical Laborem Exercens *was promulgated.*

It should never be forgotten that the true purpose of every economic, social, and political system and of every model of development is the integral advancement of the human person. Development is clearly something much more fundamental than merely economic progress measured in terms of the gross national product. True development takes as its criterion the human person with all the needs, just expectations, and fundamental rights that are his or hers. This is the central idea that I presented in my recently published encyclical, *Laborem Exercens*. Its purpose is to highlight "the man who works" and who thus contributes to the economic development and the civil progress of his own country and of the whole world. Human work constitutes, in fact, the "essential key" of the whole social question.[46]

On December 13 he prayed for the Polish nation, where General Wojciech Jaruzelski, as mandated by the Soviet Union, had just completed a coup d'état and imposed martial law.

My solicitude turns again toward the country, toward the nation, whose son I am, which, like every nation and country, has the right to

---

xi The harquebus, or arquebus, was a heavy fifteenth-century firearm.

special solicitude on the part of the Church. At this moment this solicitude embraces the whole of Poland and all the Poles. They have, as a
nation, the right to live their own life and solve their own internal
problems in the spirit of their own convictions in conformity with their
own culture and national traditions. These problems, which are certainly difficult ones, cannot be solved by the use of violence. Hence my
appeal and my request: it is necessary to return to the way of renewal,
constructed with the method of dialogue in respect for the rights of
every man and of every citizen.[47]

*At the closing of the year, once again his voice was raised in favor of the
Middle East and against every form of terrorism.*

I cannot fail to refer, even if fleetingly, to the situation in the
Middle East, in particular in beloved Lebanon, which remains fraught
with dangers and apprehension because of frequent bloodshed. Nor
do I forget beloved Northern Ireland, upon which terroristic attacks
continue to cast their fatal shadow. . . . In this context I feel it is my
duty to raise my voice against the serious and still unresolved phenomenon of international terrorism, which is a permanent threat to
the internal and international peace of peoples. President Sadat,[xii] a
courageous promoter of international understanding and of the
advancement of his ancient, noble, and strong people, has fallen victim to it. There have been innumerable victims, all over the world,
struck down when carrying out their duty and made the object of
unspeakable cowardly actions, which are really and truly acts of
murderous war, covered by the tacit complicity of a few and by the
anonymity of the cities which are becoming dehumanized and disin-
tegrating. Also, the president of the United States of America escaped
from one of these attacks.[xiii] [48]

---

xii Egyptian President Anwar Sadat (1918–1981), together with Israeli Prime Minister
Menachem Begin, signed the Camp David Peace Agreement (1971) for which they
shared the Nobel Peace Prize. Sadat's efforts toward improved relations with Israel and
the West resulted in his assassination by discontented soldiers during a military parade in
Cairo on October 6, 1981.

xiii John Hinckley Jr. attempted to assassinate President Ronald Reagan on March 30,
1981, outside the Washington, D.C., Hilton Hotel.

At the same time, he launched an appeal for the "boat people" and refugees from every part of the world.

I cannot forget the situation in which several hundred thousand Southeast Asian refugees find themselves, a situation which is being dramatically prolonged. They have been received in holding centers, especially in Thailand, but, regarding housing and work, they are waiting for a definitive solution worthy of the respect due to the human person. . . . [In the same way] it is not possible to forget the thousands of men, women, and children, including many sick and elderly, who have left Afghanistan; and I also have to mention the refugees from various African countries. There are nations that see a large part of their population flee from their territory, obliged to seek elsewhere for conditions of subsistence and the spaces necessary for freedom. Their sufferings are ours, too, and they await the generous, concrete, and effective response of international solidarity.[49]

1982: Pilgrimage to Fatima

From February 12 to 19 he carried out his pastoral visit in Nigeria, Benin, Gabon, and Equatorial Guinea.

The more than 14,000 kilometers traveled in these days have allowed me to have direct knowledge of the human and Christian situation of the countries visited . . . of the difficulties with which they are still struggling, but also of the strong will of those peoples to construct a better tomorrow by means of a generous effort at the national level and by international cooperation. I observed once again with lively satisfaction that the foundation, or rather the cement unifying those African populations, also of those not yet reached by the voice of the Gospel, is a spiritual vision of life, the idea of the Divinity as the first cause of all things, the need of respect for the dignity of man, and the family spirit. But I have been comforted still more by observing how precisely the evangelical leaven is succeeding to an ever greater extent in vivifying the values of the African tradition, and in ensuring at the same time development, renewal, and improvement.[50]

On April 18 he visited Bologna.

My visit to Bologna has begun happily and with heartfelt anticipation of being before the image of the Blessed Virgin of Saint Luke,[xiv] venerated for centuries as the principal patroness of the city and the archdiocese, and who from the hill of the Guardian has always given special protection as *Praesidium et decus civitatis* [protector and glory of the city], comforter during times of public calamities and star of hope, thus weaving in an admirable way her mysterious assistance with the history of the Bolognese. And now, I come down from that mystical hill, and with deepest emotion, come to meet the grand, fertile-soiled metropolis where pulses the life of men, where the present generation continues the journey toward future goals of an illustrious city, celebrated throughout the world for its ancient university, rooted in the Christian faith, always open to the thrilling vibrations of liberty, teacher of the ancient law.[51]

> *From May 12 to 15 he made a pastoral visit to Portugal, with a pilgrimage to Fatima to mark the one-year anniversary of the assassination attempt on his life. He recites the Act of Consecration and entrusts the world to the Immaculate Heart of Mary.*

The goal of the pilgrimage was especially Fatima, where I felt called in a particular way as a result of the attempt on my life on May 13 last year. I have said many times already that it is only to the mercy of God and the special protection of the Mother of Christ that I owe the saving of my life and the possibility of further service to the See of Peter. In the second place, this pilgrimage, just as the others, allowed me to strengthen, through the visit to the Church in Portugal, those bonds of unity with which it has from the beginning been united to the universal Church through communion with the Bishop

---

xiv The origin of the Byzantine painting of Mother and Child, known as the Madonna of San Luca, is unknown. It is believed to date to the tenth or eleventh century.

of Rome: these same bonds that I found very lively and cordial in the course of my visit.[52]

From May 28 until June 2 he carried out his pastoral visit in Great Britain and, as there was ongoing armed conflict between Great Britain and Argentina for sovereignty over the Falkland-Malvinas islands, he also visited Argentina from June 10 to 13, with a stopover in Brazil.

This trip, as the preceding trip I made to Great Britain, I carried out in my responsibility as universal Pastor of the Church. At the same time, I wish to challenge the consciences of people during these times of armed conflict, to consider reestablishing sentiments of peace that are so far removed from the mere laying down of arms. I ask the Lord to translate into a workable reality the profound conviction that we must use every means to search for a just, honorable, and lasting peace. During these journeys, I understood that the people of these two nations who sorrow for the ruins caused by war and live in anguish above all for the countless young lives lost, thrown into mourning and tears for their lost loved ones—these are the people who are anxiously awaiting and longing for peace.[53]

On June 15 he went to Geneva to speak to the International Conference on Labor and to visit the central headquarters of the International Committee of the Red Cross.

It was a meeting with the world of work in one of its historical and juridical centers, rich in so much associative and human significance. Among the many things I would have wanted to say on such an important theme, I chose one that I consider especially urgent in the present international situation: I insisted on the duty of solidarity, since it appears to me that this dimension is inscribed in the very nature of work, and everything today pushes toward its ever fuller realization. . . . I brought to the president of the International Committee of the Red Cross, and to his collaborators, my greeting, along with the expression of my hearty support in the activity they carry out with praiseworthy concern and generosity for the defense of every human person, for the relief of those in need, for the promotion of friendship, for cooperation and lasting peace among peoples. These are ideals that must be at the heart of every Christian.[54]

Newly elected Lebanese President Bachir Gemayel[xv] *was assassinated on September 14, and a massacre broke out four days later in the Palestinian refugee camps of Sabra and Shatila.*

With a heart full of grief and profound sorrow, I have learned the news of the horrible massacres perpetrated in the Palestinian camps of Beirut. There are reports of hundreds and hundreds of victims, babies, women, and old people, put to death in a merciless manner. There are no words adequate to condemn such crimes, which are repugnant to the Christian and human conscience. How can one not be gravely concerned in the presence of this terrible manifestation of the forces of evil, and of the spiral of violence which is spreading in the world?[55]

From October 31 through November 9 he carried out the pastoral visit in Spain, and at Santiago de Compostela he launched an appeal to the people of Europe.

The pilgrimage in that country brought me to the most ancient centers of the faith and of the Church in the space of almost two thousand years. This faith and the Church have borne fruit in particular measure with the saints and the blessed of all the periods. . . . And at the same time this papal pilgrimage in Spain enters into the context of the whole contemporary reality of the Church, of the People of God in the Iberian Peninsula. In the framework of the centuries-long tradition there have appeared problems and themes which make up the life of the Church and society today.[56]

I cry to you with love, ancient Europe: "Find yourself again. Be yourself." Discover your origins, revive your roots. Return to those authentic values that made your history a glorious one and your presence so beneficial to the other continents. Reconstruct your own spiritual unity in a climate of full respect for the other religions and any

---

[xv] Bachir Gemayel (1947–1982) was elected president of the Lebanese Republic on August 23, 1982, and was assassinated on September 14, 1982.

genuine freedom. *"Give to Caesar what belongs to Caesar, and to God what belongs to God"* (Mk 12:17). Do not become so proud of your achievements that you forget their possible negative consequences. Do not become discouraged because of the measurable loss of some of your greatness in the world or because of the social and cultural crises that affect you today. You can be even now the beacon of civilization and the stimulus of progress for the world.[57]

On November 26 he announced that the Holy Year of the Redemption would be celebrated from Lent 1983 until Easter 1984.

With the whole Church we are ardently preparing for the celebration of the *Jubilee of the Redemption.* . . . First of all, the jubilee year is meant to emphasize the aspect that captures the attention of those who are open "to the voice of the Spirit who speaks to the Churches" (Rev 2:29), the role that this jubilee of grace assumes, between the holy year celebrated in 1975 and the one that will be celebrated in 2000, at the dawn of the third millennium, the great holy year. It is then a jubilee of transition between these two dates, like a bridge launched toward the future that originates with the extraordinary experiences of all the happenings of eight years ago: in fact, Paul VI, of venerated memory, called all the faithful at that time to live their own "spiritual renewal in Christ and reconciliation with God."[58]

At the end of the year John Paul II denounced many tragedies, asking heads of state throughout the world to take concrete action.

I think of the countries of Central America: can we not hope that a true internal dialogue will permit the resolution of the serious problems of social miseries and internal tension, and that the parties involved not become victims of materialistic options, nor be subjected to interferences from outsiders who are trying to radicalize the opponents? One could mention a good many other places where tensions remain alive and dangerous, easily degenerating into acts of violence, as in Northern Ireland; and even situations that are apparently calm, but that hide a false peace, without progress, because legitimate rights remain unrecognized, with no possibility of a true dialogue between the social and political partners. The Holy See does not wish to believe in the inevitability of the state of war, nor of guerrilla conflict, for achieving justice. Justice and peace are ultimately on the road of a true dialogue, free and without deceit, when one has the courage to undertake it, when one prides himself on taking the risk, and when the other countries respect it.[59]

1983: Holy Year of the Redemption

The new Code of Canon Law, *which replaced the one decreed by Pope Benedict XV in 1917, was promulgated on January 25, 1983.*

Indeed, this Code is the *Code of the People of God*, in which the structure of the Church is established, in which the opening to the Spirit is facilitated, in which fidelity to the different gifts and charisms is expressed, in which authentic law is strengthened, and in which unity in communion is built up. The efforts of theologians also made an enlightened contribution to its editing by bringing to light, in the mystery of the Church contemplated with love, the essential parts willed by Christ, the Word Incarnate, its founder and head.[60]

From March 2 to 10 he carried out his pastoral visit in Costa Rica, Nicaragua, Panama, El Salvador, Guatemala, Honduras, Belize, and Haiti.

It was fitting to make a single pilgrimage to the countries of Central America, without however forgetting that they are different one from the other, and that not all the countries visited belong strictly to Central America.... It is generally known that the societies which I met in the course of this journey—particularly some of them—remain in a state of great internal tension, and some of them are even a theater of war. The tensions have their origin in the old socioeconomic structures, in the unjust structures which permit the accumulation of the greater part of the wealth in the hands of an elite few, together with the simultaneous poverty and misery of the vast majority of society. This unjust system must be changed by means of adequate reforms and by observing the principles of social democracy. Only in such a way and with respect for the individual character of the respective society should there be formed a solid international collaboration, necessary for these societies.[61]

On March 25 he opened the Holy Year of the Redemption.

Behold, the door of the special jubilee is opened, and through it we enter Saint Peter's Basilica. It is a symbol. We enter not only this venerable Roman basilica, but we also enter the holiest dimension of the Church—the dimension of the grace and salvation that the Church ever draws from the mystery of the redemption. She draws it always and constantly. And yet, during this year that begins today we wish the whole Church to be particularly conscious of the fact that the redemption endures in her as a gift of her divine Spouse.[62]

From May 20 through 22 he visited Milan.

Since the years of the construction of the unified state, your city has been the beating heart of the national economy and the generous promoter of welfare and charity initiatives. . . . Nevertheless, we cannot ignore the fact that in Milan we find also those negative phenomena which contaminate modern society and which have their matrix in a demeaning secularism. . . . In the face of the dangers of such a distorted interpretation of man and history it is necessary . . . to recover the mature awareness of the dignity and of the responsibility of man as the "apex of creation"; it is necessary to question oneself about the meaning and value, that is, about the ethics of the ever new conquests of science; it is necessary to repropose . . . the contemplative attitude of the believer, thanks to which it is possible to discover those answers to the crucial problems of existence which science and technology by themselves cannot offer.[63]

From June 16 through 23 he carried out a pastoral visit in Poland.

I consider it a special grace from God, a special sign of Providence, that I have been able to participate in this jubilee of Jasna Góra, the national jubilee; after six centuries of the presence of the Mother of

God in her image at Jasna Góra, to have been able to sing together with you Poland's *Te Deum Laudamus*; to have been able together with you to invite Christ with his Mother to this our Cana of Galilee, for the years to come and the future generations. . . . I deem it a special gift of Our Lady of Jasna Góra that I have been enabled to go on pilgrimage to her shrine, from Warsaw and Niepokalanów, Poznań, Wrocław, Góra Świętej Anny, and finally from my native Kraków. Allow me to mention, besides this, a gift from the Polish land: today I have been able to see the Tatra Mountains from nearby and to breathe the air of my youth.[64]

On August 14 and 15 he made a pilgrimage to Lourdes.

I am gratified to have finally been able to add Lourdes to the chain of Marian shrines that I have been granted to visit throughout the world, there to pray with my Christian brothers. It is a matter of a fundamental devotion of my life. I would like to draw the Church into prayer, into Marian prayer. Prayer is the primary duty and the primary mark of the Pope; it is the primary requirement of my service in the Church and in the world. For this reason, it was good that I should kneel down before the grotto of Massabielle and that I should be in every way a pilgrim to Lourdes, At the same time, I was able to have a fruitful meeting with the crowds that come from all over France and elsewhere, with priests, religious women, young people, the sick, families, and also the authorities of this country. I am very satisfied.[65]

From September 10 to 13 he carried out the pastoral visit in Austria.

In the sign of the cross we have pondered the history and mission of Europe, and in this perspective we have considered the history and mission of Austria. We again realized that the present and future of Europe needs the vigorous impulses that emanate from our Christian faith and life, and that there is need for receptive hearts to accept these impulses and to translate them into action. Those concerns were at the center of our ecclesiastical meetings and the solemn services we celebrated, but also at the center of my meetings with representatives of international, public, and cultural life.[66]

*On October 16 in Saint Peter's Square, he repeated the Act of Consecration
and once again entrusted the world to the Madonna.*

In entrusting to you, O Mother, the world, all individuals and peoples, we also entrust to you the consecration itself, for the world's sake, placing it in your motherly Heart. Oh, Immaculate Heart! Help us to conquer the menace of evil, which so easily takes root in the hearts of the people of today, and whose immeasurable effects already weigh down upon our modern world and seem to block the paths toward the future! From famine and war, deliver us. From nuclear war, from incalculable self-destruction, from every kind of war, deliver us. From sins against the life of man from its very beginning, deliver us. From hatred and from the demeaning of the dignity of the children of God, deliver us. From every kind of injustice in the life of society, both national and international, deliver us. From readiness to trample on the commandments of God, deliver us. From sins against the Holy Spirit deliver us! Deliver us!

Accept, O Mother of Christ, this cry laden with the sufferings of all individual human beings, laden with the sufferings of whole societies. Let there be revealed once more in the history of the world the infinite power of merciful Love. May it put a stop to evil. May it transform peoples' consciences. May your Immaculate Heart reveal for all the light of Hope! Amen.[67]

*On October 23 two attacks broke out in Beirut and, between October 19
and 25, on the island of Grenada, a pro-Cuban coup was crushed by a
United States military raid. John Paul II immediately expressed his deep
preoccupation.*

Last Sunday in Lebanon two terrorist acts caused more than two hundred deaths among American and French soldiers serving with the international peacekeeping force. In another part of the world, in the Caribbean area, a new crisis has arisen with serious events on the island of Grenada, the scene of a coup d'état two weeks ago, and now the scene of an invasion by military forces, both claiming more human victims. At the same time, uncertainty and apprehension increase in Europe and in the world over the delay in hoped-for positive developments in the disarmament negotiations. These crises have their own proper causes, but they can all be reduced to a common cause which is more general and very serious: the lack of mutual trust, which, as sad historical experience teaches, can lead to the most serious tensions, to the point of catastrophic wars.[68]

On December 27 he visited Ali Agca in Rebibbia prison in Rome.

Today I was able to meet my assailant and repeat to him my forgiveness, even though I had already forgiven him. It was not possible for me, however, to say it before. We met as men and as brothers, and all the happenings of our lives brought about this brotherhood.[69]

As the end of the year approached, he proposed a comprehensive look at the existing injustices on earth.

A complete view of the world requires that one focuses attention on the north-south contrast. . . . This problem touches the lives of a great part of the human race, and at stake is the life, the survival of those people who are in the grip of underdevelopment, and who are classified by the term "south," no matter to what continent they belong. . . . The enlargement of poverty zones is, in the long term, the most serious threat to peace. To the human causes which have their source among others in the inequality of the terms of exchange and in certain injustices, are to be added natural catastrophes, such as the terrible drought in the Sahel region. In the face of such huge and certainly very complex problems, the international community is called to show itself resolutely committed to effective and disinterested assistance. In doing so, it must show great respect for the cultures and for whatever is found in local traditions, with a concern for developing responsibility, free participation, and the unity of the poor countries.[70]

1984: The "Gospel of Suffering"

On February 11 the apostolic letter Salvifici Doloris *was promulgated.*

I have considered it opportune and significant in the Holy Year of the Redemption, which commemorates in an altogether special way

Jesus' salvific death on the cross, to exhort all Christians to meditate more deeply and with greater conviction on the inexplicable value of suffering for the salvation of the world. This letter is meant to be a help in looking at Christ Crucified and accepting the "Gospel of Suffering" with love and courage, in the mysterious but always loving plan of Divine Providence. In fact, what remains an unfathomable enigma for reason becomes a message of elevation and salvation for faith, in the light of the dead and risen Christ.[71]

On February 26 he visited Bari.

The name Bari today signifies a modern and vital city which, while developing its own definite role in the sphere of southern Italy and of the entire peninsula, is called besides to project itself with effective dynamism beyond its sea to reach ports and lands and peoples of the East. Bari, as it has been a recipient from neighboring peoples (and it will suffice merely to recall the cult[xvi] of that eastern saint, the great Nicholas, of whom it is very proud and because of whom it is celebrated throughout the world), so it is called to develop with clarity and farsightedness a program of long-range contacts and of exchanges, not only on an economic, but also on a cultural and moral level.[72]

On April 22 he closed the Holy Year of the Redemption.

The Church of Jesus Christ today renders solemn thanks for the particular experience of the redemption offered to us by the year now drawing to a close: the holy year, the extraordinary jubilee year which began with the commemoration of the Incarnation of the Word on March 25, 1983, and which concludes today on the Solemnity of the Resurrection. . . . In the name of the resurrection, while the stone is rolled away from the tomb of the Lord, we close the holy door of the extraordinary jubilee, so that the cry may never cease: *Open the doors to the Redeemer.*[73]

From June 12 to 17 he carried out his pastoral visit in Switzerland.

---

xvi Here the word *cult* refers to the popular devotion that grows up around a saint.

Despite the temptations to secularization or religious indifference, I find myself among a people who are believers, who are happy to express their faith with the Successor of Peter and the other bishops. Do not be afraid, dear friends. God is greater than our hesitant hearts. Open the doors to the Redeemer, who remains in your midst. Open your hearts to the Holy Spirit of Jesus Christ. May he strengthen your faith! May he give life to your prayer, without which you cannot remain faithful! May he enable you to understand and love the Church whose members you are! May he inspire fraternal love among you! May he keep you united to the universal Church! My prayer for you will be nourished by the memories of what I saw and experienced in my encounters with you all.[74]

From September 9 to 20 he made a pastoral visit in Canada.

The leading theme of the visit allowed us to refer to the beginning of evangelization and the Church in Canada. The motto "Let us celebrate our faith" implied a feeling of gratitude for those beginnings, which date back to the beginning of the seventeenth century. . . . The Church that lives in this society, characterized by the immigration of people coming from various nations, recalls the multiple cultural and religious traditions which comprise in various places the living organism of Christianity and of Canadian Catholicism. This diversity and multiplicity are the source of enrichment for both society and the Church. They constitute a constant challenge to the apostolic and pastoral activity of this Church.[75]

From October 5 to 7 he visited the Italian province of Reggio Calabria.

As I set foot in this city, I experienced great emotion from the fact that, almost two millennia ago, Paul of Tarsus did the same, and here lit the first spark of the Christian faith. This was the starting point of the journey of Christianity in Calabria. It spread out in every direction, from the Ionic coast to the Tyherrian slopes. . . . But your fascinating history and the natural beauty of your surroundings do not serve to make me forget about your daily situation, the economic and social difficulties with which the province of Reggio struggles. . . . I am here today to speak words of encouragement and hope. I urge you first of all to resist the temptation to evil, to strengthen your human virtues, to put together your energies, heart, and intelligence that are so abundant and true, and to work for a better society, one that is more just, ordered, human, a society worthy of the Christian traditions of your civilization.[76]

From October 10 to 12 he carried out a pastoral visit in Spain, the Dominican Republic, and Puerto Rico.

My thoughts go with special affection today to the stops on my brief but intense journey along the route of Christopher Columbus and the first missionaries to the Latin American continent. . . . The Episcopate of Latin America, through CELAM [Consejo Episcopal Latinoamericano, or Latin American Episcopal Council], has decided to celebrate the fifth centenary of the beginning of the proclamation of the Gospel on that continent with a "novena of years" of preparation. The purpose of this pilgrimage of mine was—accepting the invitation offered me by CELAM—to take part in the inauguration, in Santo Domingo's Olympic Stadium, of this preparatory novena, in the celebrations of the discovery and the evangelization of the New World. That discovery was an event that indeed opened a decisive stage in the history of civilization, so much so as to close one epoch and open another. But above all, it was an event of incalculable importance for the Gospel of Christ and for the Church, which received from the Divine Master the mission to proclaim the Gospel to all nations.[77]

On December 11 the apostolic exhortation Reconciliatio et Paenitentia *was published.*

I call upon all the faithful to read this document. In it the Church, aware of the profound drama of the divisions and injustices that trouble mankind, but also attentive to the consuming desire for reconciliation and peace which throbs in the soul of millions of people, with courageous frankness reproposes to modern man Christ's call to conversion of heart as a prerequisite for reconciliation with God, with oneself, with one's brethren, and with all creation. It is an appeal that demands a not-so-easy journey. The Church knows this. For this reason, in the pages of the document she also points out the practical road to take in order to reach the desired goal: it is a road on which man finds Christ, a Pilgrim who walks by his side and supports him with the word of Scripture, with the understanding and the prayer of the community, with the grace of the sacrament conferred by the Church's Minister.[78]

During his talks, Pope Wojtyła never forgot to offer a clear picture of the lights and shadows of the year.

We must consider the undeniable positive accomplishments, so as to better estimate what is possible, to strengthen the hope and the desire to undertake such gestures of peace. By way of significant example, you will understand my citing the signing of the Treaty of Peace and Friendship between Argentina and Chile, which ended the dispute over the southern zone. This was an affair which, six years ago, could have degenerated into a fratricidal war and consumed the energies of these dynamic peoples in destructive enterprises. But the two parties were determined to continue along the course of dialogue, which had reached an impasse, and they requested the mediation of the Holy See. . . . I would also like to cite as another positive sign the recent opening of discussions in Geneva between the United States of America and the Soviet Union on the limitation of nuclear arms. It was indeed necessary that the dialogue, too long frozen, be resumed on a question as vital as this. After this first meeting, it seems that one can feel a prudent optimism.[79]

I exhort you to offer a special heartfelt prayer to the Lord for all those who have died from violence. Unfortunately, they are many, and in many regions of the world. The heart is oppressed at the thought of so much human blood spilled, so much suffering, so many tears. Even these past days have been saddened by distressing news: I am thinking of Mrs. Indira Gandhi, prime minister of India,[xvii] who was

---

xvii Indira Gandhi (1917–1984) was assassinated outside her residence by two of her bodyguards in retaliation for damage done to the holiest Sikh temple in an attack against terrorists.

assassinated yesterday in New Delhi; I am thinking of the Polish priest, Father Jerzy Popiełuszko,[xviii] whose tragic death has touched the world. I am thinking of the people who have met death in the recent uprising in Chile,[xix] the victims of the repressions in South Africa,[xx] and all the numerous victims of violence in so many other countries in the world. May the great and merciful God give peace to their immortal souls and grant the living to understand that not with violence, but with love, will a future be built that is worthy of man.[80]

1985: The World Gathering of Youth

The beginning of the year saw a terrible tragedy that engaged John Paul II at the forefront.

I wish to draw attention once again to the great tragedy that has struck millions of men, women, and children in Ethiopia and in other parts of Africa. Human life is being attacked, weakened, and destroyed by widespread and enduring famine. The suffering and death that are the common lot of so many people call for a continued response of prayer, fraternal love, and human compassion from the rest of mankind.[81]

From January 26 to February 6 he carried out his pastoral visit in Venezuela, Ecuador, Peru, and Trinidad and Tobago.

The three whole days spent in Venezuela allowed me to draw near to the problems which the Church in that country is experiencing, and to take part in the apostolic tasks it must face. . . . The most important task for the future seems to be, against the background of the lively

---

xviii Jerzy Popiełuszko (1947–1984) was a charismatic Polish priest who preached against the Communist regime as an active supporter of the Solidarity workers movement. On October 19, 1984, he was abducted and murdered. Popiełuszko was beatified on June 6, 2010.

xix A popular uprising against the military dictatorship of Augusto Pinochet began in 1983, which he met with decisive repression.

xx Organized efforts against apartheid came to a head in the 1980s with a student protest. The government response was to declare a state of emergency that continued through the 1990s.

religious tradition, the strengthening of the awareness of the Christian vocation, particularly of native priestly and religious vocations. Also necessary are the preservation and development of the fine traditions with regard to the implementation of the Church's social doctrine in the various sectors of life.

Under the ecclesial aspect, we solemnly celebrated in Quito the 450th anniversary of the beginning of evangelization. . . . The Church in Ecuador—with its episcopate, the ecclesiastics, the religious (who have great merit), and with the growing lay apostolate—appears profoundly bound to the society. The preparation for the papal visit was long, as was evidenced by the numberless confessions, the crosses carried by the participants in the meetings, and finally by the large crowds in all the places of celebrations, along the streets and the roads.

The whole of Peru is Catholic, and the Church constitutes a special link among all the inhabitants of the country. The social problems exist also on a vast scale, with the Church's equally vast responsibility for a just solution. . . . It seemed that they expressed the most essential desires that overwhelm them, these were articulated by representatives of the *pueblos jóvenes*[xxi] in Lima: the desire for God and the desire for bread. The first is their spiritual wealth, and it is necessary to do everything to preserve and increase this wealth. The second is linked with the wide-ranging poverty and misfortune and also with the even more conscious cry for social justice. It is necessary to do everything to achieve this justice without having recourse to violence and totalitarianism, preserving the democratic order to which those societies are rightly bound.

The brief visit to Trinidad and Tobago was not merely an "adjunct" to the three Bolivian towns. I wish to express my joy, especially for the fact that this society, so varied in its origins, which for many centuries experienced the bitterness of slavery and colonial dependence, is today a society of free citizens and is evidently matured through this freedom. Then I express my joy for the fact that the Church, engaging in ecumenical activity and collaboration with representatives of other

---

xxi These "new towns" are shanties lacking electricity and running water built up around Lima and other cities by the poor from outlying regions who have come seeking economic and social opportunity.

religions (especially Hinduism), lives its authentic life and serves the good of the whole society.[82]

In Rome on March 30 and 31 he received the participants of the international gathering of young people.

The United Nations proclaimed 1985 the International Year of Youth. . . . On Palm Sunday of that year, representatives of the young of all five continents came to Rome. I still have before my eyes the images of my meeting with that assembly of young people of every race and territory in the square in front of Saint John Lateran, during which we prayed and reflected together, with the intimate participation of all those present, rendered one in heart and soul. . . . The Lord blessed that meeting in an extraordinary way, so much so that, for years to come, the World Day of Youth has been instituted, to be celebrated on Palm Sunday, with the substantial collaboration of the Council for the Laity.[83]

From May 11 to 21 he carried out a pastoral visit to the Low Countries, in Luxembourg and in Belgium.

The visit to the Benelux[xxii] countries reconfirmed the enormous effort put forth there by the Church, especially in the first half of this century, in various areas, first of all in the missionary field. Men and women religious, priests of the diocesan clergy, and laymen and women have worked and continue to work until today in many young Churches. . . . Another success, already in the preconciliar period, was the fully developed activity of the laity, which is evidenced by numerous organizations.[84]

On June 16 and 17 he visited Venice.

Venice has a talent all its own. Pope Roncalli[xxiii] loved to consider Venice the bridge city between the West and the East, and this

---

xxii Benelux is a term referring to the union formed by Belgium, the Netherlands, and Luxembourg and sealed in the Treaty of the Benelux Economic Union (1960), a precursor of the European Union. The term now encompasses the economic, social, and cultural cooperation among the three nations.

xxiii Angelo Giuseppe Roncalli (born near Bergamo, Italy, in 1881) was the patriarch of Venice when he became Pope John XXIII (1958–1963). He convened Vatican Council II.

vocation can be felt and seen also today. Venice is a city of peace, as a place of encounters, of dialogue, of welcome, of noble hospitality toward all.... I will remember this encounter as a great gift, also because it offers me the possibility to see the two faces of our civilization that here are truly united and interdependent. I think of the splendor of Venice and its glorious history, and I think at the same time of the city of Mestre with the industrial complex of Marghera, that indicates the modern way of living and producing. How do you make this succeed? They seem so different, almost opposites. And yet, they do unite, and this takes place in your people, in their freedom, in their rights.[85]

From August 8 to 19 he carried out his pastoral visit in Togo, Ivory Coast, Cameroon, the Central African Republic, Zaire (now the Democratic Republic of the Congo), Kenya, and Morocco.

The Church in Africa is both a missionary church and a mission church. In each of these countries she encounters, first of all, people with the traditional "animist"[xxiv] religion and goes to meet them with the Gospel. The fruits of this "first" evangelization are conversion and Baptism. . . . At the same time the Church gradually is beginning to have its own priestly and religious vocations. . . . In the same way as priestly and religious vocations, an awareness of the vocation of the apostolate of the laity, in the family as well as in the various sectors of social life, is developing. . . . The fullness of this Christian vocation is holiness, which is also the principal fruit of the Eucharist. For this reason, a significant part of my African pilgrimage was the beatification of the first daughter of Zaire, Sister Anuarite Nengapeta, who in 1964 suffered martyrdom to defend her virginity, consecrated to Christ.[86]

On September 8 he made a pastoral visit to Liechtenstein.

Full of lasting memories, I leave this beautiful and friendly country. I think of the magnificent scenery with the majestic mountains and the so carefully tilled meadows and fields, of the manifold churches and chapels, wayside and mountaintop crosses, which bear witness to the

---

xxiv Animism is the belief that all or various parts of creation have souls, i.e., plants, trees, rocks, mountains, etc.

long Christian tradition prevailing here and to the faith of the citizens. . . . Dear people of God in the principality of Liechtenstein! Due to the natural circumstances in which you live, you have a particular sensitivity to that which is small and in need of protection. Safeguard the virtues of modesty and of magnanimity. Acquire them anew if you have lost them; strengthen them if they have become weak![87]

He visited Genoa from September 21 to 22.

I have come here to say that Genoa, an extraordinarily busy city, rich in its history, must not contradict itself in the future. Do not let yourselves be swept away by the temptation, so prevalent in great modern centers, of separating faith from progress. Fill up your voids, reform your evils, overcome the opposition in a climate of renewed trust, use well your resources and your energies, construct your future as you have your past on the living foundation of the Gospel, on the security of its morals that do not degrade but elevate the individual, the family, and the society. You will contribute, in this way, to the affirmation of an authentic civilization, and you will continue to give the waiting world witness of the highest and truest riches.[88]

He visited Cagliari on October 19 and 20.

As I made my pastoral visits throughout Italy, I have desired for a while to come to Sardinia and especially to Cagliari, this city which, because of its more numerous inhabitants, its most ancient history, its position on the sea, its port, and most of all its secular Christian tradition, places it like a splendid pearl mounted in the setting of your most beautiful island. . . . Dearest citizens of Cagliari! While I am sure that you, with your spirit of initiative that leads you to use well your resources and collaborate in building [projects] to resolve well your economic and social problems, I charge you to also remain anchored to the solid and secure principles of the faith.[89]

At the end of the year there were many tragedies that he brought to the attention of world leaders.

Allow me to pause here and recall several countries or regions presently involved in conflicts, or regrettable tensions. We are always thinking of the dear Lebanese people. Some new signs and recent attempts underline their desire and will for peace. . . . We also think with sadness of the continuing murderous and destructive combats between Iran and Iraq, always hoping that the parties involved will find a reasonable way for a just peace. For the people of Afghanistan, each one of you knows in what conditions they have been living for the last six years, and moreover, the United Nations has underlined this on several occasions. . . . The situation of Cambodia, which has been so dramatic, continues to be painful and difficult. The international community is anxious, and rightly so, about finding a solution which will permit the Cambodian people to enjoy a true independence, worthy of their cultural traditions. South Africa continues to suffer from bloody racial conflicts and tribal opposition. The solution to apartheid and the beginning of a concrete dialogue between government authorities and representatives of the legitimate aspirations of the people are indispensable means for reestablishing justice and concord, and banishing fear which today provokes so much inflexibility.[90]

1986: Prayer for Peace at Assisi

From January 31 through February 10 he carried out the pastoral visit in India.

The papal pilgrimage was a *meeting with the great and highly varied historical past* of India, which goes back to the third millennium before Christ. This past is not merely a history in the ethnic sense or a manifestation of the diverse forms of sociopolitical systems. It is first of all a great *patrimony of spiritual value*, in the religious, moral, and cultural sense. The encounter with this cultural patrimony is important for Christians above all because it regards the recognition *of the primacy of the spirit* in human life and of *requirements of a moral nature*. . . . The pilgrimage in India was, therefore, among other things a providential occasion for continuing dialogue with all who believe in God and seek to orient their lives from the perspective of a transcendental reality. The quest of the Absolute and the yearning for peace are very evident in the spirituality of the various religions present in India, and they are well expressed in the thought and poetry of many celebrated figures.[91]

On April 13 he visited a synagogue in Rome.

A truly exceptional experience for me was certainly my visit to the Synagogue of Rome. The history of the Jews in Rome is a unique chapter in the history of the Jewish people, a chapter closely linked for that matter to the Acts of the Apostles. During that memorable visit, I spoke of the Jews as our *elder brothers in the faith*. These words were an expression both of the Council's teaching and a profound conviction on the part of the Church.[92]

On May 30 the encyclical Dominum et Vivificantem *(dated May 18) was promulgated.*

It will, together with the encyclicals *Dives in Misericordia* and *Redemptor Hominis*, dedicated to the Father and Son, constitute a trilogy. Thus we have a Trinitarian trilogy. I entrust this new text to the Holy Spirit; I have prepared it with great love for him and for the Church, and I wish that what I have written will help to sustain in the faithful an ever livelier devotion to the Third Person of the Blessed Trinity, to whom Christ, before he was raised into heaven, entrusted the task of guarding his Church "into all the truth" (Jn 16:13).[93]

From July 1 to 8 he carried out his pastoral visit in Colombia and the Caribbean isle of Saint Lucia.

In order that the peace that Christ brings may prevail on the paths of Colombia, it is necessary to have a complete and coordinated evangelization in the spirit of the Church's social doctrine, committed to multiple activities in favor of social justice, the safeguarding and promotion of the rights of the person, of the family, and of human communities so as to create a more balanced equality between the evident contrasts of a very rich world and another too poor. . . . The apostolic journey in Colombia was concluded with a pastoral visit to the island of Saint Lucia. It was a brief visit of a few hours, but warm and intense.

I vividly recall the Eucharistic celebration at Reduit Park in Castries, where I mentioned that faith is a precious gift, that it has formed the culture and history of that island.[94]

A pastoral visit to France was made on October 4 through 7.

From Rome to Lyons, from Lyons to Taizé and Paray-le-Monial, and then to Ars and finally to Annecy, I made a pilgrimage in the footsteps of Blessed Antoine Chevrier, Saint Francis de Sales, Saint Jane de Chantal, Saint Margaret Mary Alacoque, and especially the saintly Curé of Ars. It was precisely the occurrence of the two-hundredth anniversary of the birth of John Mary Vianney that provided the French bishops with the opportune occasion to invite me once again to their country. . . . The figure of the holy Curé of Ars does not cease to speak also to the people of today. His extraordinary life of prayer and mortification, and his heroic dedication to the Word of God and the sacraments, especially the Sacrament of Penance, continue to be an important point of reference for the priests of the contemporary Church.[95]

On October 18 and 19 he visited Florence.

Beloved Florentines . . . may you find a stronger inner impulse to witness before the world to the continuity of the ancient civil and Christian traditions of your land, and to safeguard its fundamental values. Proudly defend the brilliant and spiritual resources that have been deposited in your minds. Your cultural tradition is not, and must not be, merely an object of contemplation and pride, but a lively source of inspiration and commitment; a stimulus to strive sincerely for universal values contained in and expressed by that tradition; a studied attempt to relive and emulate the spiritual greatness of the past, and to banish every form of sterile criticism and opaque materialism.[96]

On October 27 he presided over the World Day of Prayer for Peace in Assisi. Many religious leaders from all parts of the world participated in this event.

In a word, the Catholic Church, the other churches and ecclesial communions and the non-Christian religions, by responding in their own way to the decision of the United Nations to establish 1986 as a "Year of Peace," wished to do so by using their own language, by approaching the cause of peace in the dimension which for them is the essential one: the spiritual dimension, and more precisely through prayer, accompanied by fasting and by pilgrimage. Nor was it a matter, on the part of the representatives of the great religions, of negotiating upon convictions of faith in order to arrive at a syncretistic religious consensus among ourselves. On the contrary, it was a matter of together turning, in a disinterested way, toward the capital objective of peace among men and among the peoples, or rather it was a matter of turning, all of us, toward God, in order to implore this gift from him.[97]

From November 18 through December 1 he carried out a pastoral visit in the countries of Bangladesh, Singapore, Fiji, New Zealand, Australia, and Seychelles.

The central point of every meeting was the Eucharist, and around it developed the local programs of papal service, carefully prepared by the clergy and laity under the guidance of the bishops. . . . Meetings with various groups of people had their place in the program of the visit to the Church in the Australian continent. First of all, according to the criterion of age, I met the children and youth, the adults—married couples and parents—and, lastly, the "third age" representatives. . . . The papal service in the Australian continent—as likewise in the other stages of this journey, in many places and in different ways—met with a conscious and consistent collaboration in the ecumenical field. What happened at Melbourne was symbolic. Before the great ecumenical meeting, there was the visit to the Anglican Cathedral, and the torch which was lit there was borne to the stadium, the place of the common prayer of all the Christians.[98]

Among the many tragedies of the year, in particular he elaborated on the poverty in Sudan.

I wish to call the attention of all who hear me to the tragic situation of about two million people in the southern region of Sudan. Those brothers of ours run the risk of dying from hunger if they do not receive, in the shortest time possible, food supplies and other relief. . . .

I am certain that in the face of the basic needs of life of so many human beings, all will give way to the feeling of fraternal solidarity, which should overcome every other motive or party interest.[99]

1987: A Year Dedicated to Mary

The encyclical Redemptoris Mater *was promulgated on March 25.*

This encyclical is essentially a meditation on the revelation of the mystery of salvation, which was communicated to Mary at the dawn of redemption, and in which she was called to participate and collaborate in a completely exceptional and extraordinary way. . . . The encyclical expresses the universality of Christ's redemption and the universality of the Virgin Mary's motherhood. It is addressed to the faithful of the Catholic Church who are called to celebrate the Marian Year. It also expresses the profound aspiration towards the unity of all Christians which the Second Vatican Council codified and which is the object of ecumenical dialogue.[100]

From March 31 to April 13 he carried out his pastoral visit in Uruguay, Chile, and Argentina.

The main purpose of my visit was to give thanks. Together with the two nations, I wished to give thanks to God for the peaceful solution to the conflict: as a result, Argentina and Chile were spared incalculable losses, most of all young lives, which would have been the sad outcome of engagement in conflict. . . . Because the bilateral decision not to have recourse to arms and to initiate the process of mediation was made in Montevideo, the capital of Uruguay, it seems appropriate to begin the thanksgiving journey in that city. My deepest gratitude goes to the civil authorities in Uruguay. . . . The visits to Chile and Argentina were of a pastoral nature similar to many other journeys which I have made as Successor of Peter in various countries throughout the five continents.[101]

From April 30 to May 4 he was on a pastoral visit in the Federal Republic of Germany.

"You shall be my witnesses" (Acts 1:8). These words of Christ constituted the theme of the apostolic visit which I made to the Federal Republic of Germany during the first days of May. . . . Christ's words to the apostles before the ascension should be referred particularly on this occasion to Sister Teresa Benedicta of the Cross, Edith Stein, whom I had the joy of beatifying on May 1 during the solemn liturgy at Cologne. Edith Stein perished in a death camp, sharing the fate of many millions of the sons and daughters of her race. She died as a Jew and, at the same time, as a Carmelite nun. . . . Within the scope of the appeal addressed to all, some matters were particularly emphasized during the pilgrimage. One was social justice, closely connected with the question of work and employment. . . . Underlining the value of work and the need to humanize it, I spoke of the tragedy of unemployment and referred to the dangers of technology unbridled by conscience. I did not fail to refer to the need of respect for the ecological environment.[102]

On the vigil of Pentecost, June 6, he opened the Marian Year.

This is a coincidence and a kind of convergence of events which has great significance and which deserves to be emphasized: on that historic day when the Spirit was poured out on the Church, we find Mary; on this day, which is today, when the Spirit is still being poured out, we must find Mary. On this solemn feast the Bishop of Rome joins all his brothers in the episcopate, the successors of the apostles, in order to deepen, throughout the Church, in the prospect of the new millennium, awareness of the maternal presence of the Mother of God in the mystery of Christ and of the Church.[103]

From June 8 to 14 he carried out his pastoral visit in Poland. During this time he placed himself in prayer at the tombs of Cardinal Wyszyński and Father Popiełuszko.

"Having loved his own who were in the world, he loved them to the end" (Jn 13:1). This is the text of John's Gospel on which the Church in Poland meditated during the National Eucharistic Congress. . . . Linked with the Eucharist were the sacraments administered at various places during my pilgrimage through Poland: the sacrament of

Holy Orders at Lublin, the sacrament of Matrimony (with the renewal of marriage vows by married couples) at Szczecin, the sacrament of the Anointing of the Sick at Gdańsk, First Communion to the children at Łódź?. . . . Parallel to this multiple experience of the Eucharistic mystery there developed, during the pilgrimage, another line of reflection which, in the ensemble of the Gospel message, was closely linked with the Eucharist, namely, that of moral commitment, both in the personal and community dimension—beginning with the family, through the different communities linked with the world of labor, and finally the community understood in the full sense: society and the nation.[104]

In August, tragic news arrived from India, and Pope Wojtyła immediately launched an appeal for solidarity.

I would now like to mention the people of Bangladesh and the eastern regions of India who have been struck by disastrous flooding in recent days. This calamity has claimed many victims and destroyed large amounts of goods, homes, and structures, leaving millions homeless in conditions of great difficulty. In the face of such an emergency we must express solidarity and understanding for such a sorely tried people. This situation cries out to the charity of all.[105]

A pastoral visit was carried out in the United States from September 10 through 21.

An overview of the visit leads me to direct my attention to the pluralism which was evident during this journey, above all, ethnic pluralism. The southwestern part of the United States has special bonds with the Hispanic world. In fact, the first evangelization came from the lands of the Latin American continent, and traces of this are found to the present day in the names of the principal cities and ecclesiastical centers (e.g., San Antonio, Los Angeles, San Francisco, and so many others). . . . Within the ethnic pluralism of the United States there has been developing for generations a confessional or religious pluralism. The Catholic Church constitutes about 23 percent of all Americans (i.e., more than 50 million). Besides the Catholic Church, the overall Christian population of the United States is comprised of numerous other churches and Christian communities. Ecumenical dialogue and collaboration are flourishing (except with some extremist communities and sects)....The Church and Christianity in America should be profoundly aware of the challenge of the contemporary world presented by its division into a rich *North* (the fully developed countries) and the underdeveloped *South* (the so-called Third World). In the name of the Gospel, the Church and Christianity must constantly echo this challenge. Together they should seek opportune solutions.[106]

> *In an overview at the end of the year, once again there emerged the tragedies of civil populations involved in conflicts and internal battles: from Iran to Iraq, from Mozambique to Ethiopia, and still in Angola, Afghanistan, Sri Lanka, and other areas of the Middle East and Central America.*

No one can remain indifferent in the face of these conflicts that every day threaten or extinguish human lives, destroy the social or cultural patrimony of an entire people, stifling it or hindering it from freely progressing towards its development. Certainly the first responsibility belongs to the governments directly involved. But they must know that all of humanity suffers and is humiliated by the evils which overwhelm one part of its members, and that with them it seeks a favorable and humane solution. Some of the peoples involved can invoke the reasons they have for an armed response to attacks, resorting to the morally acceptable distinction between legitimate defense and unjustified aggression. But motives are often very complex, and in any case, situations arise in which the escalation is such that it surpasses all limits and finally proves to be unjust because it is deadly and ruinous for the different parties.[107]

1988: The Encyclical on Solidarity

On March 19 the encyclical Solicitudo Rei Socialis *(dated December 30, 1987) was promulgated.*

In order to commemorate the twentieth anniversary of the encyclical of Pope Paul VI, *Populorum Progressio,* I have sent to all Christians a letter which begins with the words *Solicitudo rei socialis*. In it I have sought to emphasize the value of solidarity. It is an attitude of the mind based on a consideration of the ever closer bonds which, in fact, bind people and nations to one another in the contemporary world. However, solidarity is also a moral virtue which grows out of the awareness of the connatural interdependence which binds every human being to his own equals in the various areas of his existence: economy, culture, politics, religion. Solidarity, therefore, cannot be reduced to a vague attitude of emotional participation or to a word devoid of practical repercussions. It requires an active moral commitment, a firm and persevering determination to dedicate oneself to the common good, or rather to the good of all and of each individual. We are all responsible for one another.[108]

From May 7 to 19 the pastoral visits in Uruguay, Bolivia, Peru, and Paraguay were carried out.

The jubilee of the five-hundredth anniversary of the beginning of the evangelization of Latin America, which is approaching, sets out in relief the principal task of the new evangelization. The recent visit was carried out in the perspective of this task. Its program and the character of the liturgical and paraliturgical meetings bear witness to the happy launching of this task on the part of the church. With these aims in view, the first place was given to the family community, to the young people and children, to the elderly, the sick, and the disabled. Besides these contacts, the program also provided for meetings with persons who work in different sectors according to work, profession, and vocation. . . . With great hope and emotion I entrusted to Mary, Mother of the Church, all the efforts being undertaken for the responsible realization of this new evangelization.[109]

In Vatican City on May 21, the house of hospitality for the poor called Dono di Maria—Gift of Mary—was inaugurated and entrusted to the Congregation of Mother Teresa of Calcutta.

You can well understand the joy and emotion I feel at this moment, to see finally completed a project that has for some time been close to my heart: a house of welcome for the poorest among us here, within the walls of that city which is itself the center of the Church. Last year on June 17 I blessed the cornerstone, and look, we see it finished and ready to operate. In the limits possible, it will be able to welcome those who, here in Rome, have nowhere to stay the night, especially those who are deprived of even the minimum of family and human warmth to sustain them as they struggle through their lives.[110]

From June 23 to 27 he carried out his pastoral visit in Austria.

On this occasion I was completing the visit I made in 1983, during the so-called *Katholikentag* [Catholic Day], which was limited to Vienna, capital of Austria, and then to the Marian sanctuary of Mariazell. This time, however, Vienna was only the starting point of the program. During the following days, I was able to visit—at least indirectly—all the dioceses of the country. The slogan of the 1983 visit referred to hope; this time the organizers focused attention on the life of faith. In actual fact, there is no hope without faith. . . . They have been days full of substance, full of prayer which took on everywhere a liturgical form—especially Eucharistic—extraordinarily beautiful and mature. In the context of the beauty of nature which Divine Providence has generously bestowed on that country, and against the background of a splendid cultural and artistic patrimony, people proclaimed in that prayer, in a particularly profound way, the glory of the Creator and Redeemer, in the name of all creatures.[111]

On June 28, he signed the apostolic constitution Pastor Bonus, *for the reform of the Roman Curia.*

Everyone knows that, more than in any other era, the Church today is confronted with tasks which have an importance, extent, and multiplicity perhaps never before known. They are challenges which she must meet, and which the Holy See, in particular, feels called upon to respond to by virtue of the Petrine ministry. This has suggested a review of the structure of the Roman Curia in order to improve its functioning in relation to the Church's present needs. . . . The renewal of the laws of the Church desired by Popes John XXIII and Paul VI, and by the Second Vatican Ecumenical Council, has thus reached its final phase: The *Code of Canon Law* is already in force; the *Code of Oriental Canon Law* will be published in the near future; the apostolic constitution *Pastor Bonus* is included as an essential part of both.[112]

> *On July 2 the document* Ecclesia Dei *was promulgated. It was directed toward the supportive followers of the schismatic fraternity founded by Marcel Lefebvre who desired to remain in the Catholic Church. A few days later Pope Wojtyła received the sad news that the Anglican Communion had allowed women to be consecrated bishops.*

Shadows which bring pain and concern to the heart have not been wanting. First of all there was the unfortunately unsuccessful outcome of an attempt to avoid an objectively schismatical situation on the part of a well-known community. . . . In the second place, the enormous interest in the solution adopted by the Anglican Commission, during the Lambeth Conference, on last August 1, is well known. On that occasion it was decided that "each province should respect the decision and attitudes of other provinces regarding the ordination and consecration of women to the episcopate." Unfortunately—and it is with sincere sorrow that I speak of it here—this was a unilateral initiative which, as I wrote recently to the very dear brother Robert Runcie, archbishop of Canterbury, did not adequately take into account the ecumenical and ecclesiological dimensions of the problem, in contrast with the way always clearly followed by the Catholic Church, as well as by the Orthodox churches and the ancient Eastern churches.[113]

> *The Marian Year closed on August 15, and on September 30 the apostolic letter* Mulieris Dignitatem *(dated August 15) was promulgated.*

The Marian Year has been an incentive for the renewal of catechesis on the Blessed Virgin. Moreover, it aroused a greater interest in the Virgin in anthropological, theological, and biblical reflection. In the context of this deeper rethinking must be situated also the apostolic letter *Mulieris Dignitatem*, in which I sought to bring together the revealed message concerning woman's dignity and vocation in the Church and in society. The indications which have emerged in the course of these months lead one to persevere on the path undertaken, living *with Mary* and *like Mary* the years which separate us from the great Jubilee. On the threshold of the third Christian millennium, every local Church should engage in an effort of authentic renewal; no one, better than Mary, can be of assistance in such an undertaking. She, who first of all experienced the incarnation of the Word in her womb, can teach the believer how to accept Christ in his or her own life, and how to convey him to others, in order to introduce them to his fullness.[114]

From September 10 to 20 he carried out his pastoral visit in Zimbabwe, Botswana, Lesotho, Swaziland, and Mozambique.

It is a cause for joy that the Church implanted among the peoples of the part of Africa that I visited, are becoming autonomous and mature. The liturgy and especially participation in the Eucharist indicate how harmoniously the work of "inculturation" of the faith is being achieved in the life of these young communities. . . . The countries which I visited have been politically independent for a relatively brief time. Three of them, Zimbabwe, Botswana, and Mozambique, have a republican form of government. The other two, Lesotho and Swaziland, have preserved a monarchical regime linked to the tradition of the local dynasties. The period of the acquisition of independence, the struggle for freedom from the former colonial power, the building of their own existence as states, are all important events for the ethical dimension of international life. The various churches and episcopates have had a role to play in this process; and they must continually face up to the tasks which emerge in the case of the new societies and states. Such a task is, for example, the reconciling of opposing tribes and the promotion of integral development.[115]

From October 8 to 11 he was on his pastoral visit in France, where he also met the European institutions.[xxv]

The basic characteristic of these meetings was the proclamation of the Word of God applied to the various aspects of the Christian life.

[xxv] This refers to his historic address to the European Parliament in Strasbourg, France, on October 11, 1988, in which John Paul II argued for the formation of a united Europe open to all the nations. In this address he laid the foundation for the European Union.

Emphasis was placed on the urgent need of fidelity to the Christian patrimony so profoundly imprinted on European culture, so as not to give way to the invasion of dechristianization and always to bear witness with courage and charity to one's own faith. I sought to sow the word of God abundantly, in support of the ministry of the bishops and priests. Together with them I prayed to the Blessed Virgin, entrusting to her the hope that through her intercession, the seed which had been sown might yield a rich harvest. . . . Finally, in the programmatic discourse to the European Parliament, I reaffirmed the Church's interest and support for the integration of Europe, since Christianity is the common heritage of all its peoples. I again underlined that the Christian faith is the fundamental element of European identity, exhorting Europe to become again a beacon of world civilization through trust in God, peace among men, and respect for nature.[116]

1989: The Fall of the Wall

The Apostolic Exhortation Christifideles Laici *(dated December 30, 1988) was promulgated on January 30.*

The recent post-synodal apostolic exhortation opportunely clarifies the mission of the lay faithful as Gospel leaven in the animation and transformation of the temporal order through the dynamism of hope and Christian love. In fact, in the whole pluralistic society there is a need for a greater and more decisive Catholic presence—both as individuals and as groups—in the various areas of public life. Since the Christian vocation is by its very nature a vocation to the apostolate (cf. *Apostolicam Actuositatem*, 1), the sphere of action of the laity in the Church's mission is extended to all aspects and situations of human society.[117]

From April 28 to May 6 he carried out a pastoral visit in Madagascar, La Reunion, Zambia, and Malawi.

The historical moment in the life of each of those nations is important. The island of La Reunion continues to be an "overseas" part of the

French Republic. Madagascar, Zambia, and Malawi have achieved political independence, thanks to the process of "decolonization." Each of these countries expresses its sovereignty by resolving the problems of a social, cultural, and economic nature connected with it and also by overcoming various difficulties. The Church, on her part, seeks to collaborate effectively in this important process under the guidance of the gospel principles. . . . The countries recently visited are still in the so-called phase of first evangelization. They are mission countries where the Church's missionary work continues and remains. The beginnings of this first evangelization go back sometimes to past centuries (for example, Madagascar), but it has been put into effect more consistently in the course of the present century.[118]

From June 1 to 10 he carried out a pastoral visit in Norway, Iceland, Finland, Denmark, and Sweden.

In the ecumenical context, I undertook last June a pilgrimage of faith to the Christians of the Nordic countries. I paid homage to the Christian tradition of these peoples. Together with my Catholic and Lutheran brothers, I was able to experience intense and significant moments of spiritual ecumenism in prayer and reflection on the common mission of Christians in Europe and in the world. My pastoral journey, which up to a short time ago would have been unimaginable, has undoubtedly constituted, at a local level in the long term, an important stage along the way of ecumenism.[119]

From August 19 to 21 the pastoral visit in Spain was carried out.

"I am the Way, the Truth and the Life" (Jn 14:6). These words of Jesus Christ formed the theme of the pilgrimage to Santiago de Compostela, connected with the World Youth Day. . . . This meeting grew from the well-defined basis of the Church's pilgrimage, and particularly from the young people, who wished to take part in this pilgrimage. The pastoral care of youth bears fruit in the program of events of these days. Both the awareness and the apostolic attitude of the young people themselves bear fruit. At the same time the Youth Day is, in a certain sense, a new initiative for this apostolate and for the pastoral care which serves it. . . . Complementing the pilgrimage to Santiago de

Compostela was the visit to the Shrine of Our Lady of Covadonga,[xxvi] in the Archdiocese of Oviedo. In this very part of Spain, the Asturias, the task of freeing the country from Arab occupation was begun. At the same time, it was a struggle to defend Christian values.[120]

September 7 was set as the Day of Prayer for Peace in Lebanon.

Dear brothers, I wish to summon you—and through you all the sons and daughters of the Church—to a *day of universal prayer for peace in Lebanon.* In Italy, this day of prayer will take place on next October 4, the liturgical memorial of Saint Francis of Assisi, that holy man of gentleness and peace, who continues to invite all men and women to become "instruments of peace," so that "where there is hate, we may bring love." It will fall to each local church to select the most appropriate day for this common prayer, keeping in mind that November 22 is Lebanon's National Day. And so it will be the whole Church—as well as all those who wish to join us in this initiative—a Church at prayer, which will implore from our heavenly Father peace and salvation for Lebanon.[121]

From October 6 to 10 he carried out his pastoral visit in South Korea, Indonesia, and Mauritius.

I still have vivid memories of the impressions I received during the International Eucharistic Congress in Seoul, when, in the presence of multitudes of faithful from Korea and all parts of the world, I prostrated myself before the consecrated Host to entrust "Christ, our peace" with the hopes and concerns of the Church and of humanity. I remember, too, with great emotion, my meeting with the Christian communities of Indonesia—that immense archipelago whose population has found the way to create, in the light of the philosophical system of *Pancasila,*[xxvii] a pattern of living together that respects ethnic, cultural,

---

xxvi The victory of the outnumbered Asturians over the conquering Muslim army in 722 was attributed to the statue of the Virgin they carried with them. The first shrine was lost to a fire, but in 1901 the Basilica of Our Lady of Covadonga was built on the site of the battle.

xxvii Pancasila (literally, "five principles") is the philosophical system at the foundation of the Indonesian state: belief in one God; a just and civilized society; unity in diversity; democracy grounded by inner wisdom; and social justice for everyone. This was laid down by President Sukarno in 1945.

and religious pluralism. Significant, likewise, were my visits during that journey to the diocese of Dili on the island of Timor—so greatly tried over the last years[xxviii]—and to the churches of the Mauritius Islands.[122]

At the end of the year particular attention was given to the events in Europe.

The Holy See has welcomed with satisfaction the great transformations which have recently marked the life of many peoples, especially in Europe. The irrepressible thirst for freedom which we have witnessed there has accelerated the process of evolution; it has brought down walls and opened doors. All this has the appearance of a veritable overthrow. . . . Warsaw, Moscow, Budapest, Berlin, Prague, Sofia, and Bucharest, just to mention the capital cities, have become as it were the stages on a long pilgrimage toward freedom. We must honor those people who, at the cost of immense sacrifices, have courageously undertaken this pilgrimage; we must also honor the political leaders who have assisted it. What is admirable in the events that we have witnessed is the fact that whole peoples have spoken up: women, young people, and men have overcome their fear. The human person has shown the inexhaustible resources of dignity, courage, and freedom concealed within itself. In countries where for years a party has told people what to believe and the meaning to be given to history, these brothers and sisters have shown that it is not possible to stifle the fundamental freedoms that give meaning to human life: freedom of thought, of conscience, of religion, of expression, and of political and cultural pluralism.[123]

He spoke with great sadness of the situation in Latin America.

Unfortunately, some countries of this continent have experienced recent tragic events of bloodshed and violence. We all remember in particular the horrendous crime which happened in El Salvador with

---

xxviii The reference is to East Timor's struggle for independence, first from Portugal, then Indonesia. East Timor became independent in 2002.

the killing of the six Jesuits[xxix] and, before that, the savage assassination of the Bishop of Arauca[xxx] in Colombia. In some countries there still exists the illusion that problems can be solved through recourse to violence. Deep bitterness and strong abhorrence are stirred up in our spirit by the terrible acts of terrorism that have taken place in many regions, and no less intense is the anxiety we feel at the crimes that arrogant persons and groups still threaten to carry out in order to safeguard illegal sources of gain through drug trafficking. To these preoccupations then were added those from Panama, where there have been clashes involving innocent victims and serious inconvenience for the population.[124]

1990: Two Trips to Africa

From January 25 to February 1 he carried out a pastoral visit in Guinea-Bissau, Cape Verde, Mali, Burkina Faso, and Chad.

A central point on the schedule of the visit to each of these countries was the Eucharistic liturgy. It is the liturgy itself which makes us aware of how far the Church has come, thanks to missionary work: we have been able to testify how the communities, which grew up from the work of missionaries who came from various parts of the world, have changed into authentic African churches with their own hierarchies, with a noteworthy number of their own priests, sisters and brothers, seminarians and novices. Participation in the Eucharistic liturgy itself takes on a local character and becomes an expression of native African culture.[125]

April 21 and 22 found him on a pastoral visit in Czechoslovakia where he announced the synod of the European bishops.

[xxix] Six Jesuit priests, professors at the University of Central America in El Salvador, together with their cook and her daughter, were executed by a right-wing paramilitary group on November 16, 1989.

[xxx] Bishop Jesús Emilio Jaramillo Monsalve of Arauca, Colombia, was abducted and murdered in early October 1989 by leftist guerillas of the National Liberation Army.

During the final weeks of 1989 fundamental changes took place in the life of society in Czechoslovakia; the new government took a stance on the matter of respecting the rights of the person and society in the sovereign state which is the federation of the Czech and Slovak nations. Immediately after these changes, when President Vaclav Havel invited me to visit Czechoslovakia, I heard in this invitation the voice which we were all waiting to hear during these many years. . . . The days of April 21 and 22—the conclusion of the Easter octave in Prague, Velehrad, and Bratislava—were marked in a particularly eloquent fashion by the religious spirit of Saturday and Sunday in *albis*.[xxxi] . . . Still Velehrad remains for the Church and Slav peoples the site of the great beginning.[xxxii] At the same time this place is important in the history of Christian Europe. This spot seemed to be the most suitable one for announcing the convocation of the Synod of Bishops for Europe.[126]

From May 6 to 14 he carried out his pastoral visit in Mexico and Curaçao.

I have a real need to respond from the heart to so many enthusiastic hearts, which throughout the whole itinerary showed their faith and love for Christ and the Church. That love seems to be a special charism of the Mexican soul. Certainly it is also the fruit of so many sufferings and renunciations which the Church in Mexico went through in decades gone by. . . . At the feet of the Mother of God of Guadalupe, I have placed the humble request that the Pope's ministry may help the faithful of that Church to fulfill the mission begun almost five hundred years ago! It is a request which I renew at this moment as well. Our Lady of Guadalupe, may you bless Mexico and the entire Latin American continent which entrusts itself to you with filial affection![127]

---

xxxi The Sunday after Easter, called Low Sunday or *Dominica in albis (depositis)*, was the day on which the newly baptized put aside their white baptismal robes and took their place among the community of faithful. It is now also designated as Divine Mercy Sunday.

xxxii Velehrad, now in the Czech Republic, is the site of the cathedral and grave of Saint Methodius, who together with his brother Saint Cyril was a ninth-century missionary to the Slavic peoples. Pope John Paul II declared the brothers co-patrons of Europe, along with Saint Benedict of Nursia.

The pastoral visit to Malta was carried out from May 25 to 27.

The close contact with the Maltese people allowed me to experience the pride and the nobility of that people which in its centuries-long history was able to assimilate the values of other cultures: from the Phoenician to the Roman civilization, and from the Byzantine to the Arab.... Its small dimensions notwithstanding, Malta is a country of noteworthy international importance. Its location has made it a meeting place for diverse cultures and languages. Even today Malta maintains its vocation of mediator among peoples of the entire Mediterranean basin. My hope is that Malta will continue in what I would call a natural mission, without ever giving up its valuable inheritance of accumulated values from past generations.[128]

On August 26 he launched an appeal for peace in the Persian Gulf after an invasion of Kuwait by Iraq.

I feel the duty of inviting you to pray for peace in the Persian Gulf, where a situation has recently been created which is truly of grave concern. In reality we have been witnesses of serious violations of international rights and of the United Nations charter, as well as of the principles of ethics which must govern coexistence among peoples. Distrust seems to be increasing dramatically on both sides, and the international order, built up at the cost of painstaking effort and the sacrifice of many human lives, is severely threatened. Nor may we overlook the negative repercussions in the social and economic realm which, unfortunately, work to the detriment of the poorer nations. At this time of profound apprehension I invite you to pray fervently to God, gentle and merciful, asking him to enlighten those who are responsible for the fate of the peoples concerned, that they may be able to find just solutions to the current problems.[129]

From September 1 to 10 he carried out his pastoral visit in Tanzania, Burundi, Rwanda, and Côte d'Ivoire.

Other times in the past I have gone to different African nations to meet the local Christian communities. This time I devoted the first ten days of September to a visit to Tanzania, Burundi, and Rwanda.... The priestly ordinations held in each of the three countries are evidence of the growth of the local churches, which is proceeding apace along with the development of the lay apostolate. It is well known, in fact, how important the role of lay catechists has been since the dawn of evangelization. Today they continue to collaborate with the priests and women religious of the area, just as they did with the missionaries in past times.[130]

Once again tension exploded in Palestine, and on October 8 the Israeli army carried out a massacre in Jerusalem that left twenty people dead and one hundred fifty wounded.

The news of the sad events of the day before yesterday are cause for great sorrow, which is made greater yet due to the fact that they occurred in places considered sacred by the great religions, and in Jerusalem, the holy city for Jews, Christians, and Muslims. It is impossible to be indifferent and not condemn, along with the violence which has caused more dead and wounded, a situation of injustice which has lasted too long, and which sees two peoples, the Palestinians and Israelis, opposing one another; they are both called to live in a just and lasting peace, each in their own homeland and in that land which is so dear to them and to believers all over the world.[131]

In looking over the year that just concluded, John Paul II focused on the development of certain situations in Europe.

These days we are following with concern the political changes in certain countries of Central and Eastern Europe, including Albania. In all the societies there is upheaval and expectations are being forcefully expressed. I am thinking of the Baltic countries, especially the beloved country of Lithuania. Now that the European continent is seeking to regain its stride, it is essential that the solidarity of all should help these nations to remain faithful to their traditions and heritage and that, in dialogue and negotiation, they may find new solutions which will open doors and abolish prejudices. If 1990 was the year of freedom, 1991 should be the year of solidarity![132]

1991: The Dark Shadows of War

On January 22 the encyclical Redemptoris Missio *(dated December 7, 1990) was promulgated.*

The encyclical is intended to confirm the permanent, and therefore contemporary, validity of the missionary mandate which constitutes an inescapable duty for all who want to serve the way of the Gospel. The coming of the third millennium, moreover, arouses today even more urgent appeals for a commitment by the whole Christian world. Just as in every period of history the Church is faced with the responsibility for the mission which the risen Jesus has entrusted to her, so in our time the yearning to make Christ known cannot be diminished, but rather, with new energy and renewed trust in the word of the Lord, we should promote missionary activity. . . . The encyclical, however, is not only an appeal for missionary activity, but it is also an invitation to a new and deepened consideration of the faith convictions which should guide anyone who desires to work for evangelization. Thus, it is useful to consider above all the theological doctrine which grounds and animates the missionary duty of the people of God.[133]

The encyclical Centesimus Annus *(dated May 1) was promulgated on May 2.*

Recalling the centenary of the Leonine encyclical *Rerum Novarum*, I wanted 1991 to be the "year of the Church's social doctrine," not only properly to commemorate that historic document, but also with a timely magisterial act, to enlighten the specific problems emerging in the new circumstances which humanity experiences today in the situation of work and the development of peoples. . . . In order to emphasize the historic significance of the centenary of that encyclical, I promulgated *Centesimus Annus*, shedding light on the fruitfulness of the principles already expressed by my predecessor and examining some contemporary situations out of pastoral duty. Although taking into consideration the changing nature and complexity of the situation, in it I invited people to "look to the future at a time when we can already glimpse the third millennium of the Christian era, so filled with uncertainties but also with promises."[134]

From May 10 to 13 he carried out a pastoral visit in Portugal, ten years after the attempt on his life by Ali Agca.

The pilgrimage this year had a particular purpose: to give thanks for saving the Pope's life on May 13, 1981—exactly ten years ago. I consider this entire decade to be a free gift, given to me in a special way by Divine Providence—a special responsibility was given to me that I might continue to serve the Church by exercising the ministry of Peter. . . . My pilgrimage began with the holy sacrifice of the Mass, celebrated in Lisbon, the capital city, as a thanksgiving for the five hundred years of Portugal's participation in the Church's mission of evangelization. At the same time, this thanksgiving is an ardent appeal and prayer for a new evangelization. . . . The visit to Fatima this year is not only an occasion for thanksgiving, but at the same time is one of intense supplication. This is because the hands on the clock of time are moving toward the year 2000, and they show not only the providential changes in history of entire nations, but also new and old threats.[135]

June 1 through 9 found him on his pastoral visit in Poland.

This trip was first of all a "pilgrimage of thanks." Recent events— especially those of 1989 (fifty years after the end of World War II, which began with invasion of Poland by Hitler and Stalin)—have initiated a new state of affairs. . . . The entire course of this pilgrimage was characterized by thanksgiving. "Give thanks to God," and at the same time, by a renewal of societal life through the Church's service.[136]

From August 13 to 20 he arrived once again in Poland for World Youth Day, and then he went to Hungary.

I was able to sense the urgency and possible fruitfulness of the new evangelization in a particular way in the World Youth Day celebrated last August. We can affirm that, to a certain degree, at the shrine of Częstochowa we were allowed to experience the new situation in Europe after the breakdown of ideological and political barriers. Thousands of young people from Eastern, Central, and Western

Europe, young people from more than eighty nations, for the first time freely gathered to pray and proclaim their own faith in Christ Jesus. This event marked a step on the journey of evangelization at the end of this century, inviting us to reflect and act.[137]

"Gaude, Mater Hungaria." With these words the Church in Hungary rejoices at solemn vespers on the feast of Saint Stephen. I, too, want to express my joy today that I was able to visit Hungary precisely on August 20, the solemnity of its patron saint, and during the days preceding it. This fulfilled my desire, after so many years, of visiting a nation which, from the beginning of its recent history, has been closely tied to the See of Peter by a special bond, the sign of which is the Baptism and royal crown which the king of Hungary, Saint Stephen, received from Pope Sylvester II in the year 1000.[138]

October 12 through 21 he carried out his pastoral visit in Brazil.

Brazil is a gigantic country, one of the largest on earth. The Church lives there and fulfills her mission in 210 dioceses. The "local" program of the trip was intended to be a completion of my previous visit in 1980; [going] for the first time [to] the western part of Brazil. . . . The state of Mato Grosso is the region where new migrations, especially internal ones, are taking place and there are great ethnic differences. The Church continues to be a meeting place for all different groups. She is also a meeting place, in a notable way I would say, for the first inhabitants of this territory, for the Indians of Brazil who are defending their ethnic rights, and particularly, their right to land. . . . An unequal distribution of resources weighs on all of Brazilian life: there is a chasm between a small group of very wealthy people and the vast majority of the "underprivileged." Children, who are the victims of this injustice, must become a special focus of concern in the task of the evangelization of the society.[139]

At the beginning of the year, on January 15, the Pope sent a letter to Presidents George H. W. Bush of the United States and Saddam Hussein of Iraq, imploring them not to enter into a war in the Persian Gulf. In spite of this plea, Operation Desert Storm began two days later. By the beginning of June, war had erupted in the former Yugoslavia.

Unfortunately, 1991 was to be a year in which war played a leading role. As you recall, the so-called Gulf War broke out on January 12, only a few days after our meeting. Like every war, it left in its sinister wake the dead and wounded, devastation, hostility, and still unresolved problems. The consequences of the conflict cannot be forgotten; even today the people of Iraq continue to suffer terribly. . . . The year 1991 likewise ended amid the clash of arms. Disturbing images have shown us civilian populations literally crushed by the battles rending Yugoslavia, and particularly Croatia. Houses destroyed, inhabitants forced to flee, and economy wiped out, churches and hospitals systematically bombed; who is not appalled by these actions which reason condemns?[140]

Among the areas of the world in which Pope Wojtyła focused his attention, this year the continent of Asia stands out.

If we look to Asia, we observe the emergence of a regional identity which is becoming more obvious, thanks mostly to the constant action of regional organizations which favor the cooperation and the friendship between civilizations and peoples, often quite diverse. Thus, in the past months it has been possible to make some courageous political gestures: the two Koreas have drawn closer together, and in Cambodia an accord has been reached that permits the current factions to begin together on a journey which friendly, disinterested nations have helped to trace out. Two other nations have caught the attention of public opinion. Vast China has been particularly present on the world scene. We hope that it will be possible to establish a fruitful international cooperation with her. . . . A word also for beloved Vietnam, whose efforts towards economic openness should be supported. . . . In calling to mind the condition of these enormous populations, we must not forget the men and women who, perhaps, are the most deprived and most exposed to uncertain circumstances of every sort: exiles and refugees. We think, for example, of the tragedy being experienced by those among them who remain in camps in Hong Kong, Thailand, Malaysia, and other countries, or by those who have been forcibly repatriated.[141]

1992: The Publication of the
Catechism of the Catholic Church

From February 19 to 26 he carried out his pastoral visit in Senegal, Gambia, and Guinea.

The central moment each day was the Eucharistic liturgy. In the liturgy—through the *Opus divinum*—the Church was most fully expressed in her African rootedness. Here we can recognize that inculturation which is expressed, for example, in language, in marvelous song, in the rhythm of the offertory procession—everything was permeated with great devotion and was full of life. In the liturgy one can fully observe the special gift which the African Church brings to the common treasury of Christ's universal Church. . . . We cannot neglect another phase of this African pilgrimage, which had its own very painful eloquence. I am thinking of the time spent on Goree Island, near Dakar [Senegal]. In centuries past this basalt island witnessed the slave trade. Slaves were brutally separated from their families to be transported in humiliating conditions to America and sold as "human merchandise." . . . We want to acknowledge in a spirit of repentance all the wrongs which during this long period were perpetrated against the individuals and peoples of Africa through that shameful trade.[142]

Among the many situations of war, one in particular caught the attention of John Paul II at the beginning of the year.

For several weeks the situation in Nagorno-Karabakh, in the distant Caucasus, has continued to worry the international community, and we all feel duty-bound to express our solidarity with the families who are mourning their loved ones, dead or wounded. Together, let us pray the almighty and merciful God to take pity on the suffering and help all to make feelings of fraternity prevail. These peoples will then be able to live freedom, to enjoy growth and development without fear and with respect for their own ethnic and cultural identity.[143]

From June 4 to 10 he carried out the pastoral visit in Angola and São Tomé and Principe.

In recent decades society and the Church in Angola have passed through unusually difficult circumstances. The struggle for independence, which was to have ended the colonial period, turned into a civil war, with enormous destruction and numerous human victims: suffice it to recall the great number of young people disabled by the war. The Church was greatly threatened by the Marxist ideology that prevailed at the time. If she managed to survive in these conditions it was a gift of Divine Providence, due to truly heroic missionaries and, a fact which must be given particular mention, the result of the persevering commitment of local catechists. . . . The archipelago of São Tomé and Principe, located to the northwest of Angola, entered the colonial period at the end of the fifteenth century. . . . Here, as in Angola, a democratic regime was established following the period of Marxist domination, and contacts with the West have been intensified. The Church faces pastoral tasks and obligations similar to those in Angola. Most basic is the challenge of family and young people, as well as the problem of native vocations to the priesthood and religious life, with the related problems of seminaries and the lay apostolate.[144]

His pastoral visit in the Dominican Republic was carried out from October 9 through 14.

"*Jesus Christ is the same yesterday, today and forever*" (Heb 13:8). These words have a special meaning in connection with the date of October 12, 1492. Christopher Columbus, who left Spain heading West to search for a new route to the Indies (thus, toward Asia), discovered a new continent on that date. The discovery of America began with the island of the Antilles, and in particular, that which was then named Hispaniola. Precisely on that island the cross, the symbol of redemption, was erected for the first time—and from there evangelization began. . . . On October 12, 1992, the Bishop of Rome, together with the whole Church and especially with the American episcopate, went on pilgrimage to that cross from where—five hundred years ago—the evangelization of this new land began, first toward the south and then toward the north. This was primarily a pilgrimage of thanksgiving. The itinerary included Santo Domingo and the shrine of Our

Lady of Altagracia. . . . Through my pilgrimage to the place where evangelization began, a pilgrimage characterized by thanksgiving, we wanted at the same time to make an act of atonement before the infinite holiness of God for everything which during that advance toward the American continent was marred by sin, injustice, and violence.[145]

On December 9 the Catechism of the Catholic Church, *which had been approved in June, was promulgated.*

This new text represents a privileged tool and a pressing invitation to an appropriate Gospel formation in order to begin the new evangelization with firm conviction and apostolic foresight. Hence the urgent need for catechesis, called to break the bread of God's word, thus fostering an ever deeper understanding of it in regard to the challenges of our time. This catechesis is certainly not exhausted in merely transmitting ideas. Its task is "to advance in fullness and to nourish day by day the Christian life of the faithful, young and old," so that the believer may be "impregnated" by the mystery of Christ, and thus learn ever better "to think like him, to judge like him, to act in conformity with his commandments, to hope as he invites us to" (*Catechesi Tradendae*, no. 20). The new *Catechism*, a reference point for the catechesis of the Christian communities spread throughout the world, will provide a sure path in this direction.[146]

1993: The Encyclical on Catholic Morality

At Assisi, on January 9 and 10, he presided over the Encounter of Prayer for Peace in Europe and especially in the Balkans.

This meeting has been particularly dedicated to prayer for peace in Europe, especially in view of the grave situation of the peoples living in the Balkans. We have shared this experience together, with us have been associated the particular churches of the entire European continent. It has been our common objective to manifest and make fruitful the constant concern that fills us for those suffering because of the blindness and hardness of heart of others, for those—whether child, man, woman, elderly person, innocent civilian, individual, or whole people—who are forced to pay the sad price of a war not wanted but endured. Our interest is meant to be effective, an interest made practical in fervent and ceaseless prayer, which should be followed by selfless action consisting of help and humanitarian support. Our commitment, moreover, is meant to foster the culture of peace, through daily gestures of respect for other's rights and with patient work for reconciliation.[147]

From February 3 to 10 he carried out a pastoral visit in Benin, Uganda, and Sudan.

It was not the first time the Pope went to Africa; neither, perhaps, will it be the last. Africa is hospitable: it is glad to welcome the Pope and prepared to face any sacrifice, even a financial one, to do so. This is a noble characteristic that distinguishes it. Africa is poor, but at the same time rich with the same riches with which Christ enriched all of us, making himself poor for us. This does not mean that in Africa one can be silent as regards problems of social justice, not only in the domestic context, but also on the level of intercontinental relations; on the contrary, it is necessary to speak out. It is also necessary to talk of the problems that concern our relations with the followers of the great religion of Islam, seeking to face them with an open mind with a view to possible solutions.[148]

On April 25 he went to Albania.

For years Albania had become synonymous with the particular oppression established by a totalitarian, atheistic system in which the rejection of God was pushed to its furthest limits. There the right to freedom of conscience and religion had been trampled upon most brutally; those who simply administered Baptism or engaged in any religious practices were threatened with the death penalty. . . . A vain attempt, as events have shown: the long night was finally followed by the dawn of a new day. The Church in Albania is now living a new spring. My visit last Sunday was meant to hallow this event by consecrating new bishops in the cathedral of Shkodër, one of the most majestic churches in the Balkans. During the years of dictatorship it was turned into a sports complex; now it has returned to its original splendor, becoming the symbol of Albania's resurrection.[149]

On May 9, from Argentina, he launched a strong admonition to the Mafia.

God once said, "You shall not kill." No man, no human association, no mafia can change or trample on this most sacred right of God. The people of Sicily are a peace-loving people, a life-giving people. They cannot live forever under the pressure of a contrary civilization, a civilization of death. A civilization of life is needed. In the name of the crucified and risen Christ, of Christ who is the Way and the Truth and the Life, I say to those who are responsible for this: Repent! God's judgment will come some day![150]

On May 29 he closed the second synod for the Diocese of Rome.

With the promulgation of the *Book of the Synod*, yesterday I had the joy of crowning the long process of the pastoral synod of the Diocese of Rome, which began seven years ago. Like so many other dioceses throughout the world, the Church which is in Rome, thirty years after the first synod also wants to redesign her life and commitment in the light of the theological and pastoral perspectives offered by the Second Vatican Council. Now we are beginning the no less demanding road of its fulfillment: the indications which came from the synod's reflections must become the practice and life of the whole ecclesial community.[151]

From June 12 to 17 he carried out a pastoral visit in Spain, where he presided over the International Eucharistic Congress.

The Eucharistic Congress in Spain was closely connected with the celebrations for the fifth centenary of the evangelization of America— that is, of the evangelization that began with Christopher Columbus' discovery of the new continent. It was there, in the Spanish land of Andalucía in Seville and Huelva, that the historic expedition was prepared. It was not merely a question of technical preparations, but spiritual as well. The navigators realized that they were setting out toward the unknown. What they discovered corresponded in no way at all to what they had imagined at their departure. The places which I was able to visit—Moguer, Palos de la Frontera, La Rábida—show how with great faith and trust Columbus and his sailors had entrusted their adventure to God's hands. From these very same places—after the discovery of the new continent—the first missionaries set out to proclaim the Gospel.[152]

From August 9 to 16 he traveled to Jamaica, Mexico, and the United States for his pastoral visit.

World Youth Day takes place this year in Denver in the United States, at the foot of the Rocky Mountains. During the apostolic pilgrimage which brought me to Denver, I was able to complete my visits commemorating the fifth centenary of the evangelization of America, pausing with the African American community in the island of Jamaica and with the Indian Mexican community at Merida in the Yucatan, tracing the footsteps of the native peoples of Mexico. The participation of large groups of their descendants showed how efficient evangelization was in that country. Why did I find Denver the great surprise of 1993? Great opposition was expected, at least according to some sources of information, and instead World Youth Day was a tremendous achievement. Not an achievement of the Pope or of the Church, but first and foremost, Christ's achievement. And it was not the first time that the young people expressed so vigorously their desire to carry the Gospel into the new millennium.[153]

From September 4 to 10 he carried out a pastoral visit to Lithuania, Latvia, and Estonia.

It was finally possible to set foot in that tortured land among contemporary witnesses of Christ's cross and resurrection; there, where the missionary proclamation, branching out from Rome to the north and east of Europe, met the impetus of evangelization from Constantinople. In those lands the witness of the faith has once again become man's strength. It is difficult not to feel deeply moved at the memory of the

Hill of Crosses in Lithuania. It is difficult not to wander in mind and heart to the Dawn Gate, to Šiluva in Lithuania or to Aglona in Latvia. It is difficult not to express wonder at seeing what a sincere and cordial welcome they gave the Pope not only in Riga that has a Lutheran majority, but in Estonia itself, where the number of Catholics is not more than a few thousand. After Vilnius, Kaunas, and Riga, Tallinn too awaited the presence of Peter's Successor and his ecumenical visit to the Lutheran cathedral, as well as his words to the Estonians during the afternoon celebration in the Old City. His words, improvised at the time, turned out to be the most important moment not only for Estonia, but in some ways, for all Europe. Eleven years ago, Santiago de Compostela in Spain was the venue of the European Act. In 1993, it is as though Europe had felt the completion of that act precisely in Tallinn, after the famous events of 1989.[xxxiii] [154]

Veritatis Splendor (Splendor of Truth; dated August 6) was promulgated on October 5.

This document, greatly expected and prepared at length, is only now being published because it seemed appropriate that it be preceded by the *Catechism of the Catholic Church*, which contains a complete, systematic exposition of Christian morality. The present document examines its implications and foundations more deeply, exercising discernment regarding certain controversial problems in recent moral theology. In particular, it reaffirms the dignity and greatness of the human person created in God's image, and proposes anew the genuine concept of human freedom, showing its essential and constitutive relationship with the truth in accordance with Christ's words. "The truth will make you free!" (Jn 8:32).[155]

On November 11 he slipped and fell; the diagnosis was a dislocated right shoulder, which had to be immobilized for a month.

Last Thursday, as you know, I was obliged to stay briefly in the hospital after falling as I came down the steps of the dais to greet those

---

xxxiii On August 23, 1989, 2 million people joined hands across Latvia, Lithuania, and Estonia in protest against communist rule.

present at the end of an audience. I sincerely express my gratitude to all who offered their kind assistance, providing me with the necessary medical treatment. I also thank the numerous people who were close to me with the warmth of their sympathy and, above all, the precious comfort of prayer. It was a further opportunity for me to be united more closely with the mystery of Christ's cross, in communion with our many suffering brothers and sisters. I accept this trial too from the hands of God, who arranges everything in accordance with his providential plans, and I offer it for the good of the Church and for peace among men.[156]

1994: A Year for the Family

On January 6 he sent a letter to the Italian bishops on the responsibility of Catholics in the face of present challenges.

The present moment in history, marked by events of unique social significance, is also for Italian Catholics a powerful call to decision and commitment. Mindful of the formidable challenges which emerge from the "signs of the times," as Bishop of Rome I turn with deep affection to you, bishops of the Churches in the peninsula and on the islands, bishops of the north, the center, and the south of Italy, in order to share my concerns and hopes, in particular, to witness to that legacy of human and Christian values which is the most precious heritage of the Italian people. . . . It is, above all, a legacy of faith kindled here by apostolic preaching from the earliest years of the Christian era and soon confirmed by the blood shed by innumerable martyrs. . . . Secondly, it is a cultural legacy, which has flourished from that common stock over the course of the centuries. What treasures of knowledge, insight, and experience have followed, increasing also because of the faith. . . . Lastly, it is a legacy of unity which, even beyond its own specific political framework matured in the course of the nineteenth century, is deeply rooted in the hearts of the Italians.[157]

On January 23 he celebrated a Mass in the Vatican basilica for peace in the Balkans.

It is a day of prayer that unites the entire Church. To prepare for it, a study meeting took place in the Vatican, devoted to the theme of peace in the Balkans, in the spirit of the World Day of Peace. Those who took part tried to understand the mechanisms of the war that unfortunately is still in progress, and at the same time they sought an answer to the question of whether, how, and under what conditions peace would be possible in the former Yugoslavia. *The Pontifical Council for Justice and Peace* published an "appeal" containing reflections developed during the meeting that we wish to refer to on this day of prayer.[158]

On the occasion of the International Year of the Family, on February 22 the Letter to Families *was promulgated. On October 8 John Paul II presided over the world encounter for the family, and on December 15 he promulgated the* Letter to Children.

The United Nations proclaimed 1994 as the International Year of the Family: the Church joined in this proposal, celebrating the Year of the Family throughout the world. . . . The Church wanted at the same time to highlight the beauty and sublimity of the vocation to marriage and parenthood. She wanted to remind all people how much each of us owes our family, emphasizing anew what the Second Vatican Council expressed so appropriately in the Pastoral Constitution *Gaudium et Spes* on the Church in the modern world, where it speaks of the rightful appreciation of the dignity of marriage and the family. A specific aspect of the Church's interest in the family is certainly her concern for the child. Could the Church, who is a mother, possibly fail to have this concern when from all sides truly terrifying facts are being reported? I am thinking, in particular, of the brutal murder of street children, of children forced into prostitution, of trafficking in children by organizations in organ transplants; I am thinking of children who are victims of violence and war and who are exploited for drug dealing or for other criminal activities. These are all aberrations, the mention of which alone is enough to horrify people.[159]

On March 19 he sent a letter to the heads of state and to the secretary general of the United Nations regarding the international conference on population and development.

In the face of an attempt to demote the person and his motivations, in a sphere as serious as that of human life and solidarity, the Holy See considered that it was its duty to remind the leaders of the nations of their responsibilities, and to make them realize the risk that there could be forced on humanity a vision of things and a style of living belonging to a minority. . . . Many of those taking part in the Cairo conference were expecting this statement and this witness from the Holy See. Such in fact is the reason why the Holy See has a place in the midst of the community of nations: to be the voice which the human conscience is waiting for, without thereby minimizing the contribution of other religious traditions.[160]

On April 28 he broke his femur and had a hip replacement at Gemelli Hospital, where he stayed until May 27.

I meditated on all this and thought it over again during my hospital stay. And once again I found at my side the figure of Cardinal Wyszyński, primate of Poland (yesterday was the thirteenth anniversary of his death). At the beginning of my pontificate he said to me: "If the Lord has called you, you must lead the Church into the third millennium." He himself had led the Church in Poland into its second Christian millennium. This is what Cardinal Wyszyński said to me. I understood that I have to lead Christ's Church into this third millennium by prayer, by various programs, but I saw that this is not enough; she must be led by suffering, by the attack thirteen years ago and by this new sacrifice. Why now, why this year, why in this Year of the Family? Precisely because the family is threatened, the family is under attack. The Pope has to be attacked, the Pope has to suffer, so that every family and the world may see that there is, I would say, a higher gospel: the gospel of suffering by which the future is prepared, the third millennium of families, of every family and all families.[161]

On September 10 and 11 he carried out a pastoral visit in Croatia.

This visit of the Pope to Zagreb, Croatia, was awaited for a long time. The Catholics of Croatia have participated with enthusiasm and in great numbers. We have prayed together, thanking God for the gift of Baptism, for the gift of our Christian faith, which the Croats have been perhaps the first to receive among the Slavic nations. . . . Unfortunately, last Thursday I was not able to visit Sarajevo since in a certain sense it represents the central point in the Balkan war. I trust that one day I will be able to visit. We would thus, together with our Orthodox brothers and sisters, and also with the Muslim communities, ask from God the gift of peace in the Balkans—peace for their lands, for their peoples, and yes, peace for all of Europe.[162]

On October 8 and 9 he presided over the international encounter of families.

We are in fact convinced that society cannot do without the institution of the family for the simple reason that society itself arises from families and draws its solidity from families. Faced with the cultural and social decay presently taking place, in the presence of the spread of ills such as violence, drugs, and organized crime, what better guarantee of prevention and liberation is there than a united family, morally healthy and socially involved? It is in families like these that people are trained in the virtues and in the social values of solidarity, openness, loyalty, respect for others and their dignity. . . . In the Church and in society, now is the hour of the family. Families are called to play a primary role in the task of the new evangelization. From the heart of families devoted to prayer, to the apostolate, and to the Church's life there will develop genuine vocations not only for the formation of other families, but also for the life of special consecration.[163]

1995: The Encyclical on the Value of Life

From January 11 to 21 he carried out his pastoral visit in the Philippines, Papua New Guinea, Australia, and Sri Lanka.

The choice of Manila for the World Youth Meeting was particularly appropriate, not only geographically, but also from the historical point of view. The Church in the Philippines is celebrating the fourth centenary of her foundation precisely this year. . . . Thus it can be affirmed that the world pilgrimage of youth in the Philippines has in a certain sense resumed, after four centuries, that missionary dimension of the Church's "pilgrimage" which led to the creation of the first ecclesiastical province in the Far East. This is how the Tenth World Youth Day acquired its special historical dimension. . . . The following stages of my journey in the Far East had not only a chronological but also a logical connection with World Youth Day. If indeed it portrayed a lively image of the pilgrim Church, the beatifications in Port Moresby, Sydney, and Colombo[xxxiv] pointed out the goal toward which the Church is heading down the centuries and generations. The goal of this journey is to realize that universal call to holiness, as expressed by the Second Vatican Council.[164]

On March 30 he promulgated the encyclical Evangelium Vitae *(dated March 25).*

The fruit of a broad consultation among the bishops, it is a meditation on life considered in the fullness of its natural and supernatural dimensions; a meditation interwoven with gratitude to the Lord, the God of life, and accompanied by a strong appeal to Christians and to all people of goodwill that we generously put ourselves at the service of this basic good by proclaiming to the world the "Gospel of life." . . . The encyclical bears the date of the Annunciation. I chose this solemnity because of its highly significant value for the theme of life. At the Annunciation, the Blessed Virgin welcomed the announcement of her divine motherhood. The yes she gave is the highest example of the yes every mother gives to the life of her baby.[165]

On April 29 and 30 he visited Trento, Italy.

Trent functioned as a "bridge" and a "hinge" between two great civilizations: the Latin and the Germanic. Because of this particular feature, it had the honor of hosting the Nineteenth Ecumenical Council, which took its name from here and has profoundly marked the

---

xxxiv Those beatified were Peter ToRot (1912–1945) in Port Moresby, Papua New Guinea; Sister Mary of the Cross (Mary MacKillop) (1842–1909) in Sydney; and Joseph Vaz (1561–1711) in Colombo, Sri Lanka.

features and history of the Church and European culture. The Trent region is "a land between the mountains," a splendid but stark land, once so mean in natural resources that it taught its inhabitants diligence, sobriety, and an enterprising spirit. It is a blessed land which has found in the cross, hoisted on the highest peaks, set upon hundreds of steeples, placed at crossroads, and given the place of honor in homes, a sure guidepost in life, a stable element of civilization and progress, an ever new power for overcoming the thousands of difficulties recurring on the arduous path of its history.[166]

From May 20 to 22 he carried out a pastoral visit in the Czech Republic.

Here Christianity arrived very early, and put down roots in the ninth century among the Slavs of the kingdom of Greater Moravia. It was precisely the prince of this state who invited Saints Cyril and Methodius, who came from Byzantium, to evangelize his people. This evangelization bore fruit in the territory visited by the Pope. . . . With these historical facts clearly in mind, I would like to say that the main reason for my visit was the canonization of Blessed Jan Sarkander and Blessed Zdislava. Zdislava is linked with the history of the Church in Bohemia, and Jan Sarkander with the history of the Church in Moravia. . . . In the afternoon of the same day of the canonization, the meeting with youth took place in front of the Marian shrine of Svatý Kopeček. I would certainly describe it as one of the most beautiful and original meetings I have ever had with young people. On that occasion I wished to "consign" the Lord's Prayer to the young people, the *Our Father*, as if to mark a stage in the catechumenate of youth in that country. Only Christ, in fact, can give young people what they so thirst for, that is, the full and joyous meaning of life.[167]

On May 30 he promulgated the encyclical Ut Unum Sint *(dated May 25).*

The power of God's Spirit gives growth and builds up the Church down the centuries. As the Church turns her gaze to the new millennium, she asks the Spirit for the grace to strengthen her own unity and to make it grow toward full communion with other Christians. How is the Church to obtain this grace? In the first place, through prayer. Prayer should always concern itself with the longing for unity, and as such is one of the basic forms of our love for Christ and for the Father who is rich in mercy. In this journey which we are undertaking with other Christians toward the new millennium, prayer must occupy the first place.[168]

On June 21, in Rome, the great mosque was inaugurated, and John Paul II sent a significant greeting.

This event is an eloquent sign of the religious freedom recognized here for every believer. And it is significant that in Rome, the center of Christianity and the see of Peter's Successor, Muslims should have their own place of worship with full respect for their freedom of conscience. On a significant occasion like this, it is unfortunately necessary to point out that in some Islamic countries similar signs of the recognition of religious freedom are lacking. And yet the world, on the threshold of the third millennium, is waiting for these signs! Religious freedom has now become part of many international documents and is one of the pillars of contemporary society. While I am pleased that Muslims can gather in prayer in the new Roman mosque, I earnestly hope that the right of Christians and of all believers to express their own faith will be recognized in every corner of the earth.[169]

From June 30 to July 3 he carried out a pastoral visit in Slovakia.

The main reason for my visit to Slovakia was the canonization of the three martyrs of Košice[xxxv] [who] gave their lives for their fidelity to the Church and did not yield to the brutal pressure of the civil authorities, of the rulers who wished to force them into apostasy. . . . It should not be forgotten that the whole Church of Slovakia, situated within the communist Republic of Czechoslovakia at the time, suffered painful persecution. Almost all the bishops were unable to

---

xxxv The seventeenth century martyrs of Košice are Saints Marek Krizevcanin, Melichar Grodziecki, SJ, and Stefan Pongracz, SJ.

exercise their pastoral service. Many endured cruel imprisonment. Some ended their lives as true martyrs. . . . The Church in Slovakia has enjoyed religious freedom for only a few years, and perhaps this fact accounts for the great vitality that I could see and feel during my visit.[170]

September 9 and 10 he was in Loreto, Italy, on the occasion of the pilgrimage of youth from Europe.

From Loreto this evening, we have made a wonderful pilgrimage from the Atlantic to the Urals, to every corner of the continent, wherever there are young people in search of a "common home." I say to all, this is your house, the House of Christ and Mary, the House of God and man! Young people of Europe marching towards the year 2000, come into this House and build a different world together, a world where the civilization of love holds sway! . . . For this reason, do not forget what your roots are. The tree that wants to grow and bear fruit must draw nourishment from good soil with its roots. Young people of Europe, the Gospel is the soil in which to sink the roots of your future! Christ meets you in the Gospel. Discover his friendship and appreciate it, invite him to be your companion on your daily journey.[171]

From September 14 to 20 he went to Cameroon, South Africa, and Kenya for a pastoral visit.

I still have vivid memories of the pilgrimage which took me to Africa for the eleventh time, from September 14 to 20. How can one not be touched by the Africans' human warmth? How can one forget the colors, sounds, and rhythms of that land? . . . Unfortunately, once again I have seen with my own eyes this continent's problems. Africa bears the scars of its long history of humiliations. This continent has too frequently been considered only for selfish interests. Today Africa is asking to be loved and respected for what it is. It does not ask for compassion, it asks for solidarity. This is the message I gathered everywhere, and in particular at my meeting with Nelson Mandela, who guided the victorious struggle against apartheid, interpreting the desire of his people and the whole of Africa to be reborn in the peace and collaboration among all its children.[172]

From October 4 to 9 he carried out a pastoral visit in the United States and addressed a discourse to the General Assembly of the United Nations.

I returned to this important international assembly after sixteen years. The opportunity was given me by the fiftieth anniversary of the founding of the United Nations. My visit took place exactly thirty years after the historic address to the peoples of the world made by my predecessor, Pope Paul VI, in that place. How many events of exceptional importance have occurred in the meantime! Ancient problems have been happily solved, but dark clouds still loom on the world's horizon. In Europe, the wall that separated the East from the West has fallen, but in the world, due to the great economic differences, there is still a deep gulf between North and South. The need to banish atomic arms is noted, but often the proliferation of sophisticated and destructive weapons still lurks in the shadows; thanks to the wide-scale and constant interchange between nations and cultures, awareness of the human family's unity is deeper, but at the same time in some regions on every continent aggressive nationalism and bloody conflicts break out. In view of this situation, how can we fail to recognize the importance of the United Nations? I sincerely thank the Lord for giving me the possibility to make a contribution so that the United Nations organization may carry out ever more effectively the task for which it was founded: to be a center of harmonization that guarantees peace and safeguards the human rights of individuals and peoples, that helps men and women to build a world where the various nations may truly feel they are a "family."[173]

1996: Confiding About His Hospital Stay

On February 22, with the apostolic constitution Universi Dominici Gregis, *he reformed the rules of the Conclave.*

I have deemed it necessary to revise the form of the election itself in the light of the present-day needs of the Church and the usages of modern society. I have thus considered it fitting not to retain election by acclamation *quasi ex inspiratione* [by acclamation], judging that it is no longer an apt means of interpreting the thought of an electoral college so great in number and so diverse in origin. It also appeared necessary to eliminate election *per compromissum* [through a compromise], not only because of the difficulty of the procedure, evident from the unwieldy accumulation of rules issued in the past, but also because by its very nature it tends to lessen the responsibility of the individual electors who, in this case, would not be required to express their choice personally. After careful reflection I have therefore decided that the only form by which the electors can manifest their vote in the election of the Roman Pontiff is by secret ballot, in accordance with the rules set forth below. This form offers the greatest guarantee of clarity, straightforwardness, simplicity, openness, and, above all, an effective and fruitful participation on the part of the cardinals who, individually and as a group, are called to make up the assembly which elects the Successor of Peter.[174]

The apostolic exhortation Vita Consecrata *was promulgated on March 25.*

Beyond all superficial assessments of its usefulness, the consecrated life is important precisely in its being unbounded generosity and love, and this all the more so in a world which risks being suffocated in the whirlpool of the ephemeral. "Without this concrete sign there would be a danger that the charity which animates the entire Church would grow cold, that the salvific paradox of the Gospel would be blunted, and that the 'salt' of faith would lose its savor in a world undergoing secularization." The Church and society itself need people capable of devoting themselves totally to God and to others for the love of God. The Church can in no way renounce the consecrated life, for it eloquently expresses her inmost nature as "Bride." In the consecrated life the proclamation of the Gospel to the whole world finds fresh enthusiasm and power.[175]

On March 27 seven Trappist monks were kidnapped in Algeria by Islamic fundamentalists. On May 24 the kidnappers announced that they had beheaded them. On August 1 Bishop Pierre Claverie of Oran was assassinated.

Algeria continues to wallow in an abyss of unprecedented violence, giving a bleak impression of an entire people taken hostage. The Catholic Church in Algeria paid a heavy price last year, with the barbaric murder of the seven Trappist monks of Notre-Dame de l'Atlas,[xxxvi] and the brutal death of Bishop Pierre Claverie of Oran.[xxxvii] [176]

On April 14 Pope Wojtyła went to Tunisia and launched a firm appeal, while in North Africa there followed the tragic news of a terrorist ambush.

There is no one who can kill in the name of God; no one who can decide to put a fellow human being to death.... Despite the fact that there are difficulties and misunderstandings, go to encounter your brothers and sisters, without distinction of ethnic origin or religion.[177]

From May 17 to 19 he carried out a pastoral visit in Slovenia.

The history of Christianity for the Slovenian people is now 1,250 years old. The present configuration of the state goes back about five years.... Thus they too experienced the sufferings of the Second World War and, after the conflict, found themselves with the other peoples in the Yugoslav federation subjected to the power of the communist system. This federative link was loosed only in the '90s at the price of civil war which claimed many victims, although fortunately in the land of Slovenia less than elsewhere.... The Slovenian people's faith, sorely tried in this century, has remained unshaken, and for this we give

---

xxxvi On March 26 or 27, seven French Trappist monks of Tibhirine were kidnapped by a group of Islamic extremists, who murdered them on May 21 after demands for a prisoner exchange failed.

xxxvii The bishop of Oran and his driver were assassinated during the spate of murders of religious persons by the militants. Bishop Pierre Claverie, a native Algerian, was recognized for his promotion of dialogue between Christians and Muslims and his opposition to the military takeover and the assassination of President Mohammed Boudiaf in 1992.

thanks to God. Now there is need for a renewed missionary effort, for which spiritual support, vigilant attention, and prophetic discernment of the "signs of the times" are essential, especially on the part of those who are called to consecrate their whole life to the Gospel.[178]

From October 6 to 15 he was in Gemelli Hospital in Rome for an appendectomy. It is he himself who announced it from his window in Saint Peter's Square at the end of the Sunday Angelus prayer.

I want to confide in you. This evening I must be admitted to the hospital for surgery. In asking you to accompany me with your prayers, I greet also all those who are in hospitals or houses of rehabilitation, knowing that I can count especially on your spiritual solidarity.[179]

On November 13 he spoke to the World Summit for Nutrition organized by the Food and Agricultural Organization of the United Nations (FAO) in Rome.

The World Summit on Nutrition, held in November by FAO here in Rome, has called the attention of all to the scandal of hunger and malnutrition, which are suffered by one person in five throughout the world. As I speak to this summit, I cannot help but recall the unsupportable contrasts still existing between those who lack everything and those who squander without restraint those goods that, in the plan of the Creator, are destined to be shared by all humanity. It is urgent and necessary that all states make the effort to follow economic plans based not only on profit, but also on the sharing of goods in solidarity.[180]

In his customary reflections on the year that just concluded, the Pope said there were some signs of hope.

We must take note of the agreement reached at the end of the year in Abidjan, Côte d'Ivoire; for peace in Sierra Leone, while at the same time expressing the hope that disarmament and the demobilization of the armed forces will take place without delay. May the same come true in neighboring Liberia; itself engaged in a difficult process of normalization and of preparation for free elections. In Guatemala, peace seems finally to be at hand after too many years of fratricidal conflict. The agreement signed on last December 29, by creating a climate of trust, should favor the settlement, in unity and with courage, of the many social problems still to be resolved. Turning our gaze towards Asia, we await the date of July 1, 1997, when Hong Kong will return to the sovereignty of mainland China. By reason of the size and vitality of the Catholic community living in the territory, the Holy See will follow with very particular interest this new stage, trusting that respect for differences, for the fundamental rights of the human person, and for the rule of law will accompany this new journey forward, prepared for by patient negotiations.[181]

1997: Trips to Sarajevo and Beirut

On April 12 and 13 Pope John Paul II went to Bosnia.

Last Sunday I was in Sarajevo, a city that symbolizes our century, a land of suffering and hope. I thank the Lord for the peace process that has begun and I hope it will bring lasting fruits of reconciliation and solidarity. During my visit I had the opportunity to appreciate the activity of the ecclesial institutions, governments, international organizations, and all who have worked to alleviate that people's suffering and hardship. It is now necessary to proceed without delay in coming to the aid of those who have been sorely stricken during the tragic conflict, and to help the victims who are still suffering the consequences. This is the time for moral and material rebuilding. Let us continue to be close to the people of that beloved region with our effective solidarity.[182]

On May 10 and 11 he was in Lebanon.

Throughout the years of war, together with the whole Church, I closely followed the difficult times experienced by the Lebanese people and united myself in prayer with the sufferings which they endured. On numerous occasions, from the beginning of my pontificate, I have urged the international community to help the Lebanese people once again to live peacefully within a national territory recognized and respected by all, and to foster the rebuilding of a society of justice and brotherhood.... Henceforth all are called to commitment on behalf of peace, reconciliation, and fraternal life, by offering at their various levels signs of forgiveness and by working in the service of the national community, so that violence will never again prevail over dialogue, fear and suspicion over trust, resentment over fraternal love.[183]

On June 26 he spoke of the letters he had sent ten days previously to Israeli Prime Minister Benjamin Netanyahu and to Yasser Arafat, president of the Palestinian Authority, to solicit peace in the Middle East.

To Netanyahu: This appeal of mine is above all a moral one. I address it confidently to all those who are committed to the search for the good of their peoples. In the name of God and of the faith in him which unites us all, let everyone avoid increasing the levels of tension and frustration: history, above all in the Holy Land, teaches us that great hopes, if unfulfilled over a long period of time, can cause further unforeseen provocations and uncontrollable situations of violence.[184]

To Arafat: I am not unaware of the practical and technical difficulties involved, and which will arise at every step of the way, but I believe that they can and must be met with courage and determination, virtues proper to those who work for peace in a land that is holy, for the peoples who live there, and for the whole of humanity.[185]

From August 21 to 24 he was in Paris for World Youth Day.

Everyone is called to share in God's life, thanks to the death and resurrection of Christ. Does not our encounter at this World Youth Day reflect this truth? All of you, assembled here from many countries and continents, bear witness to the universal vocation of the People of God redeemed by Christ! ... Dear young people, your journey does not end here. Time does not come to a halt. Go forth now along the roads of the world, along the pathways of humanity, while remaining ever united in Christ's Church! Continue to contemplate God's glory and God's love, and you will receive the enlightenment needed to build the civilization of love, to help our brothers and sisters to see the world transfigured by God's eternal wisdom and love.[186]

He was in Brazil from October 2 to 6 for the World Meeting for Families.

The meeting with the world's families offered me the happy opportunity to visit the Brazilian land for the third time. Thus I have been able to meet that people again who are so dear to the Church and to me personally, a people rich in history, culture, and humanity, as well as faith and hope. . . . These meetings, which the Church arranges on a world scale, express the will and commitment of the People of God to walk united on a privileged path: the path of the Gospel, the path of peace, the path of youth, and, in this case, the path of the family. Yes, the family is eminently the path of the Church, which recognizes in it an essential and irreplaceable element of God's plan for humanity. The family is the privileged place for personal and social development. Whoever fosters the family fosters the human person; whoever attacks it, attacks the human person. Today the family and life are confronted by a fundamental challenge which affects human dignity itself.[187]

In regard to the tragedies of the Middle East, he returned to raising his voice annually.

Peace seems to have moved further away from the Middle East, since the peace process begun in Madrid in 1991 is practically at a standstill, when it is not altogether endangered by ambiguous or even violent incidents. My thoughts turn at this time to all those Israelis and Palestinians who in recent years had hoped that justice, security, peace, and a normal everyday life would finally dawn on this Holy Land. Today, what remains of this desire for peace? The principles of the Madrid conference and the guidelines of the 1993 Oslo meeting paved the way to peace. They still remain the only effective means of moving forward. There is no need at all to attempt other paths. . . . Not far from there, an entire population has become the victim of a constraint which puts it in hazardous conditions of survival. I refer to our brothers and sisters in Iraq, living under a pitiless embargo. In response to the appeals for help which unceasingly come to the Holy See, I must call upon the consciences of those who, in Iraq and elsewhere, put political, economic, or strategic considerations before the fundamental good of the people, and I ask them to show compassion. . . . We cannot pass over in silence the tragedy of the Kurdish peoples, which in these very days has drawn everyone's attention; the immediate demands of compassion towards refugees in extreme situations must not make us forget the quest of millions of their brothers and sisters who are also calling for secure and acceptable conditions of life.[188]

1998: The Encyclical on Faith and Reason

He carried out his pastoral visit in Cuba from January 21 through 26.

My visit to Cuba reminded me of my first visit to Poland in 1979. I wished for our brothers and sisters of that beautiful island that the fruits of this pilgrimage be similar to the fruits of that pilgrimage made in Poland. . . . In Havana's imposing José Martí Plaza, I saw an enormous picture depicting Christ, with the words: "Jesus Christ, I trust in you!" I gave thanks to God, because, precisely in that square named after the "revolution," there was a place for the One who brought the true revolution into the world, that of the love of God who frees man from evil and injustice and gives him peace and fullness of life.[189]

On July 7 the apostolic letter Dies Domini *(dated May 31) was promulgated.*

The rediscovery of Sunday is one of the urgent priorities in the life of the Christian community today. For many people, in fact, this day risks being considered and lived merely as the "weekend." But Sunday is quite different: it is the day of the week when the Church celebrates Christ's resurrection. It is the weekly Easter! That is why it is the "Lord's Day" par excellence, as its very name *domenica*, retained in Italian and other languages, recalls and which corresponds to the Latin *dies dominica* or *dies Domini*. In obedience to the third commandment, Sunday must be kept holy, above all by participation in Holy Mass. There was a time in traditionally Christian countries when this was made easier by the whole cultural context. Today, in order to remain faithful to Sunday practice, it is often necessary to go "against the tide."

Thus, a renewed consciousness of faith is necessary. Do not be afraid, dear friends, to open your time to Christ! Time given to him is not wasted; on the contrary, it is time gained for our humanity; it is time which fills our days with light and hope.[190]

On October 15 the encyclical Fides et Ratio *(dated September 14) was promulgated.*

This document deals with the relationship between faith and reason, a crucial theme for culture and for life itself, since faith and reason represent two different, but complementary ways to reach God. The way of reason leads, so to speak, from the world to God the Creator: it proceeds from investigation into the reality of the world to the search for its ultimate foundation. From a perception of the contingent nature of everything earthly, reason rises to the mystery of the One who is the origin and foundation of all things. In the knowledge of faith, on the other hand, the process is from God to the world: God wished to reveal himself in history, with a language and message that go well beyond that of creation. This revelation, by means of intrinsically connected words and deeds, is the event by which God reaches out to human beings and speaks to them, "in order to invite and receive them into his own company" (*Dei Verbum*, no. 2). It is an encounter which culminates in Christ, "the fullness of all Revelation" (ibid.). The "obedience of faith" must be given to God who reveals himself (ibid., no. 5). It is a commitment offered in complete freedom, that is, secure not only from external constraint but also from that blind fideism which feeds on emotions and is subject to every change of sentiment. Reason plays an important role in avoiding fideism, for it is called to discern the signs by which God made his revelation credible, so that man can accept it and fully adhere to it.[191]

On November 29 the bull Incarnationis Mysterium, *which announced the Great Jubilee Year 2000, was promulgated.*

The Great Jubilee of the Year 2000 is almost upon us. Ever since my first encyclical letter, *Redemptor Hominis*, I have looked toward this occasion with the sole purpose of preparing everyone to be docile to the working of the Spirit. The event will be celebrated simultaneously in Rome and in all the particular churches around the world, and it will have, as it were, two centers: on the one hand, the city where Providence chose to place the see of the Successor of Peter, and on the other hand, the Holy Land, where the Son of God was born as man, taking our flesh from a Virgin whose name was Mary (cf. Lk 1:27). . . . The period of the Jubilee introduces us to the vigorous language which the divine pedagogy of salvation uses to lead man to conversion and penance. These are the beginning and the path of man's healing, and the necessary condition for him to recover what he could never attain by his own strength: God's friendship and grace, the supernatural life which alone can fulfill the deepest aspirations of the human heart.[192]

> *At the end of the year the gaze of John Paul II turned toward Europe and Latin America, where there were signs of hope.*

I think especially of Ireland, where the agreement signed on last Good Friday has established the basis for a much-awaited peace, which must be founded on a stable social life, on mutual trust and the principle of equality before the law for all. Another reason for satisfaction for all of us is the peace process in Spain, which for the first time is enabling the peoples of the Basque territories to see the specter of blind violence retreat and to think seriously of a process of normalization. The transition to one currency and the enlargement towards the East will no doubt give Europe the possibility to become more and more a community with a common destiny, a true "European community"—this is in any case our dearest wish. This obviously presupposes that the member countries are able to reconcile their history with the same common project, so that they may all see themselves as equal partners, concerned only for the common good. . . . I would like to draw to your attention further grounds for satisfaction in relation to the American continent. I am referring to the agreement reached in Brasilia on last October 26 between Ecuador and Peru. Thanks to the persevering efforts of the international community—especially on the part of the guarantor countries—two sister nations had the courage to renounce violence, to accept a compromise, and to resolve their differences in a peaceful way. This is an example for so many other nations still bogged down in divisions and disagreements.[193]

Africa, instead, is a continent facing great difficulties.

Africa remains a continent at risk. Of its fifty-three states, seventeen are experiencing military conflicts, either internally or with other states. I am thinking in particular of Sudan where, in addition to a cruel war, a terrible human tragedy is unfolding; Eritrea and Ethiopia, which are once again in dispute; and Sierra Leone, where the people are still the victims of merciless struggles. On this great continent there are up to eight million refugees and displaced persons practically abandoned to their fate. The countries of the Great Lakes region still bear open wounds resulting from the excesses of ethnocentrism, and they are struggling amid poverty and insecurity; this is also the case in Rwanda and Burundi, where an embargo is further aggravating the situation. The Democratic Republic of Congo still has far to go in working out its transition and experiencing the stability to which its people legitimately aspire, as the massacres which recently occurred at the very beginning of the year near the town of Uvira testify. Angola remains in search of a peace which cannot be found and in these days is experiencing a development which causes great concern and which has not spared the Catholic Church.[194]

1999: The Opening of the Holy Door

From May 7 to 9 he carried out a pastoral visit in Romania.

These have been days of deep emotion, which I have intensely felt and which will be cherished in my heart. Let us accept the events we shared together as a gift from God's hand, confident that they will bear fruits of grace for Christians and for all the people of Romania. Your country has a unique ecumenical vocation stemming from its very roots. Because of its geographical location and long history, its culture and tradition, Romania in a way is a house where East and West meet in natural dialogue. The Church too breathes here with her two lungs in a particularly visible way, as we have seen in these days.[195]

June 5 through 17 found him on a pastoral visit in Poland.

My mind and heart are still filled with images of the places I visited, and especially of the throngs of compatriots and other faithful from various countries who gave me a moving welcome wherever I went. Memories and feelings of deep intensity come back to mind. How can I not thank the Lord for this great opportunity he gave me? Today I would especially like to offer him my gratitude.... It was an unforgettable experience of faith and brotherhood. "God is love" was the theme that marked this pilgrimage at every stage: only the Gospel of Love, the Gospel of the Beatitudes, can bring peace to hearts and make social relations tranquil and fruitful. Solidarity and peaceful understanding between individuals and peoples flow from God's love and from peace with him.[196]

With the apostolic letter Spes Aedificandi *of October 1, he proclaimed Saints Bridget of Sweden, Catherine of Siena, and Teresa Benedicta of the Cross (Saint Edith Stein) patronesses of Europe.*

The real reason then which led me to these three particular women can be found in their lives. Their holiness was demonstrated in historical circumstances and in geographical settings which make them especially significant for the continent of Europe. Saint Bridget brings us to the extreme north of Europe, where the continent in some way stretches out to unity with the other parts of the world; from there she departed to make Rome her destination. Catherine of Siena is likewise well known for the role which she played at a time when the Successor of Peter resided in Avignon; she brought to completion a spiritual work already initiated by Bridget by becoming the force behind the Pope's return to his own see at the tomb of the prince of the apostles. Finally, Teresa Benedicta of the Cross, recently canonized, not only lived in various countries of Europe, but by her entire life as thinker, mystic, and martyr, built a kind of bridge between her Jewish roots and her commitment to Christ, taking part in the dialogue with contemporary philosophical thought with sound intuition, and in the end forcefully proclaiming by her martyrdom the ways of God and man in the horrendous atrocity of the Shoah.[197]

From November 8 to 9 he carried out his pastoral visit in the Republic of Georgia.

Set between East and West, the Church in Georgia has always been open to contacts with other Christian peoples. At times, the bonds between the Georgian Church and the See of Rome have been deep and strong; and, though at other times there have been tensions, the awareness of our common Christian vocation has never faded completely. My presence among you now is a sign of how deeply the Catholic Church desires to foster communion with the Georgian Church.[198]

The evening of Christmas he opened the Great Jubilee Year of 2000.

During the Conclave, on October 16, 1978, after my election, the Primate of the Millennium (the Polish Cardinal Stefan Wyszyński) said to me: "now you must lead the Church into the third millennium."[199]

This year there is yet another reason which makes more holy this day of grace: it is the beginning of the Great Jubilee. Last night, before Holy Mass, I opened the Holy Door of the Vatican basilica. A symbolic act which inaugurates the Jubilee Year, a gesture which highlights with singular eloquence something already present in the mystery of Christmas: Jesus, born of Mary in the poverty of Bethlehem—he, the Eternal Son given to us by the Father, is, for us and for everyone, the Door! The Door of our salvation, the Door of life, the Door of peace! This is the message of Christmas and the proclamation of the Great Jubilee.[200]

A few days earlier, Pope Wojtyła had traced a quick synthesis of the recently concluded journey of preparation for the holy year.

Together with all the People of God throughout the world, in these years we have walked towards the Great Jubilee. Looking back at our journey so far, I feel it my duty to thank the Lord first of all for the Trinitarian inspiration which has marked it. From year to year, we have paused in contemplation before the persons of the Father, the Son, and the Holy Spirit. . . . Many projects have been started in the particular Churches in preparation for the Jubilee Year. On a universal level, the continental synods have been of great importance, and it is right to expect them to yield abundant fruit on the basis of the practical directives in their respective post-synodal apostolic exhortations.[201]

In his customary end of the year talk, he expanded upon the entire century.

The century just ended has seen remarkable advances in science which have considerably improved people's life and health. These advances have also contributed to our dominion over nature and made easier people's access to culture. Information technology has made the world smaller and brought us closer to one another. Never before were we so quickly informed about the daily events which affect the lives of our brothers and sisters in the human family. But one question can be asked: was this century also the century of "brotherhood"? Certainly an unqualified answer cannot be given. As the balance is made, the memory of bloody wars which have decimated millions of people and provoked massive exoduses, shameful genocides [xxxviii] which haunt our memories, as well as the arms race which fostered mistrust and fear, terrorism, and ethnic conflicts which annihilated peoples who had lived together in the same territory, all force us to be modest and in many cases to have a penitent spirit. The life sciences and biotechnology continue to find new fields of application, yet they also raise the problem of the limits imposed by the need to safeguard people's dignity, responsibility, and safety. Globalization, which has profoundly transformed economic systems by creating unexpected possibilities of growth, has also resulted in many people being relegated to the side of the road: unemployment in the more developed countries and extreme

---

[xxxviii] One of these genocides took place in Rwanda (April to June 1994) when at least 800,000 Tutsis and their sympathizers were massacred by the Hutus. Besides the Jewish Holocaust, other genocides in this century have taken place in Darfur, Armenia, Cambodia, and Bosnia.

poverty in too many countries of the Southern Hemisphere continue to hold millions of women and men back from progress and prosperity. For this reason it seems to me that the century now beginning ought to be the century of solidarity. We know one thing today more than in the past: we will never be happy and at peace without one another, much less if some are against others. . . . The men and women of the twenty-first century will be called to a more developed sense of responsibility. First, their personal responsibility, in fostering a sense of duty and honest labor: corruption, organized crime, or passivity can never lead to a true and healthy democracy. But there must also be an equal sense of responsibility toward others: an attitude of concern for the poor, participation in structures of mutual assistance in the workplace and in the social sphere, respect for nature and the environment—all these are required if we are to have a world where people live together in a better way. Never again must there be separation between people! Never again must some be opposed to others! Everyone must live together, under God's watchful eyes![202]

2000: Year of the Great Jubilee

On January 2 the Pope presided over the Jubilee for Children.

Dear children and young people! You have come to Rome from Italy and other countries in the world to form a friendship with Jesus, after the example of the young saints like Pancras and Tarcisius, who gave their lives to stay faithful to Christ! The effort and hardships that you had to face made you realize that following the Gospel requires sacrifice but fills one with joy. Have a good Jubilee! . . . At the beginning of a New Year, dear children and young people, we cannot forget all those of your own age who are suffering hunger or violence, and those who are victims of hideous forms of exploitation. How could we forget the many children who are denied even the right to be born? When people want to build a world ignoring God and his law, they are in fact giving rise to a situation of more and more suffering and injustice. With the Jubilee the Lord invites us to correct these wrongs by cooperating in the great plan he has for every person and for the whole human race.[203]

From February 24 to 26 he went on pilgrimage to Mount Sinai in Egypt.

I thank the Lord who, after the special commemoration of Abraham celebrated in the Paul VI Hall last Wednesday, enabled me in these days to make my intended pilgrimage to Egypt, the hospitable land which gave refuge to the Holy Family when fleeing from Herod, which has welcomed the Gospel since apostolic times, and which is heir to an ancient culture. . . . Now my thoughts turn to the principal goal of my pilgrimage, the ancient Monastery of Saint Catherine on Mount Sinai. There, in a simple but moving ceremony, I was able to commemorate both the moment when God spoke from the burning bush and revealed his name, "I Am," to Moses, and the moment when he made the Covenant with the People on the basis of the Decalogue. The fundamental norms of the natural law are reflected in the Ten Commandments. The Decalogue shows the way to a fully human life. Without it there is no calm or peaceful future for individuals, families, or nations.[204]

On March 12 he celebrated the Day of Pardon.

In the faith context of the Great Jubilee, today we are celebrating the Day of Pardon. This morning in Saint Peter's Basilica I presided at a moving and solemn penitential act. On this first Sunday of Lent, bishops and ecclesial communities in various parts of the world knelt before God, in the name of the entire Christian people, to implore his forgiveness. The Holy Year is a time of purification: the Church is holy because Christ is her Head and her Spouse; the Spirit is her life-giving soul; the Virgin Mary and the saints are her most authentic expression. However, the children of the Church know the experience of sin, whose shadows are cast over her, obscuring her beauty. For this reason the Church does not cease to implore God's forgiveness for the sins of her members. This is not a judgment on the subjective responsibility of our brothers and sisters who have gone before us: judgment belongs to God alone, who—unlike us human beings—"sees the heart and the mind" (cf. Jer 20:12). Today's act is a sincere recognition of the sins committed by the Church's children in the distant and recent past, and a humble plea for God's forgiveness. This will reawaken consciences, enabling Christians to enter the third millennium with greater openness to God and his plan of love.[205]

March 20 to 26 he went on pilgrimage to the Holy Land (Jordan, Independent Palestinian Territories, and Israel).

Following the path of salvation history, as narrated in the Apostles' Creed, my Jubilee Pilgrimage has brought me to the Holy Land. From Nazareth, where Jesus was conceived of the Virgin Mary by the power of the Holy Spirit, I have reached Jerusalem, where he "suffered under Pontius Pilate, was crucified, died, and was buried." Here, in the Church of the Holy Sepulcher, I kneel before the place of his burial: "Behold, the place where they laid him" (Mk 16:6). . . . . Here at the Holy Sepulcher and Golgotha, as we renew our profession of faith in the Risen Lord, can we doubt that in the power of the Spirit of Life we will be given the strength to overcome our divisions and to work together to build a future of reconciliation, unity, and peace? Here, as in no other place on earth, we hear the Lord say once again to his disciples: "Do not fear; I have overcome the world!" (cf. Jn 16:33).[206]

On April 30 he presided over the canonization ceremony of Sister Faustina Kowalska, the Apostle of Divine Mercy, who had been beatified on April 18, 1993.

Christ took upon himself the sins of us all (cf. Is 53:12), so as to make satisfaction for justice wounded by sin; in this way he maintained a balance between the justice and the mercy of the Father. It is significant that Sister Faustina saw this Son as the merciful God, yet she contemplated him not so much on the cross but rather in his subsequent state of risen glory. She thus linked her mystical sense of mercy with the mystery of Easter, in which Christ appears triumphant over sin and death (cf. Jn 20:19–23).

I have chosen here to speak of Sister Faustina and the devotion to the merciful Christ which she promoted, because she too belongs to our time. . . . The people of that time understood her message. They understood it in the light of the dramatic buildup of evil during the Second World War and the cruelty of the totalitarian systems. It was as if Christ had wanted to reveal that the limit imposed upon evil, of which man is both perpetrator and victim, is ultimately Divine Mercy. Of course, there is also justice, but this alone does not have the last word in the divine economy of world history and human history. God can always draw good from evil, he wills that all should be saved and come to knowledge of the truth (cf. 1 Tim 2:4); God is Love (cf. 1 Jn 4:8). Christ, crucified and raised, just as he appeared to Sister Faustina, is the supreme revelation of his truth.[207]

On May 1 he presided over the Jubilee for Workers.

The Jubilee offers a suitable opportunity to open our eyes to the poverty and marginalization, not only of individuals but also of groups and peoples. In the Bull of Indication [Proclamation] of the Jubilee I recalled that "some nations, especially the poorer ones, are oppressed by a debt so huge that repayment is practically impossible" (*Incarnationis Mysterium*, 12). To reduce or indeed to remit this debt: here is a Jubilee gesture which would be so desirable! This appeal is addressed to the rich and developed nations, but also to people of great wealth and to those who are in a position to foster solidarity among peoples. May it ring out at this historic encounter, at which Christian workers and nonconfessional labor organizations have united in a common effort. Workers, employers, collaborators, financiers, salespeople: join your arms, your minds, your hearts to contribute to the building of a society which respects man and his work. Man is more valuable for what he is than for what he has.[208]

On May 7 he presided at the ecumenical commemoration of the witnesses of the faith in the twentieth century.

The century just ended was marked by dark shadows, but bright lights shone in the midst of them. They are the many men and women, Christians of every denomination, race, and age who witnessed to the faith during harsh persecutions, in prison, amid privations of every kind; and many also shed their blood to remain faithful to Christ, to the Church, and to the Gospel. The light of Easter itself shines brightly in them: indeed, it is from Christ's resurrection that the disciples receive the strength to follow the Master in times of trial. This is why the commemoration is taking place in the liturgical season of Easter, on this third Sunday. And the place chosen speaks for itself: the Coliseum takes us back to the origins of Christianity, when so many early Christians bore their "beautiful witness" and became the seed of new believers. Remembering the heroic witnesses to the faith in the twentieth century means preparing the future and assuring it solid reasons for hope. The new generations must know the cost of the faith they have inherited if they are to receive the torch of the Gospel with gratitude and shed its light on the new century and the new millennium.[209]

In Rome on June 25 he presided at the Statio orbis [xxxix] *of the International Eucharistic Congress.*

Christ is the Bread of salvation for man, a wayfarer and pilgrim on earth. This is why on the feast of Corpus Christi the Eucharist is carried in procession through the streets, among the homes and buildings of daily life. In the Eucharistic mystery the Risen One, in fact, has wished to continue dwelling in our midst, so that every human being can know his true name, his true face, and experience his boundless mercy. We firmly believe that Christ is the only Savior of the world. He is the Mediator of the new and eternal Covenant (cf. Heb 9:15), which fulfilled the covenant God made on Sinai with the chosen people. It is a covenant open to all peoples, in view of the great eschatological banquet foretold by the prophets of Israel. In the light of this truth, the Church does not scorn what human beings do in their various religious expressions to approach God and to be purified by him; instead she encourages fruitful interreligious dialogue. At the same time, however, she cannot fail to state clearly that Christ is the only Redeemer, the Son of God, who became incarnate for us, died and rose again.[210]

[xxxix] *Statio orbis*, or station of the world, refers to the assembling of a large crowd of believers along with a large number of concelebrants for the celebration of the Eucharist.

On August 19 and 20 he presided over the Jubilee for Youth.

Dear friends, at the dawn of the third millennium I see in you the "morning watchmen" (cf. Is 21:11–12). In the course of the century now past young people like you were summoned to huge gatherings to learn the ways of hatred; they were sent to fight against one another. The various godless messianic systems which tried to take the place of Christian hope have shown themselves to be truly horrendous. Today you have come together to declare that in the new century you will not let yourselves be made into tools of violence and destruction; you will defend peace, paying the price in your person if need be. You will not resign yourselves to a world where other human beings die of hunger, remain illiterate, and have no work. You will defend life at every moment of its development; you will strive with all your strength to make this earth ever more livable for all people. Dear young people of the century now beginning, in saying yes to Christ, you say yes to all your noblest ideals.[211]

On October 14 and 15 he presided over the Jubilee for Families.

Dear friends, let us commit all our forces to defending the value of the family and respect for human life from the moment of conception. These are values which belong to the basic "grammar" of dialogue and human coexistence among peoples. I fervently hope that governments and national parliaments, international organizations, and, in particular, the United Nations organization will not lose sight of this truth. I ask all people of good will who believe in these values to join forces effectively so that the latter may prevail in daily life, in cultural trends and in the mass media, in political decisions and the laws of nations.[212]

At the end of these twelve months rich in Jubilee days for many diverse groups, John Paul II recounted how he himself had lived the Holy Year.

The Jubilee Year has also been for me a time in which I have felt Christ's presence more keenly. The work has been—as was foreseeable—heavier than usual, but with God's help everything has turned out for the best. Now, at the end of this special year, I would like to praise the Lord who has granted me to proclaim his name so widely, making the Apostle Paul's program fully my own: "What we preach is not ourselves, but Jesus Christ as Lord, with ourselves as your servants for Jesus' sake" (2 Cor 4:5).[213]

2001: The Attack of September 11

On January 6 Pope Wojtyła closed the Great Jubilee Year of 2000 and signed the post-jubilarian apostolic letter Novo Millennio Ineunte.

The Holy Door is about to be closed, but Christ whom it represents is "the same yesterday and today and for ever" (Heb 13:8). . . . It is in his name that we have lived this year of grace, during which so many energies have been mobilized within the Christian people, both at a universal level and in the particular churches. We have seen an enormous number of pilgrims flock here, to the center of Christianity, to the various basilicas and, especially, to the tomb of the Prince of the Apostles. Day after day, in the wonderful setting of Saint Peter's Square, they have offered ever new witnesses of faith and devotion, either participating in solemn public celebrations or moving in orderly recollection to the Holy Door. This year, Saint Peter's Square has been more than ever a "microcosm" in which the most varied human situations have come in close contact. Through the pilgrims from the different continents, the world in some way has come to Rome. From children to the elderly, from artists to sportspeople, from the disabled to families, from politicians to journalists, from bishops to priests and consecrated persons, so many people have met here, not only desiring to bring themselves to Christ, but also their work, their professional and cultural milieus, their daily life. Once again, I was able to proclaim Christ, Savior of the world and Redeemer of man, to each of these generally very large groups.[214]

From May 4 through 9 he carried out a pastoral visit in Greece, Syria, and Malta.

As my Jubilee pilgrimage comes to an end, I solemnly entrust to Almighty God's loving protection the peoples of the places I have visited. In the places linked to the two-thousandth anniversary of the Savior's birth I have hoped and prayed for a great renewal of faith among Christians. I have wished to encourage believers and all people of good will to defend life, to promote respect for the dignity of every human being, to safeguard the family against so many present-day threats, to open their hearts to the world's poor and exploited, and to work for an international order built on respect for the rule of law and on solidarity with the less fortunate.[215]

From June 23 through 27 he carried out a pastoral visit in Ukraine.

May the Lord give you peace, people of Ukraine, who with tenacious and harmonious dedication have at last recovered your freedom, and have begun the work of rediscovering your truest roots. You are committed to an arduous path of reforms aimed at giving everyone the possibility of following and practicing their own faith, culture, and convictions in a framework of freedom and justice. . . . Goodbye, my people and my friends, whom I embrace with sympathy and affection! Thank you for your heartfelt welcome and hospitality, which I shall never forget![216]

From September 22 through 27 he made a pastoral visit to Kazakhstan and Armenia.

Thank you, people of Armenia, for the warmth of your friendship, for the prayer we have shared, for your yearning for Christian unity. Thank you most of all for the witness of your faith, a faith you have not abandoned in dark times, a faith which remains deeply rooted in your families and in your national life. Throughout history, Mount Ararat has been a symbol of stability and a source of confidence for the Armenian people. Yet time and again that stability and confidence were sorely tested by violence and persecution. The Armenian people have paid dearly for their frontier existence, so much so that the words "holiness" and "martyrdom" have become almost identical in your vocabulary. The terrible events at the beginning of the last century which brought your people "to the brink of annihilation," the long years of totalitarian oppression, the devastation of a disastrous earthquake: none of these has been able to prevent the Armenian soul from regaining courage and recovering its great dignity.[217]

These three memorable days which have enabled me to meet so many people here in Astana and to experience at first hand the vitality of the Kazakh people are coming to an end. The memory of my stay in this noble country, rich in history and cultural traditions, will be with me for a long time. . . . The words which I have heard in the various moments we have spent together remain impressed on my mind. I hold dear the hopes and expectations of this dear people, which I have come to know and respect more deeply: a people that has suffered years of harsh persecution, but has not hesitated to commit itself with enthusiasm to the path of development. You are a people seeking to build a serene future for its children, marked by solidarity, because you love and seek peace.[218]

The tragic terrorist attack of September 11 on the United States, the armed reaction in Afghanistan, and the mounting tensions in the Holy Land were center stage at the end of this year.

In facing this situation, disciples of Christ, Prince of Peace (cf. Is 9:5) are called to proclaim with constancy that any form of terrorist violence dishonors God's holiness and human dignity and that religion can never become a motive for war, hatred, or oppression. I renew my pressing invitation to all people of good will to be unflagging in their efforts to find just solutions to the multiple conflicts that are tearing the world apart, and to assure a present and future of peace to one and all. . . . Before being a fruit of human efforts, however, true peace is a gift of God: in fact, Jesus Christ "is our peace, who has made us both one, and has broken down the dividing wall of hostility" (Eph 2:14). Since "fasting is the soul of prayer and mercy the life of fasting, these three things, prayer, fasting, and mercy, are a single thing, each drawing life from the others" (Saint Peter Chrysologus, *Discourse* 43, PL 52, 320), I suggested to the children of the Church a day of penance and solidarity to be celebrated last December 14.[219]

But John Paul II did not overlook the other tragedies in the world.

In the face of these outbreaks of irrational and unjustifiable violence, the great danger is that other situations will go unnoticed and leave whole peoples abandoned to their sad fate. I am thinking of Africa, and the health emergencies and armed struggles which are decimating its peoples. . . . And how can I fail to mention Latin America, which is always dear to me? In some countries of this great continent the persistence of social inequalities, drug trafficking, corruption, and armed violence can endanger the foundations of democracy and discredit the political class. Most recently, the difficult situation in Argentina[xl] has given rise to public unrest which has painfully affected people's lives. This is yet another reminder that political and economic activity at the national and international levels must always be inspired by the pursuit of the authentic good of individuals and peoples.[220]

2002: The Canonization of Padre Pio

On January 24 Pope John Paul II presided at the Day of Prayer for World Peace at Assisi.

I am still feeling intensely the emotion I experienced last Thursday on the Day of Prayer for Peace: "Violence never again! War never again! Terrorism never again! In the name of God, may every religion bring upon the earth justice and peace, forgiveness and life, and love!" This is the solemn appeal that, together with the leaders of various religions, I addressed to the men of our time, forcefully rejecting the temptation to resolve serious problems of humanity by using arms and violence. Thus we have placed another milestone on the road to building a civilization of peace and love.[221]

From May 22 through 26 he carried out a pastoral visit to Azerbaijan and Bulgaria.

I am pleased to reflect with you today on the apostolic journey I made to Azerbaijan and Bulgaria. It still lives very much in my heart.

[xl] The economic crisis in Argentina (1999–2001) led to civil unrest and the president's resignation and trial for corruption.

I give thanks first of all to the Lord who granted me the grace to undertake it. . . . The great religious traditions are part of the rich historical and cultural heritage of the Azeri people; for that reason it was important to meet in the country's capital, Baku, the representatives of politics, culture, art, and the religions. . . . My visit to Sofia, Bulgaria, coincided with the Feast of Saints Cyril and Methodius, the evangelizers of the Slavs, *Slavorum Apostoli*. From the beginning of its evangelization, a solid bridge has united the See of Peter with the Bulgar people. In the last century this bond was reinforced by the valuable service of the apostolic delegate at the time, Angelo Roncalli, Blessed John XXIII. . . . The high point of my brief but intense visit in Bulgaria was the Eucharistic celebration in the central square of Plovdiv, at which I declared "Blessed" Kamen Vitchev, Pavel Djidjov, and Josaphat Chichkov, Augustinian priests of the Assumption, shot in the prison of Sofia in 1952 by a firing squad, along with Bishop Eugene Bossilkov, beatified four years ago. These courageous witnesses to the faith, together with the other martyrs of the last century, prepare a new springtime for the Church in Bulgaria.[222]

On June 16 he presided over the canonization of Padre Pio Pietrelcina.

What is the secret of such great admiration and love for this new saint? He is first of all a "friar of the people," a traditional characteristic of the Capuchins. He is also a saint who is a miraculous healer, as the extraordinary events which are part of his life attest. However, above all Padre Pio is a religious who is deeply in love with the crucified Christ. He even shared physically in the mystery of the Cross during his life. [xli] . . . Padre Pio made his journey of demanding spiritual ascent in communion with the Church. The temporary misunderstandings he had with one or other ecclesial authority did not put a brake on his attitude of filial obedience. Padre Pio was a faithful and courageous son of the Church and in this situation following the shining example of the *Poverello* of Assisi. May this holy Capuchin to whom so many

---

[xli] Padre Pio received the stigmata, the bleeding wounds of Christ, on his hands, feet, and side on October 22, 1918. These signs of the Lord's passion continued on Padre Pio's body until a few days before his death in 1968.

people turn to from every corner of the earth point out to us the means to reach holiness which is the goal of our life as Christians.[223]

Padre Pio was a generous dispenser of divine mercy, making himself available to all by welcoming them, by spiritual direction and, especially, by the administration of the sacrament of Penance. I also had the privilege, during my young years, of benefiting from his availability for penitents.[224]

From July 23 through August 2 he traveled to Canada for World Youth Day, traveling on to Guatemala and Mexico.

Today I desire to return in thought to Toronto. The seventeenth World Youth Day brought together from every continent hundreds of thousands of young men and women who were received with warm friendliness by the people of Canada, a country characterized by a rich and varied humanism. On the banks of Lake Ontario young people relived the experience of the people of Galilee on the shores of the Lake of Tiberias when, having called to himself the crowds, Jesus entrusted to them the splendid and demanding "proclamation" of the Beatitudes. The young people gathered in Toronto realized that in Jesus' words they can find the response to the expectation of joy and hope that burns in their hearts. This answer is convincing, because Jesus did not restrict himself to proclaiming the Beatitudes, but lived them in the first person, even to the supreme gift of himself. . . . The Beatitudes are the Magna Carta of those who want to introduce into the world a new civilization. The young people understood this and set out from Canada, determined to place their trust in Christ, because they know that he "has the words of eternal life" (cf. Jn 6:68).[225]

From August 16 through 19 a pastoral visit was carried out in Poland.

Today I return in thought to the eighth journey to my native land, which happily Divine Providence allowed me to carry out in these last few days. "God, rich in mercy" (Eph 2:4): these words constantly resounded during my apostolic pilgrimage. Indeed, the main purpose of my visit was to proclaim once again God, "rich in mercy," especially by consecrating the new Shrine of Divine Mercy at Łagiewniki. The new church will be a center that will spread through the world the fire of God's mercy, according to what the Lord manifested to Saint Faustina Kowalska, apostle of Divine Mercy. "Jesus, I trust in you!" This is the simple prayer that Sister Faustina taught us, and which we can have on our lips at every moment of our lives. How often, as a worker, a student, and then as a priest and bishop, in the difficult periods of the history of Poland, I also repeated this simple and profound aspiration and experienced its efficacy and power. Mercy is one of the most wonderful attributes of the Creator and of the Redeemer; the Church lives to bring humanity to this inexhaustible wellspring, of which she is depository and dispenser. This is why I wished to entrust my homeland, the Church, and all humanity to the Divine Mercy.[226]

On October 16, with the apostolic letter Rosarium Virginis Mariae, *he proclaimed the Year of the Rosary (extending from October 2002 to October 2003) and added five mysteries from the "public life" of Jesus to this traditional Marian prayer.*

What great courage is imbued by the support of the unanimous prayer of the Christian people! I myself have been able to experience the comfort it brings. This, dear friends, is our strength. And it is one of the reasons why I wanted the twenty-fifth year of my pontificate to be dedicated to the holy rosary: to emphasize the primacy of prayer, and especially of contemplative prayer, prayed in spiritual union with Mary, Mother of the Church.[227]

On November 11 he received four thousand pilgrims from the Polish Solidarity Union in Paul VI Hall; this was the anniversary of Poland's regaining of national freedom.

Recalling the date of November 11 cannot fail to remind me of the national freedom the Republic of Poland regained that day after years of strife which cost our nation so much deprivation and so many sacrifices. This external freedom was short lived, but we have always been able to appeal to it in the fight to preserve our inner, spiritual freedom. . . . I thank God for the year 1979. In that year the sense of unity for good and the common desire for prosperity of the oppressed nation overcame hatred and the desire for revenge and became the seed of a democratic state. Yes, there were attempts to destroy this work. We all remember December 13, 1981.[xlii] We managed to survive those trials.[228]

His assessment of the year 2002 seemed particularly forceful, yet it still opened to a sense of hope.

I have been struck by the feeling of fear which often dwells in the hearts of our contemporaries. An insidious terrorism capable of striking at any time and anywhere; the unresolved problem of the Middle East, with the Holy Land and Iraq; the turmoil disrupting South America, particularly Argentina, Colombia, and Venezuela; the conflicts preventing numerous African countries from focusing on their development; the diseases spreading contagion and death; the grave problem of famine, especially in Africa; the irresponsible behavior contributing to the depletion of the planet's resources: all these are so many plagues threatening the survival of humanity, the peace of individuals, and the security of societies. Yet everything can change. It depends on each of us. Everyone can develop within himself his potential for faith, for honesty, for respect of others, and for commitment to the service of others.[229]

2003: Pontifical Jubilee and Mother Teresa

On March 5 the Pope presided at a day of prayer and fasting for peace.

I wanted this Ash Wednesday to be a day of prayer and fasting to implore peace for the world. We must ask God, first of all, for a conversion of heart, for it is in the heart that every form of evil, every impulse to sin is rooted; we must pray and fast for the peaceful coexistence of peoples and nations.[230]

With news of the imminent conflict in Iraq, on March 16 the Holy Father offered an urgent appeal and a heartfelt remembrance during his Sunday Angelus message.

---

xlii On December 13, 1981, General Wojciech Jaruzelski declared martial law in Poland and outlawed the Solidarity movement.

The political leaders of Baghdad certainly have the urgent duty to collaborate fully with the international community to eliminate every reason for armed intervention. . . . But I would also like to remind the member countries of the United Nations, and especially those who make up the Security Council, that the use of force represents the last recourse, after having exhausted every other peaceful solution. . . . I belong to that generation that endured World War II and, thanks be to God, survived it. I have the duty to say to all young people, to those who are younger than I, who have not had this experience: "No more war," as Paul VI said during his first visit to the United Nations. We must do everything possible. We know well that peace is not possible at any price. But we all know how great our responsibility is. Therefore we need prayer and penance.[231]

The tragic events in Iraq were the motivation for his announcement of a new pilgrimage.

Yesterday we celebrated the solemnity of the Annunciation, the first of the "joyful mysteries" that celebrate the incarnation of the Son of God, Prince of Peace. As we prayed the rosary, we meditated on this mystery, with our hearts oppressed by the news we are receiving from Iraq, which is at war, without forgetting the other conflicts that rage around the globe. How important it is, during this year of the rosary, that we persevere in reciting the rosary to ask for peace! I ask that it be continually recited, especially at the Marian shrines. To Mary, Queen of the Rosary, I now entrust my resolution to make a pilgrimage to her shrine at Pompeii, next October 7, for the Feast of Our Lady of the Rosary.[232]

On April 17 the encyclical Ecclesia de Eucharistia *was promulgated.*

From the time I began my ministry as the Successor of Peter, I have always marked Holy Thursday, the day of the Eucharist and of the priesthood, by sending a letter to all the priests of the world. This year, the twenty-fifth of my pontificate, I wish to involve the whole Church more fully in this Eucharistic reflection, also as a way of thanking the Lord for the gift of the Eucharist and the priesthood: "Gift and

Mystery." By proclaiming the Year of the Rosary, I wished to put this, my twenty-fifth anniversary, under the sign of the contemplation of Christ at the school of Mary. Consequently, I cannot let this Holy Thursday 2003 pass without pausing before the "Eucharistic face" of Christ and pointing out with new emphasis to the Church the centrality of the Eucharist. From this Eucharist the Church draws her life. From this "living bread" she draws her nourishment. How could I not feel the need to urge everyone to experience it ever anew?[233]

From June 5 through 9 he went to Croatia; it marked his one hundredth international trip.

The hundredth journey which I have just completed gives me the opportunity to renew my heartfelt thanks to Divine Providence who has granted me to accomplish this important pastoral project. . . . On all these journeys I have truly felt like a pilgrim on a visit to that special shrine which is the People of God. In this shrine I have been able to contemplate the face of Christ, at times disfigured on the cross and at others, shining with light as on Easter morning. . . . The great, colorful assemblies of the People of God gathered for the celebration of the Eucharist remain stamped on my mind and heart as the highlights of my visits.[234]

He traveled to Banja Luka (Bosnia and Herzegovina) on June 22 for a pastoral visit.

To you, the beloved sons and daughters of this pilgrim church in Bosnia-Herzegovina, I open wide my arms in order to embrace you and tell you that you occupy an important place in the Pope's heart. He constantly brings before the Lord in prayer the sufferings which still burden your journey, and he shares with you in hope the expectation of better days. From this city, marked in the course of history by so much suffering and bloodshed, I ask Almighty God to have mercy on the sins committed against humanity, human dignity, and freedom also by children of the Catholic Church, and to foster in all the desire for mutual forgiveness. Only in a climate of true reconciliation will the memory of so many innocent victims and their sacrifice not be in vain, but encourage everyone to build new relationships of fraternity and understanding.[235]

June 25 commemorated the fortieth anniversary of the election of Cardinal Giovanni Battista Montini to the pontificate as Pope Paul VI.

I also had the grace to participate in the Council and to live in the post-conciliar period. I personally appreciated the efforts that Paul VI unceasingly made to unfold the necessity of an "updating" of the Church to meet the demands of the new evangelization. Succeeding him in the Chair of Peter, I undertook to continue the pastoral action he initiated, taking my inspiration from him as a father and a teacher.[236]

On June 28 he signed the apostolic exhortation Ecclesia in Europa.

The Good News has been and continues to be a source of life for Europe. It is true that Christianity cannot be restricted to any particular culture, but dialogues with every culture, to help all cultures to express their best qualities in every field of knowledge and human action. The Christian roots of Europe are the main guarantee of its future. Can a tree that has no roots grow and develop? Europe, do not forget your history![237]

From September 11 through 14 he carried out a pastoral visit in Slovakia.

Faithful to Christ and to the Church: this is the characteristic that Slovakia has presented throughout its history. By going there in person, I wanted to strengthen Slovakia in this fidelity as it starts out confidently towards the future. I admired with pleasure the economic and social development that has been achieved in recent years. I am sure that the Slovak people, on entering the European Union, will also know how to make their own effective contribution to building Europe at the level of values. Thank God, in fact, they possess a rich spiritual heritage which, despite the harsh persecution of the past, they have been able to keep intact. An eloquent proof of this is found there today, a promising growth of Christian life and of vocations to the priesthood and to the religious life. I pray that this beloved nation will continue confidently in this direction.[238]

On October 7 he traveled in pilgrimage to Pompeii and the Sanctuary of the Virgin of the Rosary.

I wanted my pilgrimage to have the meaning of a plea for peace. We have meditated upon the Mysteries of Light as if to turn the beam of Christ's light on the conflicts, tensions, and dramas of all five continents. In my apostolic letter *Rosarium Virginis Mariae*, I explained why the rosary is a prayer that by its very nature is oriented to peace. This is not only because it disposes us to pray for peace, strengthened by the intercession of Mary, but also because it enables us to assimilate Jesus' plan of peace, together with his mystery. At the same time, with the tranquil rhythm of the repetition of the Hail Mary, the rosary calms our spirit and opens it to saving grace.[239]

With the month of October, the Year of the Rosary comes to an end. I am deeply grateful to God for this period of grace, in which the entire ecclesial community has been able to deepen the value and importance of the rosary as christological and contemplative prayer. "To contemplate with Mary the face of Christ" (*Rosarium Virginis Mariae*, no. 3). These recurring words have become, as it were, the "motto" of the Year of the Rosary. They sum up the authentic meaning of this prayer that is both simple and profound. At the same time, they emphasize the continuity between what the rosary proposes and the path pointed out to the People of God in my previous apostolic letter, *Novo Millennio Ineunte*.[240]

In Saint Peter's Square on October 16 he presided at the solemn commemoration of his twenty-fifth anniversary of election to the pontificate.

Today, dear brothers and sisters, I am pleased to share with you an experience that has now lasted for a quarter of a century. Every day that same dialogue between Jesus and Peter takes place in my heart. In spirit, I focus on the benevolent gaze of the risen Christ. Although he knows of my human frailty, he encourages me to answer confidently, like Peter: "Lord, you know everything; you know that I love you" (Jn 21:17). And then he invites me to take on the responsibilities that he himself has entrusted to me.[241]

"You are the Christ, the Son of the living God" (Mt 16:16). How often have I repeated these words in the twenty-five years of my pontificate! I have spoken them in the main languages of the world and in many corners of the earth. Indeed, the Successor of Peter can never forget the dialogue between the Teacher and the apostle: "You are the Christ. . . ." "You are Peter. . . ." This "you" is preceded by "you" [the plural form]: "Who do you say that I am?" (Mt 16:15). Jesus' question is addressed to the group of disciples, and Simon Peter responds on behalf of them all. The first service that Peter and his successors render to the community of believers is exactly this: the profession of faith in "Christ, the Son of the living God."[242]

> To you, Lord Jesus Christ,
> the only Shepherd of the Church,
> I offer the fruit of these twenty-five years of ministry
> at the service of the people you have entrusted to my care.
> Forgive the evil done and multiply the good:
> All is your work and to you alone belongs the glory.
> With full confidence in your mercy
> I commend to you, again today, those whom years ago
> you entrusted to my pastoral care.
> Keep them in love, gather them into your sheepfold,
> take the weak upon your shoulders,
> bind up the wounded, care for the strong.
> Be their Shepherd, so that they do not scatter.
>
> Protect the beloved Church of Rome
> and the churches of the entire world.
> Fill with the light and power of your Spirit
> those you have chosen to guide your flock:
> May they fulfill their mission
> as guides, teachers, and sanctifiers with enthusiasm,
> while they await your glorious return.

I renew, through the hands of beloved Mother Mary,
the gift of myself to you; of the present and of the future:
May all be done according to your will.[243]

On October 16 he signed the apostolic exhortation Pastores Gregis, *on the bishop, servant of the Gospel of Jesus Christ.*

I well know the multiple tasks that the Lord has entrusted to us. The office to which we are called is a difficult and serious one. Where will we find the strength to carry it out in accordance with Christ's wishes? Without doubt, we find it in him alone. Today, being pastors of his flock is particularly fatiguing and demanding; nevertheless, we must have faith *contra spem in spem*, hoping against hope (Rom 4:18). Christ walks with us and sustains us with his grace.[244]

In Saint Peter's Square on October 19 he presided over the ceremony of the beatification of Mother Teresa of Calcutta, foundress of the Missionaries of Charity.

I am personally grateful to this courageous woman whom I have always felt beside me. Mother Teresa, an icon of the Good Samaritan, went everywhere to serve Christ in the poorest of the poor. Not even conflict and war could stand in her way. Every now and then she would come and tell me about her experiences in her service to the gospel values.... With particular emotion we remember today Mother Teresa, a great servant of the poor, of the Church, and of the whole world. Her life is a testimony to the dignity and the privilege of humble service. She had chosen to be not just the least but to be the servant of the least. As a real mother to the poor, she bent down to those suffering various forms of poverty. Her greatness lies in her ability to give without counting the cost, to give "until it hurts." Her life was a radical living and a bold proclamation of the Gospel.[245]

At the same time, two great feasts were celebrated, his twenty-fifth pontifical anniversary and his forty-fifth episcopal anniversary.

Since 1958, there are already forty-five years of episcopate: that is enough! [...] Of these forty-five years, I spent twenty at Kraków, first as an auxiliary, then as vicar capitular [temporary administrator], then as metropolitan archbishop and cardinal; but twenty-five years in Rome! So by these calculations you see that I have become more Roman than "Krakóvian." But all of this is Providence.[246]

There is only one remedy for old age: it is Jesus, who is the resurrection and the life. This means that, despite old age and death, there can always be youthfulness of spirit.[247]

I would like to thank the Holy Spirit for the gift of the sacrament of the priesthood and the episcopacy, and I ceaselessly pray the Spirit to help me be faithful to it until death. . . . I renew before Christ the offer of my readiness to serve the Church as long as he wants, in total abandonment to his holy will. I leave to him the decision as to how and when he will relieve me of this service. I do not cease to invoke the intercession of Mary, Mother of Christ and our Mother and Queen— she has been my guide from my earliest years. It is to her, Mother of the Church, that I desire to entrust, in a particular way, my whole life and my service to the universal Church today and in the future.[248]

In the Christmas message, Urbi et Orbi, he burst out in one of the most heartfelt appeals of his entire pontificate.

By being born in Bethlehem, the eternal Son of God has entered into the history of each person living on the face of the earth. He is now present in the world as the one Savior of humanity. This is why we pray to him: *Savior of the world, save us!* Save us from the great evils which tear at humanity in these first years of the third millennium. Save us from the wars and armed conflicts which lay waste to whole areas of the world, from the scourge of terrorism, and from the many forms of violence which assail the weak and the vulnerable. Save us from discouragement as we set out on the paths to peace, difficult paths indeed, yet possible and therefore necessary; paths which are always and everywhere urgent, especially in the land where you were born, the Prince of Peace.[249]

2004: Gifts to Aleksy and Bartholomew

Taking his cue from the first apostolic nuncio murdered in office, Archbishop Michael Aidan Courtney (killed in Burundi on December 29, 2003), and from the massacre in the general quarters of the United Nations in Bagdad (August 19, 2003), the Pope expressed a clear condemnation of terrorism.

I would like to pay a special tribute this morning to Archbishop Michael Courtney, apostolic nuncio in Burundi, who was recently assassinated. Like all nuncios and diplomats, he wanted to serve above all the cause of peace and dialogue. I praise his courage and his concern to support the Burundian people in their journey toward peace and greater brotherhood, in the name of his episcopal ministry and his diplomatic task. I would also like to remember Mr. Sergio Veira de Mello, special representative of the United Nations in Iraq, who was killed in an attack while fulfilling his mission. I would like to mention further all the members of the diplomatic corps who have lost their lives in recent years or who have been made to suffer on account of their mandate. And how can I fail to mention the international terrorism which by sowing fear, hate, and fanaticism disgraces all the causes that it claims to serve? I shall merely say that every civilization worthy of the name presupposes the categorical rejection of violence.[250]

On March 11 a terrorist attack in the railroad station of Atocha in Madrid caused the death of 201 people and injured fourteen hundred. Also in the Middle East the continued violence produced more victims among the faithful due to the strained relationships among the three monotheistic religions.

The atrocious crime [in Madrid] stunned world public opinion. We are deeply distressed at such barbarity and wonder how the human soul can go so far as to conceive such detestable crimes. In reasserting my total condemnation of these unjustifiable acts, I once again express my participation in the grief of the victims' relatives and my closeness in prayer to the injured and their families. The wave of solidarity witnessed in every corner of Spain last Friday, with the participation of the political authorities of all Europe, caused a great reverberation through-out the world. It is precisely by relying on the united contribution of all the healthy forces of the continent that it is possible to look ahead with confidence and hope for a better future.[251]

The history of relations between Jews, Christians, and Muslims is marked by patches of light and shadow and has unfortunately known some painful moments. Today we are aware of the pressing need for sincere reconciliation among believers in the one God. . . . The unani-mous hope that we express is that people may be purified of the hatred and evil that threaten peace continuously, and be able to extend to one another hands that have never been stained by violence, but are ready to offer help and comfort to those in need. Jews honor the Almighty as protector of the human person and the God of the promises of life. Christians know that love is the reason why God enters into relations with human beings and that love is the response he demands of them. For Muslims, God is good and can fill the believer with his mercies. Nourished by these convictions, Jews, Christians, and Muslims cannot accept that the earth must be afflicted by hatred or that humanity be overwhelmed by endless wars. Yes! We must find within us the courage for peace. We must implore from on high the gift of peace. And this peace will spread like a soothing balm if we travel nonstop on the road to reconciliation.[252]

In a general audience on March 24, he once again entrusted the Church and the world to Mary.

I am thinking back to several significant moments at the beginning of my pontificate: to December 8, 1978, when I entrusted the Church and the world to Our Lady at Saint Mary Major's; and to June 4 of the following year, when I renewed this consecration at the Shrine of Jasna Góra. I am thinking in particular of March 25, 1984, the Holy Year of the Redemption. Twenty years have passed since that day in Saint Peter's Square when, spiritually united with all the bishops of the world who had been brought together beforehand, I wanted to entrust all humanity to the Immaculate Heart of Mary in response to what Our Lady asked at Fatima. Humanity was then going through difficult times that were giving rise to deep distress and uncertainty. Twenty years later, the world is still frighteningly streaked by hatred, violence, terrorism, and war. . . . The expectation of justice and peace in every part of the earth is always growing greater. How can we respond to this thirst for hope and love other than by turning to Christ through Mary? I also repeat to the Blessed Virgin today the plea I made to her then. *"Mother of Christ, let there be revealed, once more, in the history of the world the infinite saving power of the Redemption: the power of merciful Love! May it put a stop to evil! May it transform consciences! May your Immaculate Heart reveal for all the light of hope!"* [253]

On June 5 and 6 he went to Bern for the encounter of young Catholics of Switzerland.

The main reason for my apostolic pilgrimage to that beloved nation was to encounter the young Catholics of Switzerland, who held their first national meeting last Saturday. I thank the Lord who gave me the opportunity to spend moments of great spiritual enthusiasm with them, and to address a message to the new Swiss generations which I would like to extend to all the young people in Europe and across the world. I can sum up this message, so dear to my heart, in three verbs: "Arise!" "Listen!" and "Set out!" It is Christ himself, risen and alive, who repeats these words to every young man and woman of our time. [254]

On June 10 he announced the celebration of a special Eucharistic Year.

It will begin with the World Eucharistic Congress, planned to take place from October 10 to 17, 2004, in Guadalajara, Mexico, and will end with the next ordinary assembly of the Synod of Bishops, that will be held in the Vatican from October 2 to 29, 2005, and whose theme will be: "The Eucharist: source and summit of the life and mission of the Church." Through the Eucharist, the ecclesial community is built up as a new Jerusalem, a principle of unity in Christ among different persons and peoples. [255]

After the adoption of the new European Constitution, the Holy See expressed sorrow due to the opposition of some governments that failed to recognize the Christian roots of Europe. The Pope did not hesitate to express his judgments.

One does not cut away the roots from which one has grown.[256] I am thinking of a Europe whose unity is based on true freedom, whose precious fruits of freedom of religion and social freedoms have matured in the *humus*, the soil of Christianity. Without freedom there is no responsibility, either before God or before men and women. . . . The Europe I have in mind is a political, indeed, a spiritual unit in which Christian politicians of all countries act with an awareness of the human riches that faith brings: men and women who are committed to making these values fruitful, putting themselves at the service of all for a Europe centered on the human person on which shines the face of God. This is the dream I carry in my heart.[257]

> *On August 14 and 15 he went on a pilgrimage to Lourdes in view of the one hundred fiftieth anniversary of the proclamation of the dogma of the Immaculate Conception of Mary.*

Kneeling here, before the grotto of Massabielle, I feel deeply that I have reached the goal of my pilgrimage. This cave, where Mary appeared, is the heart of Lourdes. Here the Blessed Virgin asked Bernadette to recite the rosary, as she herself told the beads. This grotto has thus become a unique school of prayer where Mary teaches everyone to gaze with burning love upon the face of Christ. Lourdes is the place, then, where the Christians of France, and those from so many other nations of Europe and the world, kneel and pray. As pilgrims to Lourdes, we too wish this evening to retrace in prayer, together with Mary our Mother, the "mysteries" in which Jesus reveals that he is the "light of the world."[258]

On December 8, 1854, one hundred and fifty years ago, Blessed Pius IX proclaimed the dogma of the Immaculate Conception of the Blessed Virgin. The privilege of being preserved free from original sin means that she was the first to be redeemed by her Son. Her sublime beauty, which mirrors that of Christ, is for all believers a pledge of the victory of divine grace over sin and death. The Immaculate Conception shines like a beacon of light for humanity in all the ages. At the beginning of the third millennium, she guides us to believe and hope in God, in his salvation and in eternal life. In particular, she lights the way for the Church, which is committed to the new evangelization.[259]

On August 25 in Paul VI Hall the Pope presided at the celebration of the Word and the commissioning of a Vatican delegation to return the icon of the Theotokos of Kazan to Patriarch Aleksy II of the Russian Orthodox Church.

After passing through various countries and staying a long time at the Shrine of Fatima in Portugal, the icon providentially arrived here more than ten years ago. Since then, it has found a home with me and has accompanied my daily service to the Church with its motherly gaze. How often since that day have I called on the Mother of God of Kazan, asking her to protect and guide the Russian people who venerate her, and to hasten the moment when all the disciples of her Son, recognizing one another as brothers and sisters, will be able to fully restore our interrupted unity. From the very first, I wanted this holy icon to return to its own land of Russia, where, according to reliable historical accounts, it was for a great many years the object of profound veneration on the part of entire generations of the faithful.[260]

On September 5 he went to Loreto for the ceremony of the beatification of the Spanish priest Pere Tarrés i Claret and of the Italian laypersons Alberto Marvelli and Pina Suriano in the presence of three hundred thousand members of Catholic Action.

Today, through the beatification of these three Servants of God, the Lord is saying to you: the greatest gift you can make to the Church and to the world is holiness. May you have at heart what the Church has at heart: that numerous men and women of our time be won over by fascination for Christ; may his Gospel shine once more as a light of hope for the poor, the sick, those who hunger for justice; may Christian communities be ever more lively, open, and attractive; may our cities be hospitable and provide livelihood for all; may humanity follow the paths of peace and brotherhood. It is up to you laypeople to witness to the faith through your own specific virtues: fidelity and gentleness in the family, competence at work, tenacity in serving the common good, solidarity in social relations, creativity in doing useful deeds for evangelization, and human promotion. It is also up to you, in close communion with the pastors, to show that the

Gospel is timely and that faith does not tear the believer from history but roots him more deeply in it.[261]

On November 27 he presided over the ecumenical celebration for entrust-ing the relics of Saints Gregory of Nazienzen and John Chrysostom to the ecumenical patriarch of Constantinople, Bartholomew I.

In the transfer of such holy relics we find a blessed occasion to heal our memories in order to strengthen our journey of reconciliation, to confirm that the faith of these holy doctors is the faith of the Churches of East and West. We also see this as a favorable moment to "show in word and deed today the immense riches that our Churches preserve in the coffers of their traditions" (*Orientale Lumen*, no. 4). This is the "acceptable time" to join our prayer to their intercession, so that the Lord will hasten the arrival of the moment when we can live full communion together in the celebration of the Holy Eucharist, and thus to work more effectively together so that the world will believe that Jesus Christ is Lord.[262]

The Pope made clear reference to the many tragedies that occurred in 2004 in different parts of the world.

The enormous catastrophe[xliii] which on December 26 struck different countries of Southeast Asia and as far as the coasts of East Africa made for a painful ending of the year just past. A year troubled also by other natural calamities, such as the devastating cyclones in the Indian Ocean and the Antilles, and the plague of locusts which desolated vast regions of Northwest Africa. Other tragedies also cast a shadow on 2004, like the acts of barbarous terrorism which caused bloodshed in Iraq and other countries of the world, the savage attack in Madrid, the terrorist massacre [at a school] in Beslan, the inhuman acts of violence inflicted on the people of Darfur, the atrocities perpetrated in the Great Lakes region of Africa. These events have caused great anguish and distress, and we would feel a tragic concern

---

[xliii] The Indian Ocean tsunami of 2004 caused by a 9.1 magnitude underwater earthquake left 300,000 dead in Thailand, Indonesia, Sri Lanka, India, and surrounding countries.

for the future of humanity were it not for the fact that from the cradle of Bethlehem there comes to us a message, both divine and human, of life and more certain hope.[263]

2005: Always *Totus Tuus*

On February 13 the seer of Fatima, Sister Lúcia, died at the age of ninety-seven.

The visit of the Virgin Mary which Lúcia, as a little girl, received at Fatima in 1917 together with her cousins Francisco and Jacinta was the beginning of a unique mission to which she remained faithful to the end of her days. . . . I recall with emotion my several meetings with her and the bonds of our spiritual friendship that grew stronger with the passage of time. I have always felt supported by the daily gift of her prayers, especially during the most difficult moments of trial and suffering. . . . I like to think that it was the Blessed Virgin, the same one whom Sister Lúcia saw at Fatima so many years ago, who welcomed her on her pious departure from earth to heaven.[264]

On February 22 the founder of Communion and Liberation, Monsignor Luigi Giussani, died.

I had various opportunities to meet Monsignor Luigi Giussani, and I admired his ardent faith. He expressed this in a Christian witness that was especially inspiring among the youth. It led them to an extensive and convinced acceptance of the Gospel message. I thank the Lord for the gift of his life, spent without reserve in consistently following his priestly vocation, in listening constantly to the needs of his contemporaries, and in courageous service to the Church.[265]

He was again brought to Gemelli Hospital on February 24 due to a relapse from the influenza he had suffered the preceding week. An emergency tracheotomy was performed to resolve an acute attack of respiratory distress. Waking up from the anesthesia, he scribbled a few words on a piece of paper:

But I am always *Totus tuus.*[266]

On March 25, Good Friday, he sent a message on the occasion of the traditional Way of the Cross at the Coliseum. The meditations had been composed by Cardinal Joseph Ratzinger.

The adoration of the Cross directs us to a commitment that we cannot shirk: the mission that Saint Paul expressed in these words: "In my flesh I complete what is lacking in Christ's afflictions for the sake of his body, that is, the Church" (Col 1:24). I also offer my sufferings so that God's plan may be completed and his Word spread among the peoples. I, in turn, am close to all who are tried by suffering at this time. I pray for each one of them.[267]

John Paul II died at 9:37 P.M. on April 2, 2005. For the prayer Regina Caeli on April 3 he had prepared this last message:

Dear Brothers and Sisters,

Today the glorious Alleluia of Easter resounds. Today's Gospel from John emphasizes that on the evening of that day he appeared to the apostles and "showed them his hands and his side" (Jn 20:20), that is he showed them the signs of the painful passion with which his body was indelibly stamped, even after his resurrection. Those glorious wounds, which he allowed doubting Thomas to touch eight days later, reveal the mercy of God who "so loved the world that he gave his only Son" (Jn 3:16).

This mystery of love is at the heart of the liturgy today, the second Sunday of Easter, dedicated to the devotion of Divine Mercy.

As a gift to humanity, which sometimes seems bewildered and overwhelmed by the power of evil, selfishness, and fear, the Risen Lord offers his love that pardons, reconciles, and reopens hearts to love. It is a love that converts hearts and gives peace. How much the world needs to understand and accept Divine Mercy!

Lord, who revealed the Father's love by your death and resurrection, we believe in you and confidently repeat to you today: Jesus, I trust in you, have mercy upon us and upon the whole world.

The liturgical solemnity of the Annunciation that we will be celebrating tomorrow urges us to contemplate with Mary's eyes the immense mystery of this merciful love that flows from the Heart of Christ. With her help, we will be able to understand the true meaning of Easter joy that is based on this certainty: the One whom the Virgin bore in her womb, who suffered and died for us, is truly risen. Alleluia![268]

On the afternoon of April 4, after the first viewing in the Clementine Hall, the body of Pope Wojtyła was transferred into the Vatican Basilica. In the morning of April 8, he was carried to Saint Peter's Square for the solemn funeral, presided over by Cardinal Joseph Ratzinger who, on the afternoon of April 19 would come forward as Pope from the Conclave that was opened the previous day, taking the name of Benedict XVI.

The very young Professor Ratzinger accompanied Cardinal Joseph Frings, archbishop of Cologne, to the Council [Vatican II], as a theological expert. He then was nominated the archbishop of Munich by Pope Paul VI, who also made him a cardinal, and he participated in the Conclave that entrusted the Petrine ministry to me. When Cardinal Franjo Šeper died, I asked Ratzinger to succeed him as prefect of the Congregation for the Doctrine of the Faith. I thank God for the presence and the help of Cardinal Ratzinger, who is a trusted friend.[269]

The feeling was totally reciprocated, as was witnessed in the affectionate expressions pronounced by Cardinal Ratzinger at the conclusion of his homily for the funeral.

None of us can ever forget how in that last Easter Sunday of his life, the Holy Father, marked by suffering, came once more to the window of the apostolic palace and one last time gave his blessing *Urbi et Orbi*. We can be sure that our beloved Pope is standing today at the window of the Father's house, that he sees us and blesses us. Yes, bless us, Holy Father. We entrust your dear soul to the Mother of God, your Mother, who guided you each day and who will guide you now to the eternal glory of her Son, our Lord Jesus Christ.[270]

Beginning from March 6, 1979—and with updates always made during the course of his annual Lenten spiritual exercises of March 1, 1980;

March 5, 1982; March 1, 1985; March 5, 1990; and March 17, 2000—
John Paul II expressed his last will in a rich testament of faith and
spirituality. These are some significant passages:

Totus tuus ego sum.
In the Name of the Most Holy Trinity, Amen.

"Watch, therefore, for you do not know on what day your Lord is coming" (Mt 24:42)—these words remind me of the last call that will come at whatever time the Lord desires. I want to follow him and I want all that is part of my earthly life to prepare me for this moment. I do not know when it will come but I place this moment, like all other things, in the hands of the Mother of my Master: *Totus tuus*. In these same motherly hands I leave everything and everyone with whom my life and my vocation have brought me into contact. In these hands I above all leave the Church, and also my homeland and all humankind. I thank everyone. I ask forgiveness of everyone. I also ask for prayers, so that God's mercy may prove greater than my own weakness and unworthiness.

During the spiritual exercises I reread the Testament of the Holy Father Paul VI. It was reading it that gave me the incentive to write this Testament.

I leave no possessions of which it will be necessary to dispose. As for the things I use every day, I ask that they be distributed as seems appropriate. Let my personal notes be burned. I ask that Father Stanisław see to this, and I thank him for his help and collaboration, so understanding, for so many years. On the other hand, I leave all my other thank yous in my heart before God himself, because it is difficult to express them.[271]

Today, I would like to add just this: that everyone keep the prospect of death in mind and be ready to go before the Lord and Judge—at the same time Redeemer and Father. So I keep this continuously in my mind, entrusting that decisive moment to the Mother of Christ and of the Church—to the Mother of my hope.

The times we are living in are unspeakably difficult and disturbing. The Church's journey has also become difficult and stressful, a characteristic proof of these times—both for the faithful and for pastors. In some countries (as, for example, those I read about during the spiritual exercises), the Church finds herself in a period of persecution no less evil than the persecutions of the early centuries, indeed worse, because of the degree of ruthlessness and hatred. *Sanguis martyrum semen christianorum*: "The blood of martyrs is the seed of Christians" (Tertullian). And in addition to this, so many innocent people disappear, even in this country in which we live. . . .

I would like once again to entrust myself entirely to the Lord's grace. He himself will decide when and how I am to end my earthly life and my pastoral ministry. In life and in death [I am] *Totus tuus* through Mary Immaculate. I hope, in already accepting my death now, that Christ will give me the grace I need for the final Passover, that is, [my] Pasch. I also hope that he will make it benefit the important cause I seek to serve: the salvation of men and women, the preservation of the human family and, within it, all the nations and peoples (among them, I also specifically address my earthly homeland), useful for the people that he has specially entrusted to me, for the situation of the Church, and for the glory of God himself.[272]

When, on October 16, 1978, the Conclave of Cardinals chose John Paul II, Cardinal Stefan Wyszyński, primate of Poland, said to me: "The task of the new Pope will be to lead the Church into the third millennium." I do not know if I am repeating the sentence exactly as he said it, but this was at least the sense of what I heard him say at the time. These words were spoken by the man who went down in history as the Primate of the Millennium: a great primate. I witnessed his mission, his total confidence, his struggles, and his triumph. "When victory is won, it will be a victory through Mary": the Primate of the Millennium was fond of repeating these words of his predecessor, Cardinal Augustyn Hlond.

Thus, I was in some way prepared for the task presented to me on that day, October 16, 1978. As I write these words, the Great Jubilee of the Year 2000 is already a reality that is taking place. On the night of December 24, 1999, the symbolic Great Jubilee Door in the Basilica of Saint Peter was opened, and subsequently that of Saint John Lateran, then that of Saint Mary Major—on New Year's Day, and on January 19, the door of the Basilica of Saint Paul "Outside-the-Walls."

Particularly the latter event, because of its ecumenical character, was imprinted indelibly on memories.

As the Great Jubilee of the Year 2000 continues, the twentieth century closes behind us and the twenty-first century unfolds, from one day to the next. In accordance with the designs of Providence, I have been granted to live in the difficult century that is retreating into the past, and now in the year in which I have reached my eighties (*octogesima adveniens*), I must ask myself whether the time has come to say with Simeon of the Bible, "*Nunc dimittis*" (Lk 2:29).

On May 13, 1981, the day of the attack on the Pope during the general audience in Saint Peter's Square, Divine Providence miraculously saved me from death. He himself, who is the One Lord of life and death, extended this life of mine, and in a certain way he restored it to me. Ever since that moment it has belonged even more to him. I hope he will help me to recognize how long I must continue this service to which he called me October 16, 1978. I ask him to deign to call me to himself whenever he wishes. "If we live, we live to the Lord, and if we die, we die to the Lord; so then . . . we are the Lord's" (cf. Rom 14:8). I hope that as long as I am granted to carry out the Petrine service in the Church, God in his Mercy will grant me the necessary strength for this service. . . .

As the end of my earthly life draws close, I think back to its beginning, to my parents, my brother and my sister (whom I never knew, for she died before I was born), to the parish of Wadowice where I was baptized, to that city of my youth, to my peers, my companions of both sexes at elementary school, at high school, at university, until the time of the occupation when I worked as a laborer, and later, to the parish in Niegowić, to Saint Florian's Parish in Kraków, to the pastoral work of academics, to the context . . . to all the contexts . . . to Kraków and to Rome . . . to the persons who were especially entrusted to me by the Lord.

I want to say just one thing to them all: "May God reward you!"

In manus tuas, Domine, commendo spiritum meum.[273]

Appendix 1

Chronology

1920 On May 18 near Wadowice (Kraków), Poland, Karol Jozef Wojtyła, the future Pope John Paul II, is born. His father, also named Karol, forty years old, is an Army official. His mother, thirty-six-year-old Emilia Kaczorowska, is a housewife. His brother Edmund is almost fourteen. On June 20 he is baptized.

1926 On September 15 he begins elementary school.

1929 On April 13 his mother dies.

1930 In September he begins junior high school.

1932 On December 5 his brother dies.

1935 On December 14 he is admitted to the Marian Sodality.

1938 In May he receives Confirmation and passes his final examinations. On June 22 he enrolls in the school of philosophy at the Jagiellonian University. In the summer he moves with his father to Kraków. In the autumn, he begins to frequent the theatrical group called Studio 38.

1939 On February 6 he joins the eucharistic/charitable works sodality of the students of the Jagiellonian University. On September 1 the Second World War breaks out in Poland.

1940 In February he meets Jan Tyranowski, who gets him involved in a group called "the living rosary" and introduces Karol to the study of the mystics. In an effort to evade deportation to Germany, on November 4 he began work in the rock quarry at Zakrzówek.

1941 On February 18 his father dies. In August he is welcomed into the family of Mieczysław Kotlarczyk, the founder of the Theater of the Living Word. During the summer he is transferred to work in the factory at Solvay.

1942 In October as a seminarian, he enrolls in the clandestine theology courses in the School of Theology at Jagiellonian University.

1943 In March he appears for the last time in the theater, taking the lead role in *Samuel Zborowski* by Juliusz Słowacki.

1944 On February 29 he is hit by a car and admitted to a hospital for recovery. In August Archbishop Sapieha transfers him, along with the other clandestine seminarians, to his residence in Kraków.

1945 On January 18 the Red Army liberates Kraków from the Nazis.

1946 On November 1 he is ordained a priest in the private chapel of Archbishop Sapieha. On November 15 he leaves for Rome to pursue theological studies at the Angelicum.

1947 On July 3 he passes the examination for a degree in theology. During the summer he travels through France, Belgium, and Holland.

1948 On June 9 he presents his thesis for a degree in theology, *The Doctrine of Faith According to Saint John of the Cross.* Two weeks later he returns to Kraków. On July 8 he is appointed parochial vicar in the parish at Niegowić. On December 16 the Jagiellonian University ratifies his doctorate in theology.

1949 In August he is appointed parochial vicar in the parish of Saint Florian in Kraków.

1951 On September 1 Archbishop Baziak gives him a two-year leave of absence to prepare for the admittance examination for qualification as a university lecturer.

1953 In October he begins to lecture on Catholic social ethics in the School of Theology at the Jagiellonian University. In December he is awarded a lecturer's certificate with the presentation of his thesis, *An Evaluation of the Possibility of Constructing a Christian Ethics Based on the System of Max Scheler.*

1954 He is named professor in the Seminary of Kraków and at the Catholic University of Lublin.

1957 On December 15 he is appointed as a qualified lecturer by the Central Qualifications Commission.

1958 On July 4 he is nominated auxiliary bishop of Kraków. On September 28 he is consecrated bishop.

1960 He publishes his treatise *Love and Responsibility.*

1962 After the death of Archbishop Eugeniusz Baziak of Kraków, on July 16, Bishop Wojtyła is elected the administrative vicar. On October 5 he leaves for Rome, where he attends the first session of the Vatican Council II, from October 11 to December 15.

1963 From October 6 to December 4 he attends the second session of Vatican II in Rome. He makes a pilgrimage to the Holy Land from December 5 to 15. On December 30 he is named archbishop of Kraków.

1964 The official bull of his appointment as archbishop of Kraków is released on January 13. March 8 is the date for his solemn installation at Wawel Cathedral. From September 14 to November 21 he attends the third session of Vatican II, and immediately leaves again for a two-week pilgrimage to the Holy Land.

1965 From September 14 to December 8 he attends the fourth and last session of Vatican II.

1967 From April 13 to 20 he takes part in the first meeting of the Council for the Laity in Rome. On June 26 he receives the title of cardinal from Pope Paul VI.

1969 From October 11 to 28 he attends the first general assembly of the extraordinary Synod of Bishops. He publishes his treatise *The Person and Act.*

1971 On October 17 he presents the cause for the beatification of Maximilian Kolbe, martyr of charity in Auschwitz.

1972 On March 8 he begins the Synod of the Archdiocese of Kraków. He publishes his study of the implementations of Vatican Council II as *The Foundations for Renewal.*

1973 From March 2 to 9 he attends the Eucharistic Congress in Australia, visiting also the Philippines and New Guinea. In May he visits Belgium, and in November he travels to France.

1974 From September 27 to October 26 he attends the third Ordinary General Assembly of the Synod of Bishops, during which he is moderator for the section on doctrine.

1975 From March 3 to 8 he attends the meeting of the Council of the Secretary General of the Synod of Bishops. In September he journeys to the Democratic Republic of Germany (East Germany).

1976   From March 7 to 13 he preaches the Spiritual Exercises in the Vatican with Pope Paul VI present; the meditations are later published in a book, *Sign of Contradiction*. From July 25 to September 5 he travels through the United States and Canada, speaking at diverse conferences.

1977   On March 18 he delivers an address at the Catholic University in Milan. On June 23 he receives an honorary degree from Johannes Gutenberg University in Mainz, Germany.

1978   From August 11 to September 3 he travels to Rome for the funeral of Paul VI, the Papal Conclave, and the ceremonies following the election of John Paul I. From September 19 to 25 he travels to the Federal Republic of Germany (West Germany). On October 3 he returns to Rome for the funeral of John Paul I. On October 14 he enters the Conclave, and on October 16 at 5:15 P.M. he is elected Pope and chooses the name John Paul II. On October 22 he inaugurates his ministry as Supreme Pastor of the Catholic Church. On October 29, he makes his first pastoral visit, to the Marian sanctuary of Mentorella near Rome. On November 5 he makes a pilgrimage to Assisi and to the Basilica of Santa Maria sopra Minerva in Rome, to venerate the patrons of Italy, Saint Francis of Assisi and Saint Catherine of Siena. On November 12, as Bishop of Rome, he takes possession of the chair in Saint John the Lateran Basilica. On December 3 he makes his first visit to a Roman parish, Saint Francis Xavier's in Garbatella.

1979   From January 25 to February 1 he travels to the Dominican Republic, Mexico (where he attends the Latin American bishops' meeting at Puebla), and the Bahamas. On March 15 the publication of his first encyclical, *Redemptor Hominis* (dated March 4), is announced. From June 2 to 10 he travels to Poland. On June 30 he holds his first consistory, creating fifteen new cardinals. From September 29 to October 8 he travels to Ireland and on to the United States, where he addresses the General Assembly of the United Nations. On October 21 he visits Naples and Pompeii. On October 25 the publication of his second encyclical, *Catechesi Tradendae* (dated October 16), is announced. From November 28 to 30 he travels to Turkey, where he meets the Orthodox Patriarch Dimitrios I.

1980   On Good Friday, April 4, he hears the confessions of some of the faithful in the Vatican Basilica. On April 13 he visits Turin. From May 2 to 12 he visits Zaire, Republic of Congo, Kenya, Ghana, Upper Volta, and Ivory Coast. From May 30 to June 2 he goes to France, where he addresses UNESCO. From June 30 to July 12 he visits Brazil. From November 15 to 19 he visits the Federal Republic of Germany. On November 25 he visits Campania and Basilicata in Italy to comfort the people who had been devastated by an earthquake. On December 2 the publication of his encyclical *Dives in Misericordia* (dated November 30) is announced. With the letter *Egregiae Virtutis* of December 31 he proclaims Saints Cyril and Methodius, together with Saint Benedict, co-patrons of Europe.

1981   On January 11, Solemnity of the Epiphany, he baptizes infants in Saint Peter's Basilica. From February 16 to 27 he travels to Pakistan, the Philippines, and Japan, stopping also in the United States. On May 13 at 5:19 P.M. he is the victim of an assassination attempt in Saint Peter's Square by Mehmet Ali Agca. He undergoes emergency surgery in Rome's Gemelli Hospital followed by a 22-day stay as a patient. He returns to the Vatican June 3. On June 20 he is readmitted to Gemelli, suffering from an infection caused by a cytomegalovirus. After surgery on August 5 he remains a patient until August 14. On September 15 the publication of his encyclical *Laborem Exercens* (dated September 14) is announced. On December 15 the publication of his apostolic exhortation *Familiaris Consortio* (dated November 22) is announced.

1982   From February 12 to 19 he visits Nigeria, Benin, Gabon, and Equatorial Guinea. On April 18 he visits Bologna. From May 12 to 15 he visits Portugal, timing his visit to Fatima to coincide with the year's anniversary of the attempt on his life. He recites the Act of Consecration and entrusts the world to the Immaculate Heart of Mary. From May 28 to June 2 he visits Great Britain, and from June 10 to 13 he goes to Argentina, with a stopover in Brazil. On June 15 he visits Geneva, where he addresses the International Conference on Labor. On August 28 he visits San Marino. On October 10 he presides at the canonization of Father Maximilian Kolbe. He visits Spain from October 31 to November 9 and makes a pilgrimage to the Shrine of Santiago de Compostela, during which he announces the publication of a message to the people of Europe. On November 26 he announces the Holy Year of Redemption to be celebrated from Lent 1983 to Easter 1984.

1983   On January 25 he promulgates the new *Code of Canon Law*. From March 2 to 10 he visits Costa Rica, Nicaragua, Panama, El Salvador, Guatemala, Honduras, Belize, and Haiti. On March 25 he inaugurates the Holy Year of the Redemption. From May 20 to 22 he visits Milan. From June 16 to 23 he travels to Poland. On August 14 and 15 he makes a pilgrimage to Lourdes. From September 10 to 13 he visits

Austria. On October 16, in Saint Peter's Square, he renews the Act of Consecration of the world to the Immaculate Heart of Mary. On December 27 he visits Mehmet Ali Agca in Rome's Rebibbia prison.

1984   On February 11 the publication of the apostolic letter *Salvifici Doloris* is announced. On February 26 he visits Bari. On April 22 he concludes the Year of Redemption. From May 2 to 12 he travels to South Korea, Papua New Guinea, the Solomon Islands, and Thailand. From June 12 to 17 he visits Switzerland. From September 9 to 20 he visits Canada. From October 5 to 7 he visits Reggio Calabria. From October 10 to 12 he visits Spain, the Dominican Republic, and Puerto Rico. On December 11 the publication of the apostolic exhortation *Reconciliatio et Paenitentia* is announced.

1985   From January 26 to February 6 he visits Venezuela, Ecuador, Peru, and Trinidad and Tobago. On March 30 and 31 he welcomes the participants of the International Encounter of Young People to Rome. From March 11 to 21 he visits Luxembourg and Belgium. On June 16 and 17 he visits Venice. From August 8 to 19 he visits Togo, the Ivory Coast, Cameroon, the Central African Republic, Zaire, Kenya, and Morocco. On September 8 he visits Liechtenstein. On September 21 and 22 he visits Genoa. On October 19 and 20 he visits Cagliari. On November 17 he sends a personal message to U.S. President Ronald Reagan and Soviet President Mikhail Gorbachev regarding the upcoming summit in Geneva.

1986   From January 31 to February 10 he visits India. On April 13 he visits the Synagogue of Rome. On May 30 the publication of the encyclical *Dominum et Vivificantem* (dated May 18) is announced. From July 1 to 8 he visits Colombia and Santa Lucia. From October 4 to 7 he visits France. On October 18 and 19 he visits Florence. On October 27 he presides over the World Day of Prayer for Peace at Assisi. From November 18 to December 1 he visits Bangladesh, Singapore, Fiji, New Zealand, Australia, and Seychelles.

1987   On March 25 the publication of the encyclical *Redemptoris Mater* is announced. From March 31 to April 13 he visits Uruguay, Chile, and Argentina. From April 30 to May 4 he revisits the Federal Republic of Germany. On June 6, the Vigil of Pentecost, he opens the Marian Year. From June 8 to 14 he travels to Poland. From July 8 to 14 he visits the Dolomite Mountains at Lorenzago di Cadore for vacation. From September 10 to 21 he visits the United States. On December 3 he receives the ecumenical patriarch of Constantinople, Dimitrios I, in a private audience.

1988 On February 19 the publication of the encyclical *Solicitudo Rei Socialis* (dated December 30, 1987) is announced. From May 7 to 19 he visits Uruguay, Bolivia, Peru, and Paraguay. On May 21 he inaugurates the hospitality house *Dono di Maria* to be entrusted to the care of the Congregation of Mother Teresa of Calcutta. From June 23 to 27 he travels to Austria. On June 28 he signs the apostolic constitution *Pastor Bonus* for the reform of the Roman Curia. On July 2 the document *Ecclesia Dei*, addressed to the followers of the schismatic fraternity founded by Marcel Lefebvre who desired to remain in communion with the Catholic Church, is published. On August 15 he concludes the Marian Year. On September 30 the publication of the apostolic letter *Mulieres Dignitatem* (dated August 15) is announced. From September 10 to 20 he visits Zimbabwe, Botswana, Lesotho, Swaziland, and Mozambique. From October 8 to 11 he visits France.

1989 On January 30 the publication of the apostolic exhortation *Christifideles Laici* (dated December 30, 1988) is announced. From April 28 to May 6 he visits Madagascar, La Reunion, Zambia, and Malawi. From June 1 to 10 he visits Norway, Iceland, Finland, Denmark, and Sweden. On August 15 the publication of the apostolic exhortation *Redemptoris Custos* is announced. From August 19 to 21 he visits Spain. On September 7 he inaugurates the Day of Prayer for Peace in Lebanon. On September 30 he receives Robert Runcie, primate of the Anglican Communion, in private audience. From October 6 to 10 he visits South Korea, Indonesia, and Mauritius.

1990 From January 25 to February 1 he visits Guinea-Bissau, Cape Verde, Mali, Burkina Faso, and Chad. On April 21 and 22 he visits Czechoslovakia. From May 6 to 14 he visits Mexico and Curaçao. From May 25 to 27 he visits Malta. On August 26 he makes an appeal for peace in the Persian Gulf following the invasion of Kuwait by Iraq. From September 1 to 10 he visits Tanzania, Burundi, Rwanda, and Côte d'Ivoire. On October 8 he promulgates the new *Code of Canon Law for the Oriental Churches*.

1991 On January 15 he sends letters to the president of the United States, George H. W. Bush and the president of Iraq, Saddam Hussein, asking them to avoid war in the Gulf. On January 22 the publication of the encyclical *Redemptoris Missio* (dated December 7, 1990) is announced. On May 2 the publication of the encyclical *Centesimus Annus* (dated May 1) is announced. From May 10 to 13 he travels to Portugal. From June 1 to 9 he visits Poland. From August 13 to 20 he returns to Poland and visits Hungary. From October 12 to 21 he visits Brazil.

1992 From February 19 to 26 he visits Senegal, Gambia, and Guinea. From June 4 to 10 he visits Angola and São Tomé and Principe. From July 12 to 26 he is in Gemelli Hospital for surgery to remove a benign intestinal tumor. From October 9 to 14 he visits the Dominican Republic. On December 9 the publication of the *Catechism of the Catholic Church*, which had been approved in June, is announced.

1993 On January 9 and 10 at Assisi he presides over the Encounter of Prayer for Peace in Europe and especially the Balkan countries. From February 3 to 10 he visits Benin, Uganda, and Sudan. On April 25 he visits Albania. On May 9, from Agrigento, he issues a stern admonition to the Mafia. On May 29 he concludes the second synod for the Diocese of Rome. From June 12 to 17 he visits Spain. From August 9 to 16 he visits Jamaica, Mexico, and the United States. From September 4 to 10 he visits Lithuania, Latvia, and Estonia. On October 5 the publication of the encyclical *Veritatis Splendor* (dated August 6) is announced. On November 11 he falls and dislocates his right shoulder, which is immobilized for a month.

1994 On January 6 he sends a letter to the Italian bishops addressing responsibility of Catholics in the face of present challenges. On January 23 he celebrates a Mass for Peace in the Balkan countries in Saint Peter's Basilica. On February 22 the promulgation of the *Letter to Families* (dated February 2) is announced. On April 28 he falls and fractures his right femur. After surgery at the Gemelli Hospital, he remains there as a patient until May 27. On September 10 and 11 he visits Croatia. In October a book of interviews, *Crossing the Threshold of Hope*, is published. On October 8 and 9 he presides at the International Conference on the Family. On November 14 the publication of the apostolic letter *Tertio Millennio Adveniente* (dated October 10) is announced, and he announces the Great Jubilee of the Year 2000. On December 15 the publication of his *Letter to Children* (dated December 13) is announced.

1995 From January 11 to 21 he visits the Philippines, Papua New Guinea, Australia, and Sri Lanka. On March 30 the publication of the encyclical *Evangelium Vitae* (dated March 25) is announced. On April 29 and 30 he visits Trento. From May 20 to 22 he visits the Czech Republic. On May 30 the publication of the encyclical *Ut Unum Sint* (dated May 25) is announced. On June 3 and 4 he visits Belgium. On June 27 he receives the ecumenical patriarch of Constantinople, Bartholomew I, in private audience. From June 30 to July 3 he visits Slovakia. On July 10 the publication of his *Letter to Women* (dated June 29) is announced.

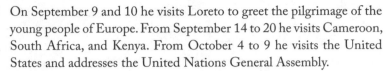

On September 9 and 10 he visits Loreto to greet the pilgrimage of the young people of Europe. From September 14 to 20 he visits Cameroon, South Africa, and Kenya. From October 4 to 9 he visits the United States and addresses the United Nations General Assembly.

1996 From February 5 to 12 he visits Guatemala, Nicaragua, El Salvador, and Venezuela. On February 22 he institutes the reform of the rules for papal Conclaves with the promulgation of the apostolic constitution *Universi Dominici Gregis*. On March 25 the publication of the apostolic exhortation *Vita Consecrata* is announced. On April 14 he visits Tunisia. From May 17 to 19 he visits Slovenia. From June 21 to 23 he visits Germany. On September 6 and 7 he visits Hungary. From September 19 to 22 he visits France. From October 6 to 15 he is a patient at Gemelli Hospital, where his appendix is removed. In November his autobiography *Gift and Mystery* is released. On November 13 he addresses the World Summit on Nutrition organized by FAO at Rome. On December 3 he receives George Leonard Carey, primate of the Anglican Communion, in private audience.

1997 On April 12 and 13 he visits Bosnia. From April 25 to 27 he visits the Czech Republic. May 10 and 11 he visits Lebanon. From May 31 to June 10 he visits Poland. On June 16 he sends a letter to Israeli Prime Minister Benjamin Netanyahu and to Palestinian Authority President Yasser Arafat to plead the case for peace in the Middle East. From August 21 to 24 he visits France. From October 2 to 6 he visits Brazil.

1998 From January 21 to 26 he visits Cuba. From March 21 to 23 he visits Nigeria. From June 19 to 21 he visits Austria. On July 7 the publication of the apostolic letter *Dies Domini* (dated May 31) is announced. From October 2 to 4 he visits Croatia. On October 15 the publication of the encyclical *Fides et Ratio* (dated September 14) is announced. On November 29 the publication of the papal bull *Incarnationis Mysterium*, which proclaims the Great Jubilee of the Year 2000, is announced.

1999 From January 22 to 28 he visits Mexico and the United States. From May 7 to 9 he visits Romania. From June 5 to 17 he visits Poland. On September 9 he sends a message to the bishops of East Timor, devastated by a civil war. On September 19 he visits Slovenia. On October 1 he publishes the apostolic letter *Spes Aedificandi*, in which he names Saint Bridget of Sweden, Saint Catherine of Siena, and Saint Benedicta of the Cross as patron saints of Europe. On October 26 the publication of his *Letter to the Elderly* (dated October 1) is announced. From November 5 to 9 he visits India and the Republic of Georgia. On Christmas Eve he inaugurates the Great Jubilee of the Year 2000.

2000   On January 2 he presides at the Jubilee for Children. From February 24 to 26 he makes a pilgrimage to Mount Sinai in Egypt. On March 12 he celebrates the Day of Forgiveness. From March 20 to 26 he makes a pilgrimage to the Holy Land (Jordan, Palestinian Territory, and Israel). On May 1 he presides at the Jubilee of the Workers. On May 7 he presides at the ecumenical commemoration of the Martyrs for the Faith of the Twentieth Century. On May 12 and 13 he makes a pilgrimage to Fatima. On May 18 he presides at the Jubilee for Priests. On June 25 he presides in Rome at the *Statio Orbis* of the International Eucharistic Congress. On August 19 and 20 he presides at the Jubilee for Youth. On October 14 and 15 he presides at the Jubilee for Families.

2001   On January 6 he concludes the Great Jubilee of the Year 2000 and signs the post-Jubilee letter *Novo Millennio Ineunte*. From May 4 to 9 he visits Greece, Syria, and Malta. From June 23 to 27 he visits Ukraine. From September 22 to 27 he visits Kazakhstan and Armenia.

2002   On January 24 he presides at the Day of Prayer for World Peace at Assisi. From May 22 to 26 he visits Azerbaijan and Bulgaria. On June 16 he presides at the canonization of Padre Pio of Pietrelcina. From July 23 to August 2 he visits Canada, Guatemala, and Mexico. From August 16 to 19 he travels to Poland. On October 16, with his apostolic letter *Rosarium Virginis Mariae*, he announces the Year of the Rosary, to extend from October 2002 to October 2003. He also announces the addition of the Mysteries of Light to this traditional Marian prayer. On November 14 he visits the Italian Parliament.

2003   On March 5 he presides at the day of prayer and fasting for world peace. On April 23 he reaches 8,959 days of his pontificate, longer than Pius VI, making John Paul II's the third-longest pontificate in Church history after Pius IX and Leo XIII, leaving out the case of Saint Peter. On April 17 the publication of the encyclical *Ecclesia de Eucharistia* is announced. On May 3 and 4 he visits Spain. From June 5 to 9 he visits Croatia, which is his 100th international trip. On June 22 he makes a pastoral visit to Bosnia and Herzegovina. On June 28 he signs the apostolic exhortation *Ecclesia in Europa*. From September 11 to 14 he visits Slovakia. On October 7 he travels to Pompeii and the Sanctuary of the Virgin of the Rosary. On October 16 he presides at the solemn concelebration commemorating the 25th year of his pontificate; he also signs the apostolic exhortation *Pastores Gregis*. On October 19, at the celebration of the beautification of Mother Teresa of Calcutta in Saint Peter's Square, a great feast is held to celebrate the 25th year of his pontificate and his 45th anniversary as a bishop.

2004 On February 28, after having visited in person 301 of the parishes in the Archdiocese of Rome, he begins to meet representatives of the remaining parishes in audiences at the Vatican. On June 5 and 6 he travels to Bern for an encounter with the Catholic young people of Switzerland. On June 10 he announces the celebration of a special year dedicated to the Eucharist. On June 29 he receives Bartholomew I, ecumenical patriarch of Constantinople, in private audience, marking the 40th anniversary of the historic meeting of Pope Paul VI with Patriarch Athenagoras. On August 14 and 15 he makes a pilgrimage to Lourdes to commemorate the 150th anniversary of the proclamation of the dogma of the Immaculate Conception of Mary. On August 25, in Paul VI Hall, he presides at the Celebration of the Word and the commission of a Vatican delegation to return the Icon of the Theotokos of Kazan to Patriarch Aleksy II. On September 5 he travels to Loreto for the beatification of the Spanish priest Tarrés i Claret and the Italian laypersons Alberto Marvelli and Pina Suriano, in the presence of 300,000 members of the Catholic Action Society.

2005 On January 30 he recites the Sunday Angelus in a personal appearance for the last time. In the evening of February 1 he is brought to the Gemelli Hospital in respiratory crisis. On February 10 he returns to the Vatican. He is again brought to Gemelli on February 24 due to a relapse of the influenza he had suffered the preceding week. An emergency tracheotomy is performed to resolve an acute attack of respiratory distress. He is a patient at Gemelli Hospital until March 13. For the first time in his pontificate, he is unable to participate personally in the solemn liturgies of Holy Week, but he manifests his spiritual union with the faithful through written messages. Around 11:00 A.M. on March 30, 2005, during the hour of the General Audience, he comes to the window of the apostolic palace to bless the thousands of pilgrims present in Saint Peter's Square: it is his last public appearance. In the afternoon of March 31, a urinary infection provokes septic shock and cardio-circulatory collapse. At dawn on April 2 he enters a coma. John Paul II dies at 9:37 P.M. on April 2, 2005, the first Saturday of the month and the Vigil of the Feast of Divine Mercy. He had lived 84 years, 10 months, and 15 days. He had been Pope for 26 years, 5 months, and 17 days.

2011 On January 14 the Vatican announced that the beatification of John Paul II would take place in the Vatican on May 1, 2011.

Appendix 2

Church Documents

An alphabetical list of Church documents referenced by their Latin titles.

Apostolicam Actuositatem

Vatican II. Decree, *On the Apostolate of the Laity*. November 18, 1965.

Catechesi Tradendae

John Paul II. Apostolic Exhortation, *On Catechesis in Our Time*. October 16, 1979.

Centesimus Annus

John Paul II. Encyclical, *On the Hundredth Anniversary of* Rerum Novarum. May 1, 1991.

Christifideles Laici

John Paul II. Apostolic Exhortation, *On the Vocation and Mission of the Lay Faithful in the Church and in the World*. December 30, 1988.

Dei Verbum

Vatican II. Dogmatic Constitution, *On Divine Revelation*. November 18, 1965.

Dies Domini

John Paul II. Apostolic Letter, *On Keeping the Lord's Day Holy*, May 31, 1998.

Dives in Misericordia

John Paul II. Encyclical, *Rich in Mercy*. November 30, 1980.

Dominum et Vivificantem

John Paul II. Encyclical, *On the Holy Spirit in the Life of the Church and the World*. May 18, 1986.

Ecclesia de Eucharistia

John Paul II. Encyclical, *On the Eucharist in Its Relationship to the Church*. April 17, 2003.

Ecclesia Dei

John Paul II. Apostolic Letter issued *Motu Proprio*, *"Ecclesia Dei."* July 2, 1988.

Ecclesia in Europa

John Paul II. Apostolic Exhortation, *On Jesus Christ Alive in His Church, the Source of Hope for Europe*. June 28, 2003.

Egregiae Virtutis

John Paul II. Apostolic Letter, *"Egregiae Virtutis."* December 31, 1980.

Evangelium Vitae

John Paul II. Encyclical, *On the Value and Inviolability of Human Life*. March 25, 1995.

Familiaris Consortio

John Paul II. Apostolic Exhortation, *On the Role of the Christian Family in the Modern World*. November 22, 1981.

Fides et Ratio

John Paul II. Encyclical, *On the Relationship Between Faith and Reason*. September 14, 1998.

Gaudium et Spes

Vatican II. Pastoral Constitution, *On the Church in the Modern World*. December 7, 1965.

Incarnationis Mysterium

John Paul II. *Bull of Indiction of the Great Jubilee of the Year 2000*. November 29, 1998.

Laborem Exercens

John Paul II. Encyclical, *On Human Work*. September 14, 1981.

Lumen Gentium

Vatican II. Dogmatic Constitution, *On the Church*. November 21, 1964.

Mulieris Dignitatem

John Paul II. Apostolic Letter, *On the Dignity and Vocation of Women*. August 15, 1988.

Novo Millennio Ineunte

John Paul II. Apostolic Letter, *At the Close of the Great Jubilee of the Year 2000*. January 6, 2001.

Octogesima Adveniens

Paul VI. Apostolic Letter, *On the Occasion of the Eightieth Anniversary of the Encyclical "Rerum Novarum."* May 14, 1971.

Orientale Lumen

John Paul II. Apostolic Letter, *To Mark the Centenary of Orientalium Dignitas of Pope Leo XIII*. May 2, 1995.

Pastor Bonus

John Paul II. Apostolic Constitution, *"Pastor Bonus."* June 28, 1988.

Pastores Gregis

John Paul II. Apostolic Exhortation, *On the Bishop, Servant of the Gospel of Jesus Christ for the Hope of the World*. October 16, 2003.

Populorum Progressio

Paul VI. Encyclical, *On the Development of Peoples*. March 26, 1967.

Reconciliatio et Paenitentia

John Paul II. Apostolic Exhortation, *On Reconciliation and Penance in the Mission of the Church Today*. December 2, 1984.

Redemptor Hominis

John Paul II. Encyclical, *The Redeemer of Man*. March 4, 1979.

Redemptoris Custos

John Paul II. Apostolic Exhortation, *On the Person and Mission of Saint Joseph in the Life of Christ and of the Church*. August 15, 1989.

Redemptoris Mater

John Paul II. Encyclical, *On the Blessed Virgin Mary in the Life of the Pilgrim Church.* March 25, 1987.

Redemptoris Missio

John Paul II. Encyclical, *On the Permanent Validity of the Church's Missionary Mandate.* December 7, 1990.

Rerum Novarum

Leo XIII. Encyclical, *On Capital and Labor.* May 15, 1891.

Rosarium Virginis Mariae

John Paul II. Apostolic Letter, *On the Most Holy Rosary.* October 16, 2002.

Salvifici Doloris

John Paul II. Apostolic Letter, *On the Christian Meaning of Human Suffering.* February 11, 1984.

Slavorum Apostoli

John Paul II. Encyclical, *The Apostles of the Slavs.* June 2, 1985.

Solicitudo Rei Socialis

John Paul II. Encyclical, *For the Twentieth Anniversary of Populorum Progressio.* December 30, 1987.

Spes Aedificandi

John Paul II. Apostolic Letter issued *Motu Proprio, Proclaiming Saint Bridget of Sweden, Saint Catherine of Siena, and Saint Teresa Benedicta of the Cross Co-Patronesses of Europe.* October 1, 1999.

Tertio Millennio Adveniente

John Paul II. Apostolic Exhortation, *On Preparation for the Jubilee of the Year 2000.* November 10, 1994.

Universi Dominici Gregis

John Paul II. Apostolic Constitution, *On the Vacancy of the Apostolic See and the Election of the Roman Pontiff.* February 22, 1996.

Ut Unum Sint

John Paul II. Encyclical, *On Commitment to Ecumenism.* May 25, 1995.

Veritatis Splendor

John Paul II. Encyclical, *The Splendor of Truth*. August 6, 1993.

Vita Consecrata

John Paul II. Apostolic Exhortation, *On the Consecrated Life and Its Mission in the Church and in the World*. March 25, 1996.

Notes

All citations attributed to John Paul II followed by a date ranging from October 16, 1978 to April 2, 2005, refer to a talk, homily, letter, or other document given by John Paul II on the date indicated.

PART ONE
Karol Wojtyła's Polish Roots

1. John Paul II, May 18, 1997, trans. Daughters of St. Paul (hereafter cited as FSP).

2. John Paul II, May 17, 1995, trans. FSP.

3. John Paul II, January 3, 1998, trans. FSP.

4. André Frossard and John Paul II, *"Be Not Afraid!": Pope John Paul II Speaks Out On His Life, His Beliefs, and His Inspiring Vision for Humanity* (Garden City, NY: Image Books, 1985), 14.

5. John Paul II, June 13, 1987, trans. FSP.

6. Cf. Carl Bernstein and Marco Politi, *His Holiness: John Paul II and the Hidden History of Our Time* (New York: Doubleday, 1996), 17.

7. John Paul II, June 7, 1979, trans. *L'Osservatore Romano* (hereafter cited as *LOR*).

8. John Paul II, May 17, 1995, trans. FSP.

9. Giovanni Paulo II, *Altzatevi, andiamo* (Vatican City: Libreria Editrice Vaticana, 2004), 31–32, trans. FSP.

10. Frossard and John Paul II, *"Be Not Afraid!"*, 30.

11. John Paul II, November 4, 1978, trans. *LOR.*

12. John Paul II, November 4, 1979, trans. FSP.

13. André Frossard and Giovanni Paolo II, *"Non abbiate paura!"* (Milan: Rusconi, 1983), 12, trans. FSP.

14. John Paul II, *The Place Within: The Poetry of Pope John Paul II* (New York: Random House, 1994), ix.

15. Frossard and John Paul II, *"Be Not Afraid!"*, 14.

16. John Paul II, April 26, 1997, trans. *LOR.*

17. John Paul II, *Crossing the Threshold of Hope* (New York: Alfred A. Knopf, 1994), 141–142.

18. John Paul II, August 14, 1991, trans. FSP.

19. John Paul II, *Crossing the Threshold of Hope*, 96.

20. John Paul II, August 14, 1991, trans. FSP.

21. Giovanni Paulo II, *Altzatevi, andiamo*, 85, trans. FSP.

22. Frossard and John Paul II, *"Be Not Afraid!"*, 163.

23. Ibid., 68.

24. Giovanni Paolo II, *Alzatevi, andiamo!*, 75, trans. FSP.

25. John Paul II, November 25, 1990, trans. FSP.

26. John Paul II, May 21, 1983, trans. FSP.

27. John Paul II, August 22, 1997, trans. FSP.

28. John Paul II, June 2, 1980, trans. *LOR.*

29. John Paul II, October 6, 1979, trans. *LOR.*

30. John Paul II, December 13, 1994, trans. *LOR.*

31. John Paul II, October 7, 1995, trans. *LOR.*

32. John Paul II, October 6, 1995, trans. *LOR.*

33. John Paul II, March 1, 1995, trans. FSP.

34. John Paul II, June 15, 1995, trans. FSP.

35. John Paul II, December 13, 1994, trans. *LOR.*

36. John Paul II, *The Place Within*, 19.

37. John Paul II, June 27, 1988, trans. FSP.

38. John Paul II, November 15, 1990, trans. FSP.

39. John Paul II, March 28, 1981, trans. FSP.

40. John Paul II, February 24, 1981, trans. FSP.

41. John Paul II, January 20, 1991, trans. FSP.

42. John Paul II, October 7, 1985, trans. FSP.

43. John Paul II, May 17, 1995, trans. FSP.

44. John Paul II, *Gift and Mystery: On the Fiftieth Anniversary of My Priestly Ordination* (New York: Image Books/Doubleday, 1996), 5.

45. John Paul II, June 22, 1983, trans. FSP.

46. John Paul II, *Gift and Mystery*, 6.

47. Giovanni Paulo II, *Altzatevi, andiamo*, 20–21, trans. FSP.

48. John Paul II, *Gift and Mystery*, 26.

49. Mieczysław Maliński, *Il mio vecchio amico Karol* (Milan: Edizioni Paoline, 1980), 37, trans. FSP.

50. John Paul II, September 15, 1987, trans. FSP.

51. Frossard and John Paul II, *"Be Not Afraid!"*, 14.

52. John Paul II, May 18, 1996, trans. FSP.

53. John Paul II, June 5, 2004, trans. *LOR*.

54. John Paul II, May 26, 1982, trans. FSP.

55. John Paul II, *Crossing the Threshold of Hope*, 119.

56. John Paul II, June 22, 1983, trans. FSP.

57. John Paul II, May 27, 1990, trans. *LOR*.

58. John Paul II, *Gift and Mystery*, 9–10.

59. Maliński, *Il mio vecchio amico Karol*, 301, trans. FSP.

60. John Paul II, March 15, 1980, trans. FSP.

61. Ibid.

62. John Paul II, June 9, 1979, trans. *LOR*.

63. John Paul II, December 9, 1978, trans. *LOR*.

64. John Paul II, February 18, 1982, trans. FSP.

65. John Paul II, March 19, 1981, trans. FSP.

66. Frossard and John Paul II, *"Be Not Afraid!"*, 14.

67. John Paul II, *Gift and Mystery*, 40.

68. Frossard and John Paul II, *"Be Not Afraid!"*, 15.

69. John Paul II, *Gift and Mystery*, 10–11.

70. Giovanni Paulo II, *Altzatevi, andiamo*, 75, trans. FSP.

71. Ibid.

72. Karol Wojtyła, *Tutte le opere letterarie: poesie, drammi e scritti sul teatro* (Milan: Bompiani, 2001), 992, trans. FSP.

73. John Paul II, May 18, 1988, trans. FSP.

74. John Paul II, *Crossing the Threshold of Hope*, 142.

75. Frossard and John Paul II, *"Be Not Afraid!"*, 122.

76. Ibid., 19.

77. John Paul II, April 1, 2004, trans. *LOR*.

78. John Paul II, November 1, 1982, trans. FSP.

79. John Paul II, June 10, 1987, trans. FSP.

80. John Paul II, June 19, 2004, trans. *LOR*.

81. John Paul II, June 10, 1987, trans. FSP.

82. John Paul II, *Gift and Mystery*, 35.

83. Frossard and John Paul II, *"Be Not Afraid!"*, 15.

84. Ibid., 17.

85. John Paul II, *Gift and Mystery*, 12.

86. Frossard and John Paul II, *"Be Not Afraid!"*, 17.

87. John Paul II, March 1, 2003, trans. *LOR*.

88. John Paul II, June 23, 1983, trans. FSP.

89. John Paul II, September 15, 1987, trans. *LOR*.

90. John Paul II, May 3, 2003, trans. *LOR*.

91. John Paul II, July 1, 1980, trans. FSP.

92. John Paul II, December 2, 1990, trans. FSP.

93. John Paul II, June 22, 1983, trans. FSP.

94. John Paul II, March 1, 2003, trans. *LOR*.

95. John Paul II, March 19, 1982, trans. FSP.

96. John Paul II, May 31, 1980, trans. *LOR*.

97. John Paul II, November 26, 1986, trans. *LOR*.

98. John Paul II, June 9, 1997, trans. FSP.

99. Maliński, *Il mio vecchio amico Karol*, 49, trans. FSP.

100. Ibid., 301, trans. FSP.

101. John Paul II, January 15, 1989, trans. FSP.

102. John Paul II, *Gift and Mystery*, 24–25.

103. John Paul II, March 20, 1999, trans. *LOR*.

104. Giovanni Paulo II, *Altzatevi, andiamo*, 105, trans. FSP.

105. John Paul II, *Gift and Mystery*, 12–13.

106. John Paul II, *Memory and Identity: Conversations at the Dawn of a Millennium* (New York: Rizzoli, 2005), 14–15.

107. John Paul II, June 22, 1983, trans. FSP.

108. John Paul II, *Gift and Mystery*, 15.

109. John Paul II, October 30, 1996, trans. FSP.

110. John Paul II, November 1, 1996, trans. FSP.

111. Giovanni Paulo II, *Altzatevi, andiamo*, 112–113, trans. FSP.

112. John Paul II, November 1, 1993, trans. FSP.

113. John Paul II, June 1, 1980, trans. *LOR*.

114. John Paul II, October 27, 1995, trans. FSP.

115. John Paul II, April 17, 2003, trans. *LOR*.

116. John Paul II, February 10, 1991, trans. FSP.

117. John Paul II, December 2, 1990, trans. FSP.

118. John Paul II, *Gift and Mystery*, 46, 49.

119. Ibid., 50–51.

120. John Paul II, June 22, 1986, trans. FSP.

121. John Paul II, December 21, 1986, trans. FSP.

122. John Paul II, March 18, 1979, trans. FSP.

123. John Paul II, November 23, 1984, trans. FSP.

124. John Paul II, *Memory and Identity*, 46.

125. John Paul II, May 19, 1985, trans. FSP.

126. Maliński, *Il mio vecchio amico Karol*, 87, trans. FSP.

127. John Paul II, March 7, 1984, trans. FSP.

128. John Paul II, April 25, 1979, trans. FSP.

129. John Paul II, March 12, 1989, trans. FSP.

130. John Paul II, *Gift and Mystery*, 59–60.

131. Ibid., 61–62.

132. John Paul II, March 12, 1989, trans. FSP.

133. John Paul II, October 21, 1990, trans. FSP.

134. John Paul II, *Gift and Mystery*, 63–64.

135. Giovanni Paulo II, *Altzatevi, andiamo*, 97, trans. FSP.

136. John Paul II, March 6, 2003, trans. *LOR*.

137. John Paul II, September 15, 1987, trans. *LOR*.

138. Giovanni Paulo II, *Altzatevi, andiamo*, 79–80, trans. FSP.

139. John Paul II, December 15, 1994, trans. FSP.

140. John Paul II, July 1, 1980, trans. FSP.

141. John Paul II, November 3, 1979, trans. FSP.

142. John Paul II, *Gift and Mystery*, 64.

143. John Paul II, January 1, 2004, trans. *LOR*.

144. Frossard and John Paul II, *"Be Not Afraid!"*, 17.

145. John Paul II, May 9, 2003, trans. *LOR*.

146. John Paul II, June 25, 1989, trans. FSP.

147. John Paul II, May 4, 1980, trans. *LOR*.

148. John Paul II, October 7, 1979, trans. *LOR*.

149. John Paul II, December 15, 1979, trans. FSP.

150. Giovanni Paulo II, *Altzatevi, andiamo*, 13, trans. FSP.

151. Ibid., 10–11.

152. Ibid., 23–24.

153. Ibid., 51.

154. Ibid., 59–60.

155. Ibid., 73–74.

156. Ibid., 76.

157. John Paul II, *Crossing the Threshold of Hope*, 98.

158. John Paul II, September 29, 1985, trans. FSP.

159. John Paul II, *Crossing the Threshold of Hope*, 157–158.

160. Giovanni Paulo II, *Altzatevi, andiamo*, 125–126, trans. FSP.

161. Ibid., 165.

162. Ibid., 59.

163. Ibid., 152.

164. John Paul II, June 6, 1979, trans. *LOR*.

165. Giovanni Paulo II, *Altzatevi, andiamo*, 96, trans. FSP.

166. Ibid., 40.

167. Ibid., 49–50.

168. John Paul II, February 21, 2004, trans. *LOR*.

169. John Paul II, February 26, 2004, trans. *LOR*.

170. Luigi Accattoli, *Man of the Millennium: John Paul II* (Boston: Pauline Books & Media, 2000), 30.

171. Maliński, *Il mio vecchio amico Karol*, 289, trans. FSP.

172. Giovanni Paulo II, *Altzatevi, andiamo*, 133, trans. FSP.

173. John Paul II, *Crossing the Threshold of Hope*, 200.

174. Ibid., 199.

175. Giovanni Paulo II, *Altzatevi, andiamo*, 71, trans. FSP.

176. Ibid., 99–100.

177. John Paul II, June 5, 1979, trans. *LOR*.

178. John Paul II, September 24, 1982, trans. FSP.

179. John Paul II, May 10, 1992, trans. FSP.

180. John Paul II, November 5, 1978, trans. *LOR*.

181. John Paul II, April 25, 1987, trans. FSP.

182. John Paul II, January 24, 1979, trans. *LOR*.

183. John Paul II, *Memory and Identity*, 83.

184. Giovanni Paulo II, *Altzatevi, andiamo*, 44–45, trans. FSP.

185. John Paul II, June 6, 1979, trans. *LOR*.

186. John Paul II, *Crossing the Threshold of Hope*, 212–213.

187. John Paul II, December 8, 2003, trans. FSP.

188. John Paul II, June 7, 1997, trans. *LOR*.

189. John Paul II, August 17, 2002, trans. FSP.

190. John Paul II, June 7, 1997, trans. *LOR*.

191. John Paul II, August 16, 2002, trans. *LOR*.

192. Giovanni Paulo II, *Altzatevi, andiamo*, 106, trans. FSP.

193. Ibid., 174–175.

194. Maliński, *Il mio vecchio amico Karol*, 332, trans. FSP.

195. Ibid., 323, trans. FSP.

196. Ibid., 331, trans. FSP.

197. Ibid., 335, trans. FSP.

198. Ibid., 377, trans. FSP.

199. John Paul II, August 27, 2003, trans. *LOR*.

200. Giovanni Paulo II, *Altzatevi, andiamo*, 60, trans. FSP.

Part Two
Successor to Peter, Heir to Paul

1. John Paul II, October 16, 1978, trans. *LOR*.

2. John Paul II, March 4, 1979, trans. FSP.

3. John Paul II, *The Place Within*, 103–104.

4. John Paul II, June 6, 1979, trans. *LOR*.

5. John Paul II, October 16, 1998, trans. *LOR*.

6. John Paul II, April 8, 1994, trans. *LOR*.

7. John Paul II, October 16, 2003, trans. *LOR*.

8. Ibid.

9. John Paul II, August 26, 1979, trans. FSP.

10. John Paul II, July 16, 1988, trans. FSP.

11. John Paul II, February 13, 1999, trans. *LOR*.

12. John Paul II, March 4, 1979, trans. FSP.

13. John Paul II, November 5, 1978, trans. *LOR*.

14. John Paul II, *Memory and Identity*, 141–142.

15. Ibid., 142.

16. Ibid., 143.

17. John Paul II, November 5, 1978, trans. *LOR.*

18. Ibid.

19. Giovanni Paulo II, *Altzatevi, andiamo*, 40, trans. FSP.

20. John Paul II, April 20, 1986, trans. FSP.

21. John Paul II, January 23, 1979, trans. *LOR.*

22. John Paul II, October 23, 1978, trans. FSP.

23. John Paul II, February 16, 1982, trans. *LOR.*

24. John Paul II, October 23, 1978, trans. *LOR.*

25. Ibid.

26. John Paul II, October 17, 1993, trans. FSP.

27. John Paul II, *Crossing the Threshold of Hope*, 218–219.

28. John Paul II, November 12, 1978, trans. *LOR.*

29. Frossard and John Paul II, *"Be Not Afraid!"*, 22.

30. John Paul II, September 8, 1979, trans. *LOR.*

31. John Paul II, May 29, 1980, trans. FSP.

32. John Paul II, May 21, 1984, trans. *LOR.*

33. John Paul II, January 22, 1989, trans. FSP.

34. Giovanni Paulo II, *Altzatevi, andiamo*, 124, trans. FSP.

35. John Paul II, January 7, 1980, trans. *LOR.*

36. John Paul II, February 21, 1980, trans. *LOR.*

37. John Paul II, February 21, 1980, trans. FSP.

38. John Paul II, October 22, 1978, trans. *LOR.*

39. John Paul II, February 2, 1983, trans. FSP.

40. John Paul II, March 1, 1987, trans. FSP.

41. John Paul II, April 26, 1987, trans. FSP.

42. John Paul II, June 1, 1980, trans. *LOR.*

43. John Paul II, September 12, 2003, trans. *LOR.*

44. John Paul II, October 25, 1978, trans. *LOR.*

45. John Paul II, October 21, 1979, trans. FSP.

46. John Paul II, January 1, 1979, trans. *LOR.*

47. John Paul II, May 2, 1980, trans. *LOR.*

48. John Paul II, March 3, 1984, trans. FSP.

49. John Paul II, March 17, 1985, trans. FSP.

50. John Paul II, July 4, 1998, trans. *LOR.*

51. John Paul II, May 2, 1980, trans. *LOR.*

52. John Paul II, March 19, 1981, trans. FSP.

53. John Paul II, October 2, 1979, trans. *LOR.*

54. John Paul II, June 2, 1980, trans. *LOR.*

55. Frossard and John Paul II, "*Be Not Afraid!*", 194.

56. Ibid., 193–194.

57. John Paul II, August 3, 1980, trans. FSP.

58. John Paul II, June 28, 1982, trans. FSP.

59. John Paul II, October 15, 1989, trans. FSP.

60. Mieczysław Maliński, *Le radici di Papa Wojtyła* (Rome: Borla, 1979), 168, trans. FSP

61. John Paul II, December 9, 1984, trans. FSP.

62. John Paul II, November 5, 1995, trans. FSP.

63. Giovanni Paulo II, *Altzatevi, andiamo*, 124–125, trans. FSP.

64. John Paul II, June 11, 1980, trans. FSP.

65. John Paul II, May 6, 1990, trans. FSP.

66. John Paul II, February 14, 1988, trans. FSP.

67. John Paul II, June 6, 1988, trans. FSP.

68. John Paul II, September 25, 1984, trans. FSP.

69. John Paul II, December 9, 1985, trans. FSP.

70. John Paul II, March 10, 1985, trans. FSP.

71. John Paul II, June 28, 1980, trans. FSP.

72. John Paul II, May 12, 1982, trans. FSP.

73. John Paul II, May 15, 1982, trans. FSP.

74. John Paul II, July 8, 1980, trans. *LOR.*

75. John Paul II, June 7, 1988, trans. FSP.

76. John Paul II, December 22, 1979, trans. *LOR.*

77. John Paul II, February 24, 1981, trans. *LOR*.

78. John Paul II, May 18, 1986, trans. FSP.

79. John Paul II, February 19, 1989, trans. FSP.

80. John Paul II, May 19, 1990, trans. FSP.

81. John Paul II, March 6, 1988, trans. FSP.

82. Frossard and John Paul II, *"Be Not Afraid!"*, 28.

83. John Paul II, November 25, 1990, trans. FSP.

84. John Paul II, November 8, 1978, trans. *LOR*.

85. John Paul II, October 12, 2003, trans. *LOR*.

86. John Paul II, November 18, 1990, trans. FSP.

87. John Paul II, April 27, 1986, trans. FSP.

88. John Paul II, February 18, 1981, trans. *LOR*.

89. John Paul II, November 29, 1978, trans. *LOR*.

90. John Paul II, November 7, 1979, trans. FSP.

91. John Paul II, May 24, 1992, trans. FSP.

92. John Paul II, June 7, 1988, trans. FSP.

93. John Paul II, May 15, 1988, trans. FSP.

94. John Paul II, March 3, 1983, trans. FSP.

95. John Paul II, February 18, 1988, trans. FSP.

96. John Paul II, February 26, 2004, trans. *LOR*.

97. John Paul II, January 25, 1998, trans. FSP.

98. John Paul II, January 28, 1990, trans. FSP.

99. John Paul II, June 7, 1998, trans. FSP.

100. John Paul II, March 5, 1995, trans. FSP.

101. John Paul II, June 10, 1987, trans. FSP.

102. John Paul II, April 19, 1991, trans. FSP.

103. John Paul II, June 5, 1988, trans. FSP.

104. John Paul II, November 5, 1989, trans. FSP.

105. John Paul II, November 22, 1986, trans. *LOR*.

106. John Paul II, March 7, 1984, trans. FSP.

107. John Paul II, June 23, 1990, trans. FSP.

108. John Paul II, February 18, 1982, trans. FSP.

109. John Paul II, March 1, 1992, trans. FSP.

110. John Paul II, April 28, 1991, trans. FSP.

111. John Paul II, June 3, 1988, trans. FSP.

112. John Paul II, June 19, 1998, trans. FSP.

113. John Paul II, September 26, 1993, trans. FSP.

114. John Paul II, November 15, 1992, trans. FSP.

115. John Paul II, March 26, 1995, trans. FSP.

116. John Paul II, January 18, 1998, trans. FSP.

117. John Paul II, January 22, 1998, trans. FSP.

118. John Paul II, March 29, 1998, trans. FSP.

119. Luigi Accattoli, *Karol Wojtyła: l'uomo di fine millennio* (Milan: Edizioni San Paolo, 1998), 121, trans. FSP.

120. John Paul II, November 24, 1984, trans. FSP.

121. John Paul II, June 1, 1980, trans. *LOR*.

122. John Paul II, October 29, 1978, trans. *LOR*.

123. John Paul II, June 5, 1979, trans. *LOR*.

124. John Paul II, December 17, 1978, trans. FSP.

125. John Paul II, *Crossing the Threshold of Hope*, 19, 20.

126. Giovanni Paulo II, *Altzatevi, andiamo*, 26, trans. FSP.

127. John Paul II, *Crossing the Threshold of Hope*, 23.

128. Giovanni Paulo II, *Altzatevi, andiamo*, 56–57, trans. FSP.

129. John Paul II, March 13, 1982, trans. *LOR*.

130. John Paul II, October 29, 1978, trans. *LOR*.

131. John Paul II, March 20, 1988, trans. FSP.

132. John Paul II, October 27, 1995, trans. FSP.

133. John Paul II, July 7, 1980, trans. FSP.

134. John Paul II, February 11, 1979, trans. FSP.

135. John Paul II, June 30, 2002, trans. *LOR*.

136. Frossard and John Paul II, *"Be Not Afraid!"*, 80–81.

137. Giovanni Paulo II, *Altzatevi, andiamo*, 61–62, trans. FSP.

138. John Paul II, December 21, 1980, trans. FSP.

139. Giovanni Paulo II, *Altzatevi, andiamo*, 139, trans. FSP.

140. John Paul II, May 12, 1980, trans. FSP.

141. John Paul II, August 29, 1982, trans. FSP.

142. John Paul II, October 5, 1986, trans. FSP.

143. John Paul II, February 11, 2005, trans. FSP.

144. John Paul II, February 13, 2005, trans. FSP.

145. John Paul II, June 2, 1997, trans. *LOR.*

146. John Paul II, May 21, 1985, trans. FSP.

147. John Paul II, October 14, 1981, trans. FSP.

148. John Paul II, May 29, 1994, trans. FSP.

149. John Paul II, October 13, 1996, trans. FSP.

150. John Paul II, October 13, 1996, trans. FSP.

151. John Paul II, October 21, 1979, trans. FSP.

152. John Paul II, August 19, 2002, trans. *LOR.*

153. John Paul II, August 19, 2002, trans. *LOR.*

154. John Paul II, March 8, 2003, trans. FSP.

155. John Paul II, September 8, 2004, trans. FSP.

156. John Paul II, *Roman Triptych: Meditations* (Washington, DC: USCCB Publishing, 2003), 25.

157. John Paul II, December 26, 1994, trans. FSP.

158. John Paul II, *The Place Within*, 13.

PART THREE
Twenty-Seven Years in the Heart of History

1. John Paul II, December 22, 1979, trans. FSP.

2. John Paul II, October 25, 1978, trans. *LOR.*

3. John Paul II, October 29, 1978, trans. FSP.

4. John Paul II, November 5, 1978, trans. *LOR.*

5. John Paul II, December 3, 1978, trans. *LOR.*

6. John Paul II, December 22, 1978, trans. FSP.

7. Ibid.

8. John Paul II, January 12, 1979, trans. *LOR.*

9. Ibid.

10. Giovanni Paulo II, *Altzatevi, andiamo*, 46–47, trans. FSP.

11. John Paul II, February 18, 1979, trans. *LOR.*

12. John Paul II, February 21, 1979, trans. *LOR.*

13. John Paul II, *Memory and Identity*, 5.

14. John Paul II, March 11, 1979, trans. *LOR.*

15. John Paul II, June 17, 1979, trans. FSP.

16. John Paul II, June 2, 1979, trans. *LOR.*

17. John Paul II, June 10, 1979, trans. *LOR.*

18. John Paul II, July 4, 1979, trans. FSP.

19. John Paul II, October 17, 1979, trans. *LOR.*

20. John Paul II, January 14, 1980, trans. *LOR.*

21. John Paul II, October 21, 1979, trans. *LOR.*

22. Ibid.

23. John Paul II, December 5, 1979, trans. *LOR.*

24. John Paul II, December 22, 1979, trans. *LOR.*

25. Ibid.

26. John Paul II, March 26, 1980, trans. *LOR.*

27. John Paul II, April 13, 1980, trans. FSP.

28. John Paul II, December 22, 1980, trans. *LOR.*

29. John Paul II, June 11, 1980, trans. *LOR.*

30. John Paul II, December 22, 1980, trans. *LOR.*

31. John Paul II, September 24, 1980, trans. *LOR.*

32. John Paul II, November 26, 1980, trans. *LOR.*

33. John Paul II, December 22, 1980, trans. *LOR.*

34. John Paul II, November 30, 1980, trans. *LOR.*

35. John Paul II, *Memory and Identity*, 5–6.

36. John Paul II, December 22, 1980, trans. *LOR*.

37. John Paul II, January 21, 1981, trans. *LOR*.

38. John Paul II, December 22, 1981, trans. *LOR*.

39. John Paul II, March 5, 1982, trans. FSP.

40. John Paul II, May 19, 1994, trans. FSP.

41. John Paul II, May 17, 1981, trans. FSP.

42. John Paul II, February 19, 1982, trans. FSP.

43. Frossard and John Paul II, *"Non Abbiate Paura!"*, 318, trans. FSP.

44. John Paul II, October 7, 1981, trans. FSP.

45. John Paul II, November 3, 1981, trans. *LOR*.

46. John Paul II, November 13, 1981, trans. *LOR*.

47. John Paul II, December 16, 1981, trans. *LOR*.

48. John Paul II, December 22, 1981, trans. *LOR*.

49. John Paul II, January 16, 1982, trans. *LOR*.

50. John Paul II, February 19, 1982, trans. *LOR*.

51. John Paul II, April 18, 1982, trans. *LOR*.

52. John Paul II, May 19, 1982, trans. *LOR*.

53. John Paul II, June 12, 1982, trans. FSP.

54. John Paul II, June 16, 1982, trans. *LOR*.

55. John Paul II, September 19, 1982, trans. *LOR*.

56. John Paul II, November 17, 1982, trans. *LOR*.

57. John Paul II, November 9, 1982, trans. FSP.

58. John Paul II, December 23, 1982, trans. *LOR*.

59. John Paul II, January 15, 1983, trans. *LOR*.

60. John Paul II, November 21, 1983, trans. *LOR*.

61. John Paul II, March 16, 1983, trans. *LOR*.

62. John Paul II, March 25, 1983, trans. *LOR*.

63. John Paul II, May 20, 1983, trans. *LOR*.

64. John Paul II, June 23, 1983, trans. *LOR*.

65. John Paul II, August 15, 1983, trans. *LOR*.

66. John Paul II, September 13, 1983, trans. *LOR*.

67. John Paul II, October 16, 1983, trans. *LOR*.

68. John Paul II, October 26, 1983, trans. *LOR*.

69. John Paul II, December 27, 1983, trans. FSP.

70. John Paul II, January 14, 1984, trans. *LOR*.

71. John Paul II, February 8, 1984, trans. *LOR*.

72. John Paul II, February 26, 1984, trans. *LOR*.

73. John Paul II, April 22, 1984, trans. *LOR*.

74. John Paul II, June 17, 1984, trans. FSP.

75. John Paul II, September 26, 1984, trans. *LOR*.

76. John Paul II, October 7, 1984, trans. *LOR*.

77. John Paul II, October 17, 1984, trans. FSP.

78. John Paul II, December 16, 1984, trans. *LOR*.

79. John Paul II, January 12, 1985, trans. *LOR*.

80. John Paul II, November 1, 1984, trans. *LOR*.

81. John Paul II, January 9, 1985, trans. *LOR*.

82. John Paul II, February 13, 1985, trans. *LOR*.

83. John Paul II, December 20, 1985, trans. *LOR*.

84. John Paul II, May 29, 1985, trans. *LOR*.

85. John Paul II, June 16, 1985, trans. FSP.

86. John Paul II, August 21, 1985, trans. *LOR*.

87. John Paul II, September 8, 1985, trans. *LOR*.

88. John Paul II, September 21, 1985, trans. FSP.

89. John Paul II, October 19, 1985, trans. FSP.

90. John Paul II, January 11, 1986, trans. *LOR*.

91. John Paul II, February 26, 1986, trans. *LOR*.

92. John Paul II, *Crossing the Threshold of Hope*, 98–99.

93. John Paul II, May 18, 1986, trans. *LOR*.

94. John Paul II, July 16, 1986, trans. *LOR*.

95. John Paul II, October 15, 1986, trans. *LOR*.

96. John Paul II, October 18, 1986, trans. *LOR*.

97. John Paul II, January 10, 1987, trans. *LOR*.

98. John Paul II, December 3, 1986, trans. *LOR*.

99. John Paul II, September 24, 1986, trans. *LOR*.

100. John Paul II, March 25, 1987, trans. *LOR*.

101. John Paul II, April 15, 1987, trans. *LOR*.

102. John Paul II, May 6, 1987, trans. *LOR*.

103. John Paul II, June 6, 1987, trans. *LOR*.

104. John Paul II, June 17, 1987, trans. *LOR*.

105. John Paul II, August 23, 1987, trans. *LOR*.

106. John Paul II, September 23, 1987, trans. *LOR*.

107. John Paul II, January 9, 1988, trans. *LOR*.

108. John Paul II, March 19, 1988, trans. *LOR*.

109. John Paul II, May 25, 1988, trans. *LOR*.

110. John Paul II, May 21, 1988, trans. FSP.

111. John Paul II, July 6, 1988, trans. *LOR*.

112. John Paul II, December 22, 1988, trans. *LOR*.

113. Ibid.

114. Ibid.

115. John Paul II, September 21, 1988, trans. *LOR*.

116. John Paul II, October 12, 1988, trans. *LOR*.

117. John Paul II, March 2, 1989, trans. *LOR*.

118. John Paul II, May 10, 1989, trans. *LOR*.

119. John Paul II, December 22, 1989, trans. *LOR*.

120. John Paul II, August 23, 1989, trans. *LOR*.

121. John Paul II, September 7, 1989, trans. *LOR*.

122. John Paul II, December 22, 1989, trans. *LOR*.

123. John Paul II, January 13, 1990, trans. *LOR*.

124. John Paul II, December 22, 1989, trans. *LOR*.

125. John Paul II, February 7, 1990, trans. *LOR*.

126. John Paul II, April 25, 1990, trans. *LOR*.

127. John Paul II, May 16, 1990, trans. *LOR*.

128. John Paul II, May 30, 1990, trans. *LOR*.

129. John Paul II, August 26, 1990, trans. *LOR*.

130. John Paul II, September 12, 1990, trans. *LOR*.

131. John Paul II, October 10, 1990, trans. *LOR*.

132. John Paul II, January 12, 1991, trans. *LOR*.

133. John Paul II, April 11, 1991, trans. *LOR*.

134. John Paul II, December 23, 1991, trans. *LOR*.

135. John Paul II, May 15, 1991, trans. *LOR*.

136. John Paul II, June 12, 1991, trans. *LOR*.

137. John Paul II, December 23, 1991, trans. *LOR*.

138. John Paul II, August 28, 1991, trans. *LOR*.

139. John Paul II, October 23, 1991, trans. *LOR*.

140. John Paul II, January 11, 1992, trans. *LOR*.

141. Ibid.

142. John Paul II, March 4, 1992, trans. *LOR*.

143. John Paul II, March 18, 1992, trans. *LOR*.

144. John Paul II, June 17, 1992, trans. *LOR*.

145. John Paul II, October 21, 1992, trans. *LOR*.

146. John Paul II, December 6, 1992, trans. *LOR*.

147. John Paul II, January 10, 1993, trans. *LOR*.

148. John Paul II, December 21, 1993, trans. *LOR*.

149. John Paul II, April 28, 1993, trans. *LOR*.

150. John Paul II, May 9, 1993, trans. *LOR*.

151. John Paul II, June 27, 1993, trans. *LOR*.

152. John Paul II, June 23, 1993, trans. *LOR*.

153. John Paul II, December 21, 1993, trans. *LOR*.

154. Ibid.

155. John Paul II, October 3, 1993, trans. *LOR*.

156. John Paul II, November 14, 1993, trans. *LOR*.

157. John Paul II, January 6, 1994, trans. *LOR*.

158. John Paul II, January 23, 1994, trans. *LOR*.

159. John Paul II, December 22, 1994, trans. *LOR*.

160. John Paul II, January 9, 1995, trans. *LOR.*

161. John Paul II, May 29, 1994, trans. *LOR.*

162. John Paul II, September 14, 1994, trans. FSP.

163. John Paul II, October 8, 1994, trans. *LOR.*

164. John Paul II, February 1, 1995, trans. *LOR.*

165. John Paul II, March 26, 1995, trans. *LOR.*

166. John Paul II, April 29, 1995, trans. *LOR.*

167. John Paul II, May 24, 1995, trans. *LOR.*

168. John Paul II, May 25, 1995, trans. *LOR.*

169. John Paul II, June 21, 1995, trans. *LOR.*

170. John Paul II, July 5, 1995, trans. *LOR.*

171. John Paul II, September 9, 1995, trans. *LOR.*

172. John Paul II, September 24, 1995, trans. *LOR.*

173. John Paul II, October 11, 1995, trans. *LOR.*

174. John Paul II, February 22, 1996, trans. *LOR.*

175. John Paul II, March 25, 1996, trans. *LOR.*

176. John Paul II, January 13, 1997, trans. *LOR.*

177. John Paul II, April 14, 1996, trans. FSP.

178. John Paul II, May 22, 1996, trans. *LOR.*

179. John Paul II, October 6, 1996, trans. FSP.

180. John Paul II, December 21, 1996, trans. FSP.

181. John Paul II, January 13, 1997, trans. *LOR.*

182. John Paul II, April 20, 1997, trans. *LOR.*

183. John Paul II, May 10, 1997, trans. *LOR.*

184. John Paul II, June 16, 1997, trans. *LOR.*

185. Ibid.

186. John Paul II, August 24, 1997, trans. *LOR.*

187. John Paul II, October 8, 1997, trans. *LOR.*

188. John Paul II, January 10, 1998, trans. *LOR.*

189. John Paul II, January 28, 1998, trans. *LOR.*

190. John Paul II, July 5, 1998, trans. *LOR.*

191. John Paul II, September 12, 1999, trans. *LOR.*

192. John Paul II, November 29, 1998, trans. *LOR.*

193. John Paul II, January 11, 1999, trans. *LOR.*

194. Ibid.

195. John Paul II, May 9, 1999, trans. *LOR.*

196. John Paul II, June 20, 1999, trans. *LOR.*

197. John Paul II, October 1, 1999, trans. *LOR.*

198. John Paul II, November 8, 1999, trans. *LOR.*

199. John Paul II, June 2, 1997, trans. FSP.

200. John Paul II, December 25, 1999, trans. *LOR.*

201. John Paul II, December 21, 1999, trans. *LOR.*

202. John Paul II, January 10, 2000, trans. *LOR.*

203. John Paul II, January 2, 2000, trans. *LOR.*

204. John Paul II, February 27, 2000, trans. *LOR.*

205. John Paul II, March 12, 2000, trans. *LOR.*

206. John Paul II, March 26, 2000, trans. *LOR.*

207. John Paul II, *Memory and Identity*, 54–55.

208. John Paul II, May 1, 2000, trans. *LOR.*

209. John Paul II, May 7, 2000, trans. *LOR.*

210. John Paul II, June 25, 2000, trans. *LOR.*

211. John Paul II, August 19, 2000, trans. *LOR.*

212. John Paul II, October 14, 2000, trans. *LOR.*

213. John Paul II, December 21, 2000, trans. *LOR.*

214. Ibid.

215. John Paul II, May 9, 2001, trans. *LOR.*

216. John Paul II, June 27, 2001, trans. *LOR.*

217. John Paul II, September 27, 2001, trans. *LOR.*

218. John Paul II, September 25, 2001, trans. *LOR.*

219. John Paul II, December 22, 2001, trans. *LOR.*

220. John Paul II, January 10, 2002, trans. *LOR.*

221. John Paul II, January 27, 2002, trans. *LOR.*

222. John Paul II, May 29, 2002, trans. *LOR*.

223. John Paul II, June 17, 2002, trans. *LOR*.

224. John Paul II, June 16, 2002, trans. *LOR*.

225. John Paul II, August 4, 2002, trans. *LOR*.

226. John Paul II, August 21, 2002, trans. *LOR*.

227. John Paul II, October 22, 2003, trans. *LOR*.

228. John Paul II, November 11, 2003, trans. *LOR*.

229. John Paul II, January 13, 2003, trans. *LOR*.

230. John Paul II, March 5, 2003, trans. *LOR*.

231. John Paul II, March 16, 2003, trans. *LOR*.

232. John Paul II, March 26, 2003, trans. *LOR*.

233. John Paul II, April 17, 2003, trans. *LOR*.

234. John Paul II, June 12, 2003, trans. *LOR*.

235. John Paul II, June 22, 2003, trans. *LOR*.

236. John Paul II, June 25, 2003, trans. *LOR*.

237. John Paul II, June 28, 2003, trans. *LOR*.

238. John Paul II, September 17, 2003, trans. *LOR*.

239. John Paul II, October 7, 2003, trans. *LOR*.

240. John Paul II, October 29, 2003, trans. *LOR*.

241. John Paul II, October 16, 2003, trans. *LOR*.

242. John Paul II, October 22, 2003, trans. *LOR*.

243. John Paul II, October 16, 2003, trans. *LOR*.

244. Ibid.

245. John Paul II, October 19, 2003, trans. *LOR*.

246. John Paul II, March 6, 2003, trans. *LOR*.

247. John Paul II, August 17, 2002, trans. FSP.

248. John Paul II, May 17, 1995, trans. *LOR*.

249. John Paul II, December 25, 2003, trans. *LOR*.

250. John Paul II, January 12, 2004, trans. *LOR*.

251. John Paul II, March 14, 2004, trans. *LOR*.

252. John Paul II, January 17, 2004, trans. *LOR*.

253. John Paul II, March 24, 2004, trans. *LOR*.

254. John Paul II, June 9, 2004, trans. *LOR*.

255. John Paul II, June 10, 2004, trans. *LOR*.

256. John Paul II, June 20, 2004, trans. *LOR*.

257. John Paul II, March 24, 2004, trans. *LOR*.

258. John Paul II, August 14, 2004, trans. *LOR*.

259. John Paul II, December 8, 2004, trans. *LOR*.

260. John Paul II, August 25, 2004, trans. *LOR*.

261. John Paul II, September 5, 2004, trans. *LOR*.

262. John Paul II, November 27, 2004, trans. *LOR*.

263. John Paul II, January 10, 2005, trans. *LOR*.

264. John Paul II, February 14, 2005, trans. *LOR*.

265. John Paul II, February 22, 2005, trans. *LOR*.

266. John Paul II, February 24, 2005, trans. FSP.

267. John Paul II, March 25, 2005, trans. *LOR*.

268. John Paul II, April 3, 2005, trans. *LOR*. Delivered posthumously by Archbishop Leonardo Sandri.

269. Giovanni Paulo II, *Altzatevi, andiamo*, 127, trans. FSP.

270. Joseph Ratzinger, April 8, 2005, trans. *LOR*.

271. John Paul II, March 6, 1979, trans. *LOR*.

272. John Paul II, March 1, 1980, trans. *LOR*.

273. John Paul II, March 17, 2000, trans. *LOR*.

Bibliography

Accattoli, Luigi. *Karol Wojtyła: l'uomo di fine millennio*. Milan: Edizioni San Paolo, 1998.

———. *Man of the Millennium: John Paul II*. Boston: Pauline Books & Media, 2000.

Bernstein, Carl, and Marco Politi. *His Holiness: John Paul II and the Hidden History of Our Time*. New York, NY: Doubleday, 1996.

Maliński, Mieczysław. *Le radici di Papa Wojtyła*. Rome: Borla, 1979.

———. *Il mio vecchio amico Karol*. Milan: Edizioni Pauline, 1980.

Frossard, André, and Giovanni Paolo II. *Non abbiate paura!* Milan: Rusconi, 1983.

———. *"Be Not Afraid!": Pope John Paul II Speaks Out on His Life, His Beliefs, and His Inspiring Vision for Humanity*. Gordonsville, VA: St. Martin's Press, 1984.

John Paul II. *Altzatevi, andiamo*. Vatican City: Libreria Editrice Vaticana, 2004.

———. *Crossing the Threshold of Hope*. New York, NY: Alfred A. Knopf, Inc., 1994.

———. *Gift and Mystery: On the Fiftieth Anniversary of My Priestly Ordination*. New York, NY: Doubleday, 1996.

———. *Memory and Identity: Conversations at the Dawn of a Millennium*. New York, NY: Rizzoli International Publications, Inc., 2005.

————. *The Place Within: The Poetry of Pope John Paul II.* New York, NY: Random House, 1994.

————. *Roman Triptych: Meditations.* Washington, DC: USCCB Publishing, 2003.

Wojtyła, Karol. *Tutte le opere letterarie: poesie, drammi e scritti sul teatro.* Milan: Bompiani, 2001.

Pauline
BOOKS & MEDIA

The Daughters of St. Paul operate book and media centers at the following addresses. Visit, call or write the one nearest you today, or find us on the World Wide Web, www.pauline.org.

CALIFORNIA
3908 Sepulveda Blvd, Culver City, CA 90230	310-397-8676
935 Brewster Avenue, Redwood City, CA 94063	650-369-4230
5945 Balboa Avenue, San Diego, CA 92111	858-565-9181

FLORIDA
145 S.W. 107th Avenue, Miami, FL 33174	305-559-6715

HAWAII
1143 Bishop Street, Honolulu, HI 96813	808-521-2731
Neighbor Islands call:	866-521-2731

ILLINOIS
172 North Michigan Avenue, Chicago, IL 60601	312-346-4228

LOUISIANA
4403 Veterans Memorial Blvd, Metairie, LA 70006	504-887-7631

MASSACHUSETTS
885 Providence Hwy, Dedham, MA 02026	781-326-5385

MISSOURI
9804 Watson Road, St. Louis, MO 63126	314-965-3512

NEW YORK
64 W. 38th Street, New York, NY 10018	212-754-1110

PENNSYLVANIA
Philadelphia—relocating	215-676-9494

SOUTH CAROLINA
243 King Street, Charleston, SC 29401	843-577-0175

VIRGINIA
1025 King Street, Alexandria, VA 22314	703-549-3806

CANADA
3022 Dufferin Street, Toronto, ON M6B 3T5	416-781-9131

¡También somos su fuente para libros, videos y música en español!